WHY SWITZERLAND?

Switzerland is a special and fascinating place. Its unique institutions, its direct democracy, multi-member executives, absence of strikes, communal autonomy, its universal military service, its wealth, and four national languages make it interesting in itself. But it has wider significance, in representing the 'Europe that did not happen', the Europe that escaped the centralisation of state and economy associated with the modern world. Today, there is a new special feature. Switzerland is an island surrounded by the European Union, and resists membership.

Why Switzerland? attempts to answer three related questions: why has such an exception to European norms survived? Why should outsiders notice its peculiarities and what can they learn from them? Finally, can so unusual a society continue to exist when many of the conditions in which it evolved have disappeared? *Why Switzerland?*, which was first published in 1976, has been completely revised (with new illustrations) to try to answer these questions for the present generation.

Cartoon from *Revue économique franco-suisse*, 1991

WHY SWITZERLAND?

Second edition

JONATHAN STEINBERG

Reader in Modern European History
University of Cambridge, and
Fellow of Trinity Hall

CAMBRIDGE
UNIVERSITY PRESS

PUBLISHED BY THE PRESS SYNDICATE OF THE UNIVERSITY OF CAMBRIDGE
The Pitt Building, Trumpington Street, Cambridge, United Kingdom

CAMBRIDGE UNIVERSITY PRESS
The Edinburgh Building, Cambridge CB2 2RU, UK
40 West 20th Street, New York, NY 10011–4211, USA
10 Stamford Road, Oakleigh, VIC 3166, Australia
Ruiz de Alarcón 13, 28014 Madrid, Spain
Dock House, The Waterfront, Cape Town 8001, South Africa

http://www.cambridge.org

First published 1976
Reprinted with corrections 1978
First paperback edition 1980
Reprinted 1984, 1985, 1987, 1991
Second edition 1996
Reprinted 1998, 2000

Printed in the United Kingdom at the University Press, Cambridge

A catalogue record for this book is available from the British Library

Library of Congress Cataloguing in Publication data
Steinberg, Jonathan.
Why Switzerland? / Jonathan Steinberg. – 2nd edn
p.   cm.
Includes bibliographical references and index.
ISBN 0 521 48170 8 (hc) – ISBN 0 521 48453 7 (pb)
1. Switzerland – Civilization. 2. National characteristics, Swiss.
I. Title.
DQ17.S7 1996
949.4 – dc20   95-43246 CIP

ISBN 0 521 48170 8 hardback 2nd edition (0 521 21139 5 1st edition)
ISBN 0 521 48453 7 paperback 2nd edition (0 521 28144 X 1st edition)

For
Matthew, Daniel and Peter

I pastori che passano l'estate sulle *alpi*, discendono di tanto in
tanto nel villaggio a rinnovar le proviste, e le proviste sono:
pane, vino, sale e giornali. E in alcuna di quelle alte capanne,
simile a tante trogloditiche, in quell'odore acre di latte
cagliato, di fumo, di sterco, più d'una volta mi è accaduto di
trovar chi sapeva fin'ultime minuzie della politica cantonale
e mondiale, chi, a me che parlavo dialetto, si studiava di
rispondere in lingua letteraria.

Francesco Chiesa

Überhaupt ist nicht gross oder klein, was auf der Landkarte so
scheint: es kommt auf den Geist an.

Johannes von Müller

Trois Suisses vont à la chasse aux escargots et ils comparent
leurs prises en fin de journée. – 'Moi', dit le Genevois rapide,
'j'en ai cent.' – 'Moi', dit le Bernois, 'j'en ai attrapé quatre.' –
'Et moi', dit le Vaudois (imaginez l'accent), 'j'en ai bien vu un,
mais il m'a échappé.'

Denis de Rougemont

Contents

Illustrations

Photographic permissions
2, *26*: Gemeindekanzlei Flühli; *3*, *9a*, *9b*, *13*; Archivio cantonale,
Bellinzona; *6a*: PTT-Museum, Bern; *6b*: Ottica Vicari, Lugano;
7, *22*: Bernisches Historisches Museum; *14*: Kunstmuseum, Bern;
15: Öffentliche Kunstsammlung Basel, Kupferstichkabinett
(Photo: Martin Bühler); *16–20*: Hans Kohler-Bally, Grenchen;
21: Zentralbibliothek, Zürich; *23*: Photostudio Hans Preisig, Sion;
24: Atelier Hegner, Solothurn; *25*: CIRIC, Lausanne; *27*, *28*: Swiss
Defence Office, London

MAPS

FIGURES

Preface to the second edition

When *Why Switzerland?* appeared twenty years ago, I asked my readers to understand its title as two questions: why a place as idiosyncratic as Switzerland existed, and why non-Swiss should care. Today, a third, much more ominous, question joins the first two: why Switzerland should continue to exist. Twenty years ago, Switzerland saw itself threatened from within and without by the Soviet empire. The still living experience of the second world war with its 'fortress mentality' reinforced Swiss defensiveness. Yet inside Switzerland the Swiss felt good about themselves. They believed that their will to resist had forced Hitler to drop his plans to invade them. They were proud of their historic liberties, their institutions, their religious peace, their wealth, their efficiency and their social harmony. Switzerland had, they believed, no strikes, no slums and no debts.

That complacency has vanished. Switzerland has drugs, AIDS, unemployment, huge public debts and one of the highest adult male rates of suicide in Europe. As former Federal Councillor René Felber said in 1990, Switzerland has become 'normal'. Yet if Switzerland has really become 'normal', then why have a Switzerland at all? The European Union asks 'why Switzerland?' almost every day. Switzerland obstructs the final integration of Europe. Its peculiar laws interfere with road traffic. Its government can never promise to fulfil treaties because the citizens say 'No'. Brussels sees Switzerland as tedious, and unreliable. But it is not Norway. The EU cannot ignore the fact that Swiss trade matters to the EU and that Switzerland controls vital land routes across the Alps.

Europe threatens Switzerland but in a new way. For the first time in seven centuries, Switzerland is surrounded by 'friends'. Beyond every frontier the Swiss see peaceful, capitalist democracies not unlike their own. The only significant difference – and it matters more each day – is that they are members of the European Union and Switzerland is not. The Swiss at the geographical centre of Europe have become politically peripheral. They stand in queues at airports with the non-European 'others'. They have no voice in the debate on European integration.

The internal structures of Swiss identity no longer seem self-evident. The Swiss maintain the second largest land army in Europe and almost all adult males have to serve in it. To fight whom? In November 1989, a third of those who turned out voted in a popular initiative to abolish the army. The shock felt even by those who supported the initiative still reverberates in Swiss society. The uncertainty about the army undermines the historic assumptions about neutrality. For nearly five hundred years Swiss neutrality has been 'armed'. It rested on the importance of territory and foot soldiers in warfare. In 1991 Switzerland tried to be traditionally 'neutral' in the Gulf War and succeeded in looking clumsy. Its citizenry have rejected government proposals to join the United Nations and to send 'blue berets' for UN service. They rejected the European Economic Area proposals in 1992 and a proposal to free Swiss property to foreign buyers in 1995. A kind of 'isolationism' has replaced 'armed neutrality' in the minds of many Swiss citizens.

Direct democracy – that thicket of initiatives, referenda, town meetings, elected bodies, corporate structures of land ownership and cartelisation which makes Switzerland utterly unlike anywhere else – looks incompatible with the *acquis communautaire*, the fourteen hundred or so regulations and directives, which membership of the European Union demands. Even at home citizens trust their system less than they used to do. Pressure groups and single-issue parties have turned direct democratic instruments into devices to cripple government. The government itself, the unique Swiss executive, has lost prestige alarmingly. A public opinion poll in the spring of 1995 showed that more than a third of those questioned had no confidence in their executive, three times more than in 1979. The executive itself – the reader might think of it as the American presidency turned into a seven-member committee – functions less well than it used to do. Both inside and outside the national parliament in Bern proposals for radical change to the Swiss executive multiply. 'Why Switzerland?' has now become a question the Swiss ask themselves.

This revised edition attempts to answer the third question as well as the two original ones. To the first, original question it replies that Switzerland exists in its present form for good historic reasons and that Switzerland provides a model of the Europe that did not become the norm, that is, a Europe without the national state. To the second question it urges foreign readers to take the Swiss state and society seriously, to look at its systems for resolving conflict as possible devices to be used elsewhere and to see in Swiss specialness some useful correctives to the 'naturalness' of any other system. In answering the third question I hope to show that Switzerland is not, as many Swiss fear, a *Willensnation*, a fragile historic antique, which will fall apart if the Swiss stop willing themselves to be Swiss. Switzerland enjoys a robust, rooted and extremely functional set of human institutions which will have a future no matter what happens elsewhere.

The political environment around Switzerland has also begun to change. It has been clear since the early 1990s that 'Eurocrats' like Jacques Delors have failed. The European Union cannot survive in its present *dirigiste*, centralised form. Each new member state makes it harder for Brussels to govern from above. The European Union will be forced by its own inner logic to become more 'Swiss', more federal, more transparent and, above all, more democratic. The Swiss have nothing to fear from or in such a Europe.

This revised edition also reflects other changes that have occurred since 1976: the emergence of unsolved environmental questions, social plagues like drugs and AIDS, the explosion of means of communication, the medical revolution. Swiss observers, partly in response to these changes, have been re-examining every aspect of Swiss life from William Tell to the provision of free needles to addicts. As a result I know more about Switzerland than I did when I wrote the first edition two decades ago. I have added a chapter on 'religion' because I now see the resolution of religious conflict as a central constituent in the establishment of the equilibrium that became modern Switzerland.

In the first edition I thanked a great many people, including members of my wife's Swiss family. To all of those who then helped and have helped since I extend my thanks again. They know how much I owe them. In preparing the revised edition I made two extended trips to Switzerland, one in 1991 and one in 1995. The 1991 trip was arranged through the Swiss Embassy in London by the then ambassador His Excellency Franz Muheim and the cultural counsellor, M. Livio Hürzeler. My thanks to them are profound. My stay in Bern turned into one of the most exciting experiences of my life. The then British ambassador, His Excellency Christopher Long and his wife Patricia, let me stay in the Residence and gave me their grand official car and chauffeur to carry me to my appointments. During that trip I was granted (and allowed to record) interviews with members of the Swiss government, and senior civil servants. They spoke to me frankly and at length. This edition bears the imprint of their views, if imperfectly. If I list them, I do so with deep gratitude and with unforgettable memories of the time they generously gave me: consigliere federale Flavio Cotti, at that time President of Switzerland and Minister of the Interior; conseiller fédéral René Felber, then Federal Minister of Foreign Affairs; Bundesrat Otto Stich, then Federal Minister of Finance; Staatssekretär Franz Blankart, director of the Federal Office for Foreign Economic Affairs in the Ministry of Economic Affairs and principal negotiator with the European Union; Ambassador Jenö Staehelin, then political director of the Department of Foreign Affairs; and M. Marc Salamin, section chief. I am also grateful to Sign. Marco Cameroni, then press officer at the Federal Department of Foreign Affairs, for his guidance and suggestions.

On that same trip, I recorded and profited from interviews with a great many other distinguished Swiss citizens in the world of politics, the arts, industry, government on cantonal level, journalism, the army and the two great churches. The Pro Helvetia Stiftung helped both to arrange some of these interviews and to finance my trip. I am grateful to the Stiftung, to Frau Hanne Zweifel-Wütrich in its offices, and to my conversation partners: Professor Dr Urs Altermatt of the Université de Fribourg; M. Pierre Baudère, architect in Fribourg; Dr Albert Bodmer, then Deputy Chairman of Ciba-Geigy, Basel; Professor Iso Camartin, Professor of Romansch Literature, University of Zürich; Dr Raffaele Ceschi, historian, Bellinzona; Professor Dr Victor Conzemius, church historian, Luzern; Divisionär a.D. Gustav Däniker, formerly chief of staff for operational training; Herr Max Frenkel of the *Neue Zürcher Zeitung*; Herr J. Frey, synodal legal officer of the Evangelical and Reformed Church of Canton Bern; Regierungsrat a.D. Dr Walter Gut, Luzern; Dr Max Hofer, episcopal vicar and chairman of the Diocesan Pastoral Office and Dr Markus Ries, then archivist, in the Bishopric of Basel; Dr A. M. Schütz, former president of Eterna Watches; Ständerrätin Rosemarie Simmen, who represents Canton Solothurn in the Upper House; Dott. Federico Spiess, Vocabolario dei dialetti della Svizzera Italiana; Landschreiber Dr Hans Windlin, Canton Zug; Sign. Flavio Zanetti, press officer of Radiotelevisione della Svizzera Italiana; Herr Egon P. S. Zehnder, Egon Zehnder and Partners, Inc., management consultants, Zürich.

In 1995 I retraced some of my steps. I spoke to the Rotary Club of Entlebuch in Canton Luzern which I had addressed in 1973 and had interviews with communal officers in Malters (Luzern) and Grenchen (Solothurn). My thanks go, first of all, to Herr Benno Baumeler, architect in Willisau, Luzern, the president of the Rotary Club and to Herr Kantonsförster a.D. Otto Bättig for the invitation and to the members of the Rotary for letting me try my thoughts on them. I am grateful to Dr Markus Dürr, Gemeinderatspräsident and Herr Josef Geisseler, Gemeindeschreiber in Malters; Herr Rolf Enggist, Stadtschreiber in Grenchen; Dr Yves Fricker, department of sociology, University of Geneva; Herr Hans Christen, press officer of the Union of Swiss Machine Industrialists, Zürich; Herr Ernst Flammer, Federal Office for Education and Science and, as always, Dr Anton Meinrad Meier and Erna and Seppi Seeberger, my wife's cousins, who arranged interviews both in 1991 and 1995 and provided a base of operations for my Swiss research. I am extremely grateful to my copy-editor, Mrs Virginia Catmur, whose eye for detail, sense of style and passion for accuracy have made this a much better book.

Much of the research on which a book like this depends involves reading newspapers. Switzerland can be proud of the high level of many of its newspapers, but it has one that I must mention. *Die Neue Zürcher Zeitung* has been serving its readers in the German-speaking world for more than two centuries. Its international and domestic reporting, the breadth of its cultural, financial and scientific interests, make it the complete daily newspaper. I could not have assembled this portrait of Switzerland without it, and I take this occasion to say 'thank you' to the *NZZ* for its superb journalism.

Finally, I am grateful to the citizens of Willisau in Canton Luzern, although they do not know it. Willisau with a total population of about 8,000 voters is divided into Willisau-Stadt and Willisau-Land, two separate self-governing communes. In Willisau-Stadt the Liberal Party and in Willisau-Land the Conservative

Party dominates local politics and favours its own party members in giving contracts and making public appointments. Each party has its own pubs, singing and gymnastic clubs and local organisations. A Willisau architect, who belongs to the Conservative Party, told me in 1995 that in seventeen years in practice he had never been engaged by a Liberal, except one who was a cousin. This historic, deeply rooted, polarisation of politics occurs all over the world and reminds me of Belfast. Nobody outside Switzerland would associate it with such practices. When I told Professor Sir John Plumb about Willisau in 1969, he urged me to write a book about Switzerland. A generation later I offer Willisau-Stadt and Willisau-Land my belated but sincere thanks.

Trinity Hall, Cambridge   JONATHAN STEINBERG

Preface to the first edition

Switzerland is a hard country to get to know. Many tourists never see the 'real' Switzerland behind the neat façade of the tourist industry. I happened to be lucky. I married into a very large, very real, Swiss family. My father-in-law, Mr O. A. Meier, his nine brothers and sisters, and the horde of cousins in different parts of the country provided my introduction to Swiss life. I hope that they will forgive me for not mentioning each by name but I must make two exceptions. Seppi and Erna Seeberger-Krummenacher owned one of the last unspoilt Alpine hotels, Kurhaus Seewenalp. There was no electricity and no motor road to ruin the hiker's paradise until the army commandeered it for manoeuvre grounds. They, their friends and the lively assortment of hotel guests from all over Switzerland put up with a lot of questions. They know how much I owe them. The other exception is also a cousin; Dr Anton M. Meier, theologian and Director of the Kinder- und Erziehungsheim St Josef in Grenchen, has been the *spiritus rector* of this entire operation. He allowed me to use his flat in Grenchen during an extended visit in 1972, arranged many fascinating interviews for me and set exacting intellectual standards for the enterprise. I know that I have fallen short of them, but, rather like the Alps themselves, I have known that his standards were there as a permanent background and goal.

Professor J. H. Plumb of Christ's College first gave me the idea that there was a book in my fascination with the idiosyncrasies of Swiss life and has kept me cheerful during some bad moments. Dr John Barber of King's College noticed that I had left out the most important piece of the argument, the economic substructure of the special Swiss political and social framework. Dr J. A. Cremona of Trinity Hall served as my Virgil in the *selva oscura dei dialetti*. Professor Frederick P. Brooks Jr of the University of North Carolina

xvii

let me have his only copy of his fascinating study of computer software at a crucial moment in the writing and reassured me that the historian can understand the world of high technology, if he has a good guide. Mr C. A. A. Rayner, formerly of Ciba-Geigy (UK) Ltd in Duxford, drew my attention to aspects of the chemical industry in Basel. Mrs Leonard Forster saved me from making a silly mistake about Gottfried Keller. Professor James Joll read the first draft of the manuscript and gave me a good deal of good advice about what was wrong with it. Miss Marjorie Shepherd helped me in preparing the manuscript and listened to my complaints when things were not going well. I owe them all my thanks.

Many people in Switzerland in every walk of life have been generous with their time and trouble. It would illustrate much of the variety of Swiss life if I paused by each to describe how he or she had opened new areas of Swiss reality to me. I hope that they will forgive me if I list them by name without further comment. My thanks and respect are theirs: Herr Dr Franz Birrer of the Swiss Embassy in Bonn, formerly cultural attaché in London; Herr Paul Adler of the Pro Helvetia Stiftung, Zürich; Dr Alfred Rötheli, Staatsschreiber of Canton Solothurn; Dr A. M. Schütz, President, Eterna Ltd; Professor Dr Adolf Gasser, Basel; Professor Dr Dietrich Schindler, Zürich; Dr R. J. Schneebeli, Director of the Volks-hochschule, Zürich; Colonel Dr Walter Schaufelberger, editor of the *Allgemeine Schweizerische Militärzeitschrift*; Professor Dr Peter Stadler, Zürich; Professor Dr Arthur Rich, Zürich; Herr Ulrich Kägi of *Die Weltwoche*, Zürich; Dott. Flavio Zanetti, Corrispondenza Politica Svizzera, Lugano; Dott. Federico Spiess and Dott. Rosanna Zeli, Vocabolario dei dialetti della Svizzera italiana, Lugano; Professor Giuseppe Martinola, Lugano; Dr Alfred Peter, *National-Zeitung*, Basel; Herr Frank A. Meyer, Büro Cortesi, Neuchâtel; Mme Lise Girardin, Députée du Conseil des Etats, Geneva; M. Claude Monnier, *Journal de Genève*; M. Ambassadeur Pierre Micheli, Geneva; Professor Dr Erich Gruner, Bern; Herr Rolf Siegrist, Schweizerische Politische Korrespondenz, Bern; Herr Benedikt von Tscharner formerly of Integration Section, Federal Political Department, Bern, and now Counsellor of Embassy (Economic and Labour) at the Swiss Embassy, London; Herr Peter Erni, Information and Press Officer, Federal Political Department, Bern; Sign. Piero Bianconi, Minusio; sign. Enzio Canonica, Consigliere nazionale and president of the Federazione Svizzera dei Lavoratori edili e del legno, Zürich; Herr Otto Bättig, Kreis-förster, Schüpfheim, Luzern.

I am grateful to the following publishers for permission to quote: *Die Weltwoche* for the table by Ulrich Kägi, copyright *Die Weltwoche*; *Schweizer Zeitschrift für Volkswirtschaft und Statistik* for the table by Peter Gilg; Francke Verlag, Bern, for the tables by E. Gruner; Huber & Co. AG for extracts from *Allgemeine Schweizerische Militärzeitschrift*.

J.S.

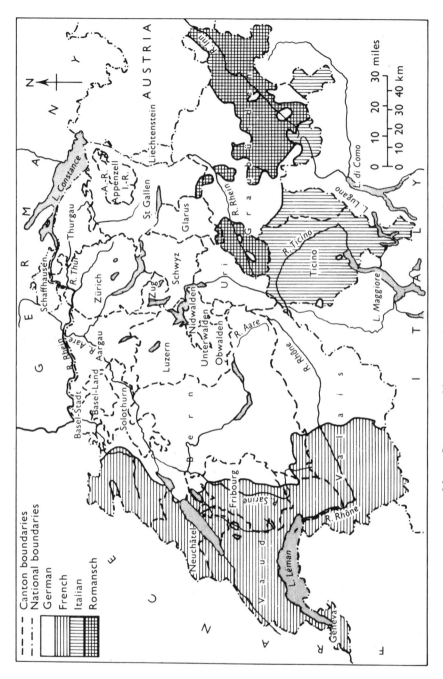

Map 1 Cantons and languages in contemporary Switzerland

CHAPTER I

Why Switzerland?

'Why Switzerland?' is really two questions not one. The first is the understandable question which any English-speaking reader who picks up a book on Switzerland must ask: 'Why should I read about Switzerland, when there are so many other things to read about?' The second, less obvious question is why there is a Switzerland at all. The present chapter will try to answer the former question; the whole book is devoted to the latter. What you have in your hands is not a guidebook. You will not find places to eat in Solothurn nor the height of the Matterhorn here. It is not a conventional history. The chapter called 'History' starts in the middle, goes backward in time and only after that does it proceed in the usual way. It is not journalism either, although most of the raw material which has been worked into the argument is drawn from our own day. If it has any clear claim to be any specific category of literature, I suppose that *Why Switzerland?* is a latter-day version of those eighteenth-century philosophical histories in which the thinkers of the Enlightenment thought they discerned underlying laws. It is a history in the way that Dr Johnson thought of history, 'contrary to minute exactness, a history which ranges facts according to their dependence on each other, and postpones or anticipates according to the convenience of narration'.[1]

If the book is odd, so is its subject. There is no place like Switzerland and hence any attempt to catch its meaning must be pretty odd too. The sheer variety of Swiss life, what I think of as its 'cellular' character, makes it hard to write a coherent account of the place. Then there are the various institutions, habits and customs unique to Switzerland: its unbelievably complicated electoral procedures, its referenda and initiatives, its specialised economy with its banks and watches, its cheese and chocolates, its citizen-soldiers with their guns in the downstairs cupboards, its complicated federalism of central government, cantons and communes, its three official and four national languages, its neutral status, its astonishing wealth per head, its huge proportion of foreign workers, its efficient public services, its enormous number of very small newspapers, its religious divisions, and until February 1971 its exclusion of women from the vote on the federal level. That is an impressive list of oddities for a country of only six million souls. But there is more.

In a world shaken by industrial unrest, Switzerland has been an island of labour peace. During 1974, there were six industrial disputes, three of which led to strikes of a day or more. The total number of days lost was 2,777. In Great Britain during the same year, the figure was 14.7 million. Nor was 1974 unusual in Swiss labour relations. The *Statistisches Jahrbuch der Schweiz 1995* reports that between 1975 and 1993 there was a grand total of twenty-seven strikes or lockouts which lasted for at least twenty-four hours or more, or just under three a year. In 1987 and 1993 there were no strikes at all and in 1986 and 1991 only one. The worst year for disputes was 1980 when five strikes and 330 firms were involved, costing 5,718 lost days of work.[2] A modern state which had done nothing else but achieve a truce in the battle between employer and employee would deserve close attention for that accomplishment alone.

Most people know that Switzerland is a country of many languages. There are in fact four national languages: German, French, Italian and Raeto-Romansch. The first three are official languages, which means that all official documents, railway time-tables or postal notices must be published in each. According to the 1990 census, 63.6% of the population speak German, 19.2% French, 7.5% Italian, 0.6% Romansch and 8.9% 'other languages'.[3] The operation of a country so constituted would be fascinating enough if that were the whole story. The reality is much more complicated, indeed bewilderingly so. Here are some facts about language in Switzerland. The 40,000 people who speak Romansch as mother-tongue divide into those who speak the Ladino of the Upper Engadin and that of the Lower Engadin – each of which has its own written language – the Surselva of the Upper Rhine valley also with a literary tradition, and the non-literary dialects of Surmeirisch and Sutselvisch. The 63.6% who speak 'German' are actually bilingual, for they speak a language they do not read or write, and read and write in a language which they sometimes speak but not as a mother-tongue. The language of the Swiss Germans, *Schwyzerdütsch*, divides itself into almost as many versions as there are valleys in the Alps, some of which, such as those of the Bernese Oberland and Oberwallis, are incomprehensible to most *Schwyzerdütsch* speakers. There is one canton, Ticino, where Italian is the official language and another, Graubünden, in which three valleys and a few communes also use it as the official tongue. What sort of Italian? Let me cite a passage from Fritz René Allemann's *25 mal die Schweiz*, where he describes the village of Bivio in Canton Graubünden:

The census of 1960 recorded a total of 188 inhabitants for Bivio . . . with an Italian majority (it is the only commune north of the main chain of the Alps which belongs to the Italian linguistic area), an old-established Raeto-Romansch minority and also some German enclaves, with a Catholic and a Protestant Church, which have co-existed in 'parity' for centuries. (Both pastors look at the congregation first before deciding which language to preach in.) But that is not all. If one listens closely, one can hear three different dialects of Italian: the native dialect which is closely related to the Raetolombardic used in the Bregaglia; the Bergamasco dialect spoken by shepherd families who during the centuries wandered over the Alps from Northern Italy; and written, 'High', Italian.[4]

Religious divisions cut deeply into Swiss life. As Urs Altermatt puts it, until recently Swiss Roman Catholics lived in a ghetto. There were Catholic bookshops, Catholic employment offices and Catholic old people's homes:

A Catholic might be born in a Catholic hospital, attend Catholic schools from kindergarten to university, read Catholic newspapers and magazines, vote for the Catholic party and take part in Catholic clubs or associations. It was not unusual for a Catholic to insure himself against sickness or accident with a Catholic company and put his savings in a Catholic savings bank.[5]

Even the Swiss Constitution played a part in making Swiss Catholics feel themselves to be second-class citizens by forbidding Jesuits to live and work in the country. The provision was altered by referendum in May 1973.

Here then are three bits of Swiss reality, chosen more or less randomly from the thickets of Helvetic oddity. They seem to point in entirely different directions. There is evidently a national pattern in labour relations. All Swiss shun the strike, not just Swiss

Germans or Swiss Catholics. Yet the other evidence illustrates the extreme particularism, the divisions within divisions or the 'cellular' quality of Swiss life. How can a place so varied have national behaviour patterns? How are the complex layers of identity (language, region, creed, party, class, occupation, age) reconciled in Swiss heads? These seem to me to be interesting questions which in a way hold up a mirror to our own less dramatic equivalents.

Switzerland is a useful place to look at some other European problems. It is small enough to be studied conveniently, odd enough to be an abbreviation for the whole of European life and advanced enough to be fully integrated into all the trends of the era. In looking at the way the Swiss cope with mass culture, modern transportation, technological change, inflation, urbanisation, population growth, secularisation, environmental pollution and violence by extremist groups, we can see in a small arena what faces Europe in the large one. Can the 'Swissness' of Switzerland adapt to the great levelling trends of the time? If it can, there is reason to hope that the Europe of the twenty-first century will not have doused national characteristics in bureaucratic grey. Particular identity will still be the essential feature of European identity, as the particularity of Switzerland is its most striking general characteristic.

The oddest thing about Switzerland is how little most foreigners know about it. No country is more frequently visited but less known. Switzerland has two faces, the smooth, expressionless, efficient surface which the tourist glides by without noticing and the turbulent, rich, inside surface which he or she never sees. The average English-speaking person, if asked to choose a few adjectives to describe Switzerland, would probably end up with a list containing the following: 'beautiful', 'efficient', 'expensive' and 'boring'. The last one crops up so frequently that I find myself shrieking 'Switzerland *is* interesting' over and over again, just to be heard. I know that Switzerland is in many ways a fascinating country but, if I mention the word 'Swiss', eyes glaze and attention wanders. In a lecture course on European history of the nineteenth century, I once announced that I intended to devote the next lecture to the Swiss civil war, and halved my audience. Not only will a Swiss question never 'come up' in an examination but even a civil war, if it happened in Switzerland, cannot be interesting.

Plate 1 Poster for the Exposition nationale suisse, 1914

Part of this is sheer prejudice, and not new either. In 1797 the exiled French aristocrat Chateaubriand observed bitterly: 'Neutral in the grand revolutions of the states which surround them, they enrich themselves by the misfortunes of others and found a bank on human calamities.'[6] The following year French troops swept away the old Swiss Confederation and the Swiss revolution began. Chateaubriand should have waited a little. Like so many foreigners he was tempted to generalise because Switzerland sometimes seems changeless. How many of those who say flatly that nothing ever happens in Switzerland would recognise this picture of the country, taken from a letter of Prince Metternich, the Austrian Chancellor, in 1845?

Switzerland presents the most perfect image of a state in the process of social disintegration . . . Switzerland stands alone today in Europe as a republic and serves troublemakers of every sort as a free haven. Instead of improving its situation by appropriate means, the Confederation staggers from evils into upheavals and represents for itself and for its neighbours an inexhaustible spring of unrest and disturbance.[7]

Another reason why Switzerland is unknown abroad is that it is hard to know. Centuries of tourism have left a mark. The Swiss simply do not reveal themselves easily to foreigners. An alien can live in some Swiss cities for years and never be invited to a Swiss home. Geneva is notorious for this but not unique. There are barriers everywhere to easy contact. It is also hard to know intellectually. There are so many puzzles and difficulties. Take the problem of frontiers. How does an artificial line drawn through a continuous stretch of countryside or marked on a bridge make everything change: table silver, foods, smells, customs, appearance of the buildings and so on? For the frontier watcher, Switzerland is a paradise. Cross the language border in Canton Fribourg (this is one not even marked by an outward sign) on the road from Bern to the city of Fribourg, and the streets become dirtier, and the window boxes of flowers less frequent. It is Francophone territory. Why are French-speaking communities less neat than German-speaking ones? Travel the road from Biel–Bienne to Porrentruy (all French-speaking) and watch the 'Jura libre' slogans painted on walls appear and disappear as the car passes from Catholic to Protestant community and back again. How can one make sense of the invisible barriers which seem to divide otherwise identical settlements? The

Plate 2 The ski resort of Sörenberg

answers to such questions are extremely difficult to devise; it is not always clear what the question is. Understanding Switzerland is so hard that few ever try.

There are modest satisfactions for those who do, and I hope that you will end up sharing my delight in the variety and exuberance of Swiss life, as I try to sketch it for you. There are also some grander rewards for anybody who takes the case of Switzerland seriously, as Dr Johnson pointed out:

Let those who despise the capacity of the Swiss, tell us by what wonderful policy or by what happy conciliation of interests, it is brought to pass, that in a body made up of different communities and different religions, there should be no civil commotions, though the people are so warlike, that to nominate and raise an army is the same.[8]

CHAPTER 2

History

Switzerland has no natural frontiers. The mountains and valleys of the Alps continue to the east and west into what is now Austria and France as they do on the southern slopes into what is now Italy. That the Bregaglia and the valley of Poschiavo are Swiss, while the Valtellina or the county of Bormio are Italian, can only be understood historically. Every Swiss frontier represents an historic act or set of events. Vorarlberg is Austrian because the Great Powers in 1919 refused to accept a plebiscite of its people for union with Switzerland. Geneva's borders on Lac Léman were settled by the Vienna Congress. Canton Ticino was conquered by Uri and later by other Swiss cantons. Constance, the 'natural' capital of the Thurgau, is German, partly because the Swiss Diet lacked the nerve in 1510 to accept another city-state into the Federation for fear of upsetting the urban–rural balance. Canton Schaffhausen contains one parcel of 41 hectares in its midst which is, in fact, German territory, and has three substantial enclaves, which cannot be reached without passing through German territory. Nor is the picture more coherent within Switzerland. Boundaries between cantons wander irregularly and unexpectedly over the landscape. Bits and pieces of Canton Solothurn lie embedded in Canton Bern, two of which, Kleinlützel and Mariastein, have borders with France as well. In Kleinlützel when people go shopping in one of the neighbouring larger towns, they tend to say 'we're going up to Switzerland'. Campione d'Italia on the eastern shore of Lago di Lugano is a chip of Italy, precisely 2.1 kilometres long and just over 1 kilometre deep at its widest point. The territory, much of which is actually lake surface, is entirely surrounded by the Swiss Canton Ticino. The complex overlapping of political authority, the jagged nonsense of frontiers and boundaries, the bits and pieces of territory lying about the map, resemble a jigsaw puzzle constructed

8

by a whimsical providence. Part of the key to the puzzle is what did not happen in Switzerland, rather than what did. The Swiss escaped the full consequences of three characteristic European trends: the trend toward rational centralisation, the growth of nationalism and the violence of religious conflict. Let us look at each in turn.

The French and their fellow travellers tried to make sense of Switzerland in the period between 1798 and 1802. During those years in Switzerland and other parts of Europe, the French installed enlightened, rational, benevolent, centralised, puppet governments. The Helvetic Republic, as the Swiss version was called, introduced the latest achievements of the French Revolution: equality before the law, uniformity of weights and measures, and a uniform code of justice. It liberated large tracts of subject territory in Ticino, Vaud, Aargau and Thurgau and raised former subjects to the dignity of citizens. The French and their supporters intended to put an end to the fantastic array of tiny republics, prince–bishoprics, princely abbeys, counties, free cities, sovereign cloisters and monasteries, free valleys, overlapping jurisdictions, guilds, oligarchies and city aristocracies. On 12 April 1798, Switzerland received a new, modern constitution. Article 1 declared it to be 'a unitary and indivisible Republic. There are no longer any borders between cantons and formerly subject territories nor between cantons.'[1]

The Swiss themselves had other ideas. At the time that unity was being proclaimed, the formerly subject communities of the old Confederation were asserting their diversity. In the area of the modern Canton St Gallen alone, eight independent republics had sprung up ranging in size from the Toggenburg valley with 50,000 citizens to the tiny republic of Sax with 1,000.[2] The mountain cantons rejected the Helvetic Republic emphatically. Napoleon needed stability along the approaches to the great Alpine passes, and he saw the armed resistance of the Swiss as a military nuisance. The Helvetic Republic existed on paper; the reality was chaos. In 1802 he summoned the representatives of the cantons and the Helvetic Senate to Paris and, speaking to them as a man 'born in a land of mountains who understands how mountain people think', he charged them to work out a new constitution.[3]

These deliberations resulted in what was called the Act of Mediation of 19 February 1803, which effectively restored political sovereignty to the old cantons under a loose, federal constitution.

Napoleon, who had been much impressed by the *Landsgemeinden*, the popular assemblies of the mountain cantons, believed them to be the characteristic Swiss institution and insisted that they be restored. The *Landsgemeinden* were conservative but democratic, though not in the modern sense. Rousseau's 'general will' was not quite what emerged from the deliberations of the *Landsgemeinden* where *Praktizieren und Trölen* (electoral bribery and corruption) were the rule, and where the *Hintersässen* (residents who lacked full civic rights) had no vote at all but, if that was the system the mountaineers wanted, Napoleon was prepared to return it to them, together with traditional Swiss federalism. The *Mediationsverfassung*, the constitution which he proposed, elevated many of the previously subject or allied (*zugewandte*) territories to full cantonal equality, and St Gallen, Graubünden, Aargau, Thurgau, Ticino and the Vaud took their places as full members of a federal union of nineteen cantons. Neuchâtel, which together with the prince–bishopric of Basel and the princely abbey of St Gallen had been one of the *zugewandte Monarchien* (allied monarchies) of the old Confederation, was not returned to it and, indeed, after the battle of Jena in 1806, Napoleon deposed the King of Prussia as Count of Neuchâtel-Valangin altogether. Geneva and the republic of Valais were annexed to France. Napoleon's intervention had paradoxical consequences. Elsewhere in Europe French armies swept aside petty sovereignties and abolished the lingering traces of 'feudalism'. In Switzerland they were preserved. Why were Swiss institutions tougher than those elsewhere in resisting French reforms?

Why was Switzerland not destroyed by another, more violent, child of the French Revolution, nationalism? Take the case of the Italian-speaking Canton Ticino, whose links to the Swiss began in 1478 when the German-speaking canton of Uri, the Gotthard Pass canton, annexed the Valle Leventina on the other side of the pass. The move brought both slopes approaching the Gotthard under one political authority and provided a base for further military expansion. Together with Schwyz and Nidwalden, the Urner extended their control during the following thirty years into the Riviera, Val Blenio and the city of Bellinzona, which remained under a tri-dominium of the three cantons until 1798. The rest of what is today Ticino, the cities of Lugano, Locarno, and the valleys around them, became joint property of twelve of the thirteen

Plate 3 St Gotthard's Pass, 1801

cantons of the old Confederation. (Appenzell got nothing because, by 1513 when it joined the Confederation, all these territories had been conquered.)

For more than 250 years these Italian-speaking communities were subject to alien rule by ignorant, corrupt, German-speaking bailiffs. Karl Viktor von Bonstetten, a Bern patrician, who made an official inspection of the areas of Ticino ruled by the twelve cantons in 1795–6, was appalled by a regime which seemed to him to be 'organised ideally for evil, where the good is impossible. If a common meadow or a common field will be badly tended, how much more a commonly held, subject territory.'[4] It is hardly surprising that many Ticinese, organised into groups called *i Patriotti*, welcomed the French intervention which put an end to centuries of misrule. Liberty, the rights of man and the citizen, the liberation of their ethnic identity as Italian-speakers, all seemed to lie in union with the new Napoleonic Cisalpine Republic, an Italian-speaking sister of the Helvetic. On 15 February 1798, the Patriots attempted a *coup d'état* and proclaimed the union of Ticino and the Cisalpine Republic. A huge and surprisingly unfriendly crowd

gathered in the Piazza Grande in Lugano. The insurgents who had
seized the representatives of Unterwalden as hostages, in the face
of the hostility of the crowd, were forced to release them. In
exchange for a promise of free passage out of Lugano, the Patriots
withdrew in confusion. That evening two lawyers from Ponte Tresa,
Annibale Pellegrini and Angelo Stoppani, led a group of armed men
to the representatives from Unterwalden whose presence had
forced the hands of the Patriots and demanded 'Swiss Liberty': 'We
demand our sacred rights; we desire Swiss liberty; finally, after
centuries of subjection, we are mature enough to govern ourselves.'
The delegates from Unterwalden announced that they would
support the request and left Lugano. In a delirium of popular
celebration, the people planted a liberty tree with a William Tell
hat on it and proclaimed themselves 'Liberi e Svizzeri'. During the
next few days all the other subject territories in the area followed
the Lugano example and declared themselves 'Free and Swiss'.[5]

Why were former subjects so loyal to former masters? Against the
powerful trends toward unified national communities why was
Switzerland able to remain a multilingual exception? Throughout
the nineteenth century, as passions stirred during the heroic days
of Italian nationalism, the Ticinese remained overwhelmingly loyal
to the Confederation. How 'unnatural' this was may be seen in the
evidence of two very different sorts of witnesses. The first of these,
the greatest Swiss historian of his time, Jacob Burckhardt, offers us
a vivid glimpse into the mind of a cultivated nineteenth-century
observer. In a letter to a friend, written in 1845, Burckhardt argued:

Among better educated, thinking, German-speaking Swiss, if only quietly
for the moment, the feeling of belonging to Germany, of our inner,
original unity, is spreading as they are less and less able to convince
themselves sincerely of the existence of Swiss nationality. They consider
themselves lucky that no dialect raised to the dignity of a written language
separates them from Germany as the Dutch are . . . Are we really one
nation with the Genevese or Ticinese as is repeatedly asserted?[6]

Very similar sentiments were expressed by Teresina Bontempi,
the fiercely irredentist editor of *L'Àdula*, the leading Italianising
journal in Ticino, on the eve of the first world war. In a leader
entitled 'Una Sintesi' of 18 April 1914, Miss Bontempi wrote: 'We
are Italians by soil and by soul, even if from the one we are divided
by a customs barrier and from the other by the blindness which it
creates.'[7]

Plate 4 Map of Canton Ticino, 1812

Nationalism was not the only force which might have torn Switzerland apart. Religious conflict was another. The Confederation has often seemed a compact with the devil. Writing in 1525 Ulrich Zwingli, the great Protestant reformer, had no doubt of it: 'I prefer a league united by faith to one in which the members putrefy. Alliances are more fruitful when faith makes them lasting than those into which treaties force us.'[8] Religious warfare divided the Swiss again and again between the sixteenth and the nineteenth centuries, and religious divisions inflamed the Jura crisis in the 1970s. It was only in 1973 that the paragraph of the Swiss constitution banning the Jesuits from the Confederation was finally annulled by the voters. To the political, ethnic and religious divisions of the past, the twentieth century added class conflict, and there was a moment in 1918, during the General Strike, when that too threatened the unity of the state and of society.

Why has Switzerland survived these threats to the unity of the Confederation? Some observers, struck by all the exceptions to the rules, have been tempted to see Switzerland as simply *sui generis*, as if the general trends of European development had no purchase there, but that is too easy. The Swiss have been affected by all the great events of history. Admittedly, for four hundred years they have been a neutral state in a continent more or less continuously at war, but that neutrality itself raises the problem of Swiss uniqueness in another form. The neutrality of the Swiss suited most of the European powers most of the time, but it has not always suited the Swiss. Zwingli's view is at least as common in Swiss history as the cautious circumspection of officials. Neutrality would have collapsed had there been no internal cohesion, no collective will to survive specifically as Swiss. The difficulty lies in defining what is specifically Swiss and what belongs to more general European currents and movements. As Perry Anderson points out in his study of feudalism, the Swiss cantonal movement was 'in many respects a *sui generis* historical experience' – in many but not in all.[9] The struggle of peasantries against feudal magnates was general throughout Europe; the specifically Swiss question is how and why the peasants won.

The answer to that question today looks very different from the one which would have been given fifty years ago. Swiss historians such as Jean-François Bergier, Guy P. Marchal, Werner Meyer and Hans-Conrad Peyer have shaken the established myths of Swiss history and the accompanying assumptions of Swiss uniqueness. In Bergier's book *Guillaume Tell*, the most he will concede to the great founder of Swiss liberty is that 'his personage has too natural and too evident a place in the stories to have been invented after the event'.[10] Whereas Bergier allows that a Swiss confederate entity may have been in some sense 'founded', Werner Meyer will not accept even that. In his 'Twelve Theses on the Emergence of the Helvetic Confederation' he asserts that 'the Swiss Confederation was not founded but grew gradually' and that 'neither in 1291 nor at any other time was there a resistance movement in central Switzerland against the Habsburgs. As a result neither the Rütli oath nor the storming of the fortress can have taken place.'[11] Hans-Conrad Peyer argued in a commemorative article in 1991 entitled 'Was the Swiss Confederation Founded?' that, while the alliance of 1291 among the central valley communities was certainly not 'unique', it acted as a kind of 'precursor' of subsequent Swiss sovereignty.[12]

The controversy which such views have aroused can be imagined. Historians who question the myths of Swiss history have been attacked as 'revisionists', 'left-wing', or as 'a kind of mysterious fifth column' in the country.[13] Both the revisionism and the violent reaction to it express that crisis of Swiss identity which has gradually seeped into public consciousness in the last twenty years. The denial of William Tell and questioning the significance of the 'foundation' of Switzerland in 1291 coincided with the 700th anniversary celebrations in 1991 that were themselves not free of controversy. Nothing solid apparently remains. Even the past has been taken from beneath the institutions of modern Switzerland. Without a proud past, anxious critics seem to say, can Switzerland have a future? As in all historical debates the present sets the agenda; the past provides the stuff for debate.

The traditional mythology of the Swiss Confederation owes a great deal to Schiller's drama *Wilhelm Tell*, first performed in Weimar in March 1804. Schiller set himself

an extremely high poetic task; an entirely local, limited folk in a remote age and – this is the main thing – an entirely local and, indeed, almost individual and unique phenomenon must be revealed to have the character of the highest necessity and truth.[14]

The great philosopher Hegel, who saw the play on the first night, overheard some Swiss grumbling because the characters 'weren't authentic Swiss',[15] but it was not long before Schiller's images and verses became part of Switzerland's own self-representation. Switzerland's history as an expression of Schiller's 'highest necessity and truth' was flattering. Schiller had also managed to turn what might have been a dangerous act of peasant insubordination into a safe, conservative restoration of an older order, which was convenient. Images of heroism and Alpine liberty played an iconographic role in the struggle to unify Switzerland in the nineteenth century and to defend it against fascism in the twentieth.

At the end of the twentieth century heroic acts by single, male figures have lost their fascination. For us history consists of long, often anonymous, processes in which the wills of individuals get bent by circumstances into unexpected consequences. Our explanations must look like scientific models, have logical structures and be susceptible to refutation. For our generation the past is a lost reality, only imperfectly recaptured by our imaginations, not a series of deeds by great men.

It seems obvious to me that the revisionists must be 'right'. Switzerland exists today because it grew out of a complex set of historic circumstances. If Switzerland became a 'special case' in European history, it was not because the Swiss were more virtuous or heroic in the thirteenth century than they are today nor because the laws of history stopped functioning in the Alps. Every crisis in Europe from the fall of the Roman Empire to the enlargement of the European Union has affected the area we know now as Switzerland. The unique elements in Swiss history make up small but in the end decisive catalytic factors in the complex chemistry of historical growth. The Swiss have preserved certain features of premodern Europe no longer found elsewhere. These features will not disappear if the myth of William Tell is dismantled. Swiss identity neither depends on the myths created in the late eighteenth century nor will it disintegrate under the hammers and chisels of revisionists in the late twentieth. The revisionist controversy tells us about the crisis in Swiss self-awareness but it cannot alter those features which make Switzerland 'Swiss'. Switzerland undoubtedly exists today and is unique in Europe. If it was not 'founded' in an heroic act, how did it develop?

No important myths are ever entirely without real content. The Alps really were important in early Swiss history. By the twelfth century the evidence suggests the existence of a distinctive 'Alpine society' characterised by what Guy Marchal calls 'the herdsman culture'. These herdsmen of the Alpine slopes lived an archaic, independent, quasi-aristocratic form of life. They were free of feudal servitudes and, as a sign of their liberty, these mountain peasants bore arms and demanded 'honour' even from nobles. This ancient pastoral world continued to use words and phrases bequeathed to them from the Roman occupation and to practise ancient forms of pasturage.[16] Even today the *Trieb*, when the herdsmen drive their cattle up to high pasturages in late May, has ceremonial character, although the long lines of frustrated motorists may not fully appreciate the traditions. The drovers wear traditional *Kuhier* short jackets and the women wear floral gowns. Their medieval clan structures had little to do with our images of democratic forms but these peasants were 'free' and not all that different from the smaller nobility of the uplands in their way of life. A second, characteristic feature of 'Alpine society' was its communalism, the extensive network of communes and valley corporations, which regulated economic activity and social life. It used to be thought that Swiss communalism was a survival of primitive Germanic tribal custom. Hans-Conrad Peyer argues instead that the settlement of the high Alpine valleys was part of the dynamic expansion of the feudal economy in the twelfth and thirteenth centuries, a 'movement almost never entirely spontaneous nor without specific leadership'.[17] Physical circumstances undoubtedly combined to promote the formation of communal modes of enterprise. As Professor Adolf Gasser suggests, conditions in the Alpine valleys dictated a social organisation of a special kind.[18] The population organised itself naturally into extended valley communes and these rapidly turned into unified, enclosed cooperatives. Raising cattle implied the maintenance of common pastures, the *Allmenden*, common marketing of animal and dairy products, common activity on the important passes and roads, the regulation of mercenary service and the purchase of weapons.

In the case of roads, this still goes on today; many extremely well travelled roads, such as that from Entlebuch in Canton Luzern over the Glaubenberg Pass to Sarnen in Canton Obwalden, are maintained by compulsory payments to a road cooperative by all the property owners who benefit from it.

Alpine conditions preserved the non-hierarchical, undivided,

that is, non-feudal valley communities, even where, as was
frequently the case, the valley was subject to noble or clerical
feudal lords. The case of the prince–abbot of St Gallen is characteristic of the kind of 'social contract' which powerful feudal princes
observed in dealing with their subject territories. In his study of
the legal codes of the abbey, Walter Müller found that all of them,
even those made during the height of absolutist practice in the
eighteenth century, give some lip service to the 'fiction of a mutual
agreement'.[19] The idea of a contract between free but not equal
entities is, of course, a general characteristic of feudalism: the
nature of the contracting parties is the peculiarly Swiss feature of
it.

The establishment of valley communities, the *Talgenossenschaften*,
was accelerated by rapid improvements in trade, commerce and
economic specialisation during the twelfth and thirteenth centuries. Between 1100 and 1300 grain prices increased by 300% and
trading communities sprang up to deal with the new traffic.[20]
Switzerland became important for the first time as the number of
people crossing the Alps increased. Some time during the early
years of the thirteenth century the way along the spectacular
Schöllenen gorge, the key to the Gotthard Pass, was opened and
the city of Luzern, established where the waters flow out of the
Vierwaldstättersee into the River Reuss, grew astonishingly.
Between its foundation in the late twelfth century and the middle
of the next century, Luzern grew to very nearly its nineteenth-
century size.[21] Since Switzerland has twenty-two major and thirty-
one minor passes, the general movement of trade produced a wave
of urban foundations, a struggle among the various existing cities,
their feudal overlords and the valley communities for control of
customs, tolls and carrying trade along the routes. As Anderson
remarks, the 'penetration of the countryside by commodity
exchange had weakened customary relationships'.[22] It had also
produced economic specialisation. The Alpine communities concentrated increasingly on cattle and dairy products. Cereal
production declined in the mountain cantons, except in bad years,
to such an extent that by the early sixteenth century Canton
Schwyz had to send to Zürich for help in a particularly bad year
because they no longer had any corn seeds ('mit samen nit
verfasst').[23] The process of economic differentiation had its
counterpart in a political and social differentiation, very much

accelerated by the great struggle between the Hohenstaufen Emperors and the Popes. Partisans of each protagonist often fought out local vendettas in the name of grander causes, and the fluctuating fortunes of the Emperors enabled agile families, especially in the valley communities, to bargain for 'freedoms' in exchange for allegiance. The interregnum caused by the death of the last Hohenstaufen in 1250, the 'schreckliche, kaiserlose Zeit', added to the political turbulence as the swarm of small lords, petty city-republics and valley communities scurried to find protectors among the remaining great lords. Even powerful, prosperous cities like Bern felt the winds of change and, together with the Free Hasli valley and the imperial city of Murten, begged Peter of Savoy in 1255 to become their protector. Yet another element in the background was the extinction of so many of the important feudal families in the area in rapid succession, the Lenzburg in 1173, the Zähringer in 1218, and the Kyburg in 1264.

The emergence of Rudolf of Habsburg in 1273 as the new King of Germany changed the picture sharply. The Habsburgs were substantial local lords in their own right, and the combination of royal and local authority made Rudolf look dangerously strong. One of the most important of the Alpine valley communities, Uri, had taken advantage of its strategic position as the keeper of the keys to the Gotthard Pass and by exploiting the desperate financial circumstances of the last Hohenstaufen Emperor, Frederick II, managed to purchase back in 1231 the overlordship of their valley which had been pawned. The valley became *reichsfrei*, that is, subject to no lord save the Emperor. The neighbouring community, Schwyz, obtained a similar charter of freedom in 1240, but the legality of this, unlike that of Uri, was not unchallenged. Rudolf of Habsburg was apparently prepared to confirm the freedom of Uri but not that of Schwyz. The *Talgenossenschaften* had by now become well established communities of largely free peasants under the direction of several powerful families (the Stauffacher and Ab Yberg in Schwyz, the Attinghusen, Meier von Silenen and von Moos in Uri, the Hunwil and Wattersburg in Obwalden and the Wolfenschiessen in Nidwalden).[24] The administration of justice under feudalism was their most important civic activity. As Perry Anderson points out, since feudalism had neither articulated legislative nor executive functions, justice came close to being 'the ordinary name of power'.[25] The *Ammann*, the valley head and generally one of the oligarchs, judged in the name of the Emperor, whose direct subject the community claimed to be. As the increasingly self-conscious valley communities extended their claims to feudal sovereignty over the ecclesiastical institutions within their territories, armed clashes occurred (between Uri and the monastery at Engelberg in 1275 and a running feud between Schwyz and the cloister at Einsiedeln). Jean-François Bergier believes that the death of Rudolph of Habsburg in 1291 and the fear of another dreadful interregnum may have led the oligarchs of the valley communities to unite. 'As to possible sites', he writes, 'we have, alas, to discard the too romantic meadow of Rütli'.[26] A sober Latin parchment could hardly have been composed in a meadow. The actual text survives, dated formally 'primo incipiente mense augusto'. It contains a variety of provisions; among the most famous are the following assertions:

> In view of the evil times the men of the valley of Uri, the *Landsgemeinde* of Schwyz and the community of the lower valley of Unterwalden, in order to preserve themselves and their possessions . . . in common council have with one voice sworn, agreed and determined that in the above named valleys we shall accept no judge nor recognise him in any way if he exercise his office for any reward or for money or if he is not one of our own and an inhabitant of the valleys.[27]

This particular clause, which internal evidence (especially the use of the first person plural) suggests was probably added later, is the one feature which distinguishes the eternal alliance of 1291 from a variety of similar leagues and treaties (often very short-lived in spite of the use of the term 'eternal' or 'perpetual') which can be identified in the era. Unquestionably the idea of a union to which the individual members of a collective community adhered in their own persons reflected the special social context of the *Talgenossenschaft*. The valley dwellers, rugged, independent mountain peasants and shepherds, possessed vigorous and warlike customs. They were used to sharing in public discussions and they conferred a special force of will to the league of 1291, neatly, if untranslatably expressed in the name they gave themselves: *Eidgenossen*, 'comrades (with a strong communal overtone – a cooperative is a *Genossenschaft*) of the oath'. *Eidgenossenschaft* is still the Swiss German expression for the federal union and comes close to being a synonym for 'Swiss' in official usage.

The event which took place 'incipiente mense augusto' in 1291 is hard to assess. As Walter Ullmann pointed out, concepts of sovereignty were still fluid in the thirteenth century; the transition from personal to abstract sovereignty was not yet complete.[28] Hence, while the actual parchment of the 1291 document, the *Bundesbrief*, survives, its precise historical significance to contemporaries must remain uncertain. The *Eidgenossen* of 1291 were not ideal types. They were something much more interesting – armed, free (or mostly so) peasants who had embarked on an alliance which they regarded as more than ordinarily solemn. Their own characteristics and the complex currents of historical development were to give that act permanent meaning. What they were doing was not uncommon; that it lasted was.

As so often in subsequent history, the key to the survival of the little league of mountain valleys has to be sought in general features of the era, and their interaction with Swiss realities. The first and most obvious point is the importance of geography, and its relationship to the general state of military technology. An example can be seen in the history of medieval Raetia, today's Canton Graubünden. Medieval Raetia, the eastern neighbour of medieval Helvetia, was a loose association of three leagues of equally loosely allied sovereign valley communities. In his history of Raetia, Benjamin Barber notes that the canton contains 150 distinct valleys in an area of 7,113 square km and that 188 of its 221 communes lie above the 700 metre line. In the conditions of medieval or early modern warfare, Raetia was simply impossible to control: 'To control Raetia would mean to control through military occupation every valley and village and village "fraction" in the land. An army occupying Chur no more controls Graubünden than does one in Milan or Vienna.'[29]

A second and fascinating element is the physical prowess of the mountaineers. Evidence is hard to get, but it would appear that a diet unusually high in protein, a well-established system of warlike sports and games and the nature of his work made the Alpine peasant a formidable opponent in warfare.[30] Certainly the excellence of Swiss soldiery accounts for a great deal of the unique course of the subsequent events. The medieval Swiss soldiery used spears, axes, hammers and especially the halberd, a weapon consisting of an axe-blade balanced by a pick with an elongated pike-head fixed at the end of a five- or six-foot staff. This nasty object, which was the Swiss weapon *par excellence*, had the advantage that in skilled hands it could deal a mortal, cleaving blow on a mounted, armoured opponent. During the Burgundian wars Swiss infantry added the *Langspiessen* or long pikes to their armoury and advanced in rows, the so-called *carré suisse*, with sticks pointed at the opponents. The long pikes broke the enemy line of battle and the halberdiers chopped through the armour of the disorganised enemy. Swiss cohorts won victory after victory on their own soil during the fourteenth century, especially at Morgarten in 1315 and in the Sempach War of 1386, the war in Oberwallis in the 1380s and the Appenzell War of the first decades of the fifteenth century.[31]

The special significance of the military victories of the Swiss can be better appreciated if they are seen against the background of the economic and social crisis of the century. Almost at the same time as the Swiss *Eidgenossen* were winning their first victories, the supply of silver from Bohemian, German and French mines began to dry up as the technical constraints of medieval mining made deeper shafts impossible. The shortage of currency led to frequent debasements and rapid price rises. The extension of area under cultivation to less good soils produced lower yields and in the middle of the century, to complete the calamity, the Black Death ravaged the European population.[32] Under these circumstances, it is not surprising that in the 1350s and 1360s waves of peasant revolt swept Europe of which the *grande Jacquerie* of 1358 was the most dramatic. Switzerland did not escape the troubles, but in a paradoxical way they strengthened the tendency for Swiss development to deviate from the European norms. Revolts in the *Landsgemeinde* cantons attacked the powers of the prominent families and extended the communal features of the *Talgenossenschaft* at the expense of the oligarchical. In the lowlands, the wave of urban unrest of the 1330s strengthened the guild movement and widened the circle of those able to participate in civic affairs. In 1336 the assembly of Luzern was enlarged to become a 'Council of 300'. In 1353 the city of St Gallen introduced full guild participation in the Large and Small Councils. In the Small Council, the masters and vice-masters of the six guilds held twelve of the twenty-four seats, though, in practice, the guilds controlled all the seats, since nine of the remaining twelve were elected by the Large Council, whose complicated procedures ensured that some eighty of the ninety members belonged to one of the guilds.[33] The system eventually turned into a labyrinth of ever smaller oligarchical circles, but in the fourteenth century the victory of the guilds provided a strong democratic impetus, for within guild chapters themselves a communal expression of opinion could take place not unlike that of the *Landsgemeinde* in the countryside. The Swiss towns could meet the mountain communities on terms of political equality.

During the middle of the fourteenth century, leagues with over-lapping membership gradually formed between the principal free mountain valleys and urban communities, so that by 1353 the three Forest Cantons had been joined by Luzern (1332), Zürich (1351), Glarus (1352), Zug (1352) and Bern (1353) to form a union of 'eight places'. In neighbouring Raetia by a similar process during the 1370s the League of the House of God (*Gotteshausbund*) united the city of Chur, the surrounding villages, the Domleschg, Schams, Poschiavo and Müstair valleys.[34] North of the Rhine similar leagues and alliances emerged, especially the League of the Swabian cities of 1331; the only difference was that the Swiss and Raetian leagues survived and the German did not.

The spread of the Helvetic and Raetian leagues owed a lot to aristocratic bankruptcy. As the economic crisis deepened, small feudal lords collapsed under their debts and frequently pawned their feudal rights, dues or tolls. The still prosperous cities of the Swiss Confederation took the chance to buy up pawned territories, as in the case of Bern's purchase of a mortgage held by the impoverished lords of Weissenburg in 1334. This particular mortgage covered the Hasli valley, an Imperial Free Valley, in theory the equal of *reichsfrei* Uri or Schwyz. By buying the *Reichspfandschaft* over the Hasli, the city of Bern came into all the privileges formerly owed directly to the Emperor, as well as substantial feudal dues and payments. Characteristically, Bern confirmed the traditional 'freedoms' of the Hasli valley dwellers, reserving for itself the right to name the *Ammann* and to demand a military levy.[35] These relationships remained unaltered until 1798. In July 1393 the eight cantons and the city of Solothurn concluded an agreement to cooperate and share spoils called the *Sempacher-brief*,[36] and in the following year the second of the three leagues of Raetia, the so-called Grey League or *Grauer Bund* (from which modern Graubünden takes its name) was founded. What these leagues and associations have in common is not so much their origins as their success against foes more numerous and reputedly stronger. At the same time that the Swiss communal forces were defeating the feudal nobility at Sempach, Näfels and Visp, the nobility of south Germany and the Rhineland won decisive victories over the cities at Doffingen and Alzey in 1388. The hitherto seamless Upper German world began to divide. North of the Rhine the free city and free peasantry fell ever more firmly into the control of the larger princely and aristocratic authorities; south of the river a complicated network of autonomous, allied communities developed. As Bernhard Stettler writes, 'the traditional framework of order was called into question without a new one replacing it at once'.[37]

During the fifteenth century Switzerland began to swell to the proportions of a European great power. Her military superiority was marked. Although the Confederation could afford to expand abroad, it continued to carry on civil wars at home. In 1436 and 1450 the city-state of Zürich, under the shifting influences of its commercial and artisan oligarchies, fought bitter battles against its neighbours, mainly for control of valuable territories and trade. The economic foundations of Swiss power expanded very rapidly. Figures are difficult to come by for the Middle Ages, but in Fribourg surviving notarised contracts of sale show a sharp recovery of trade after the fourteenth-century depression. The growing point of the Swiss economy was cloth, wool and linen. By 1413 the average annual sale of Fribourg cloth pieces had reached 8,000; it exceeded 10,000 by the 1420s and achieved a level of 12,500 in the 1430s.[38] The causes of the growth of the cloth industry in Swiss cities are not simple to explain. Severe control of the quality would appear to have played a crucial part. The famous 'G' or *Mal* on every piece of St Gallen linen is the first example of the 'made in Switzerland' image. Another element must have been the high degree of urbanisation itself. The city of St Gallen was a geographical oddity. In its centre, surrounded by a wall four feet thick and thirty feet high, stood the sovereign abbey of St Gallen, very like the modern Vatican City. Outside the walls of the city the prince–abbot ruled the traditional *Landschaft*, the hereditary lands of the abbey. The city, which was a separate republic entirely independent of the abbey, had a plot of land about two kilometres square as its entire territory outside the walls. Its seven or eight thousand inhabitants had no other occupations than commerce, artisan production and marketing.[39] This unusually marked disproportion between economic and political power (one of the striking features of Swiss economic life today, which I shall examine in a later chapter) would appear to have funnelled the entire civic energy into dominating markets not lands. By the end of the fifteenth century, an enormous trading network was carrying St Gallen linen to all parts of Europe. In Zürich it was silk which played the role of linen. In all the Swiss cities the merchants, organised in large, complex joint stock companies, became very rich, often at the expense of urban artisans and craftsmen and the peasants in the surrounding country districts who frequently did much of the actual spinning and weaving. Niklaus von Diesbach, who died in 1436, left 70,000 gulden and was known as the richest man in Bern. He had begun as an artisan, risen to power as a merchant and died a *Twingherr*, a quasi-federal landowner.[40] Swiss wealth and commerce benefited from the great importance of through traffic, and not only north–south. The east–west route, with its unusually favourable chain of easily navigable waterways, linked the Habsburg domains through the flourishing mercantile community of Geneva on Lac Léman to western Europe.

South of the Alps trade expanded rapidly into the Lombard plain and brought Swiss traders into constant, not always harmonious, relations with the wealthy city and duchy of Milan. The Swiss cantons invaded the territories of the Dukes of Milan with regularity and the fairs at Bellinzona and Chiasso were often marked by violence. Complaints about corruption and arbitrary impositions forced the Swiss representative to intervene. In effect, trade sucked the Swiss cantons into conflict with the Milanese to protect the rights and duty-free privileges of merchants under their aegis. In 1422, 1426, 1441 and 1467 agreements were made on the rights of Swiss merchants and the powers of Milanese courts to try violations. Just as regularly the agreements broke down, leaving the Swiss further engaged in Italian affairs.[41]

The gradual movement to reform and strengthen the institutions of the Holy Roman Empire encouraged sovereigns to try to tighten their hold on their subjects. In Neuchâtel, the counts tried to reduce the rights and privileges of their subjects by citing the laws of the Holy Roman Empire against what their subjects insisted were their 'libertés traditionnelles'. Whereas the count rested his claim on imperial law, the citizenry based theirs on the more ancient 'plaid de mai', an annual convocation which went back to the thirteenth century, at which the rights of the citizenry were annually proclaimed and accepted by the feudal authorities. As Maurice de Tribolet puts it, the citizenry had recourse to 'une conception plus archaïsante pour marquer l'origine régalienne de leurs franchises'.[42] This recourse to ancient liberties became part of the ideological battle which marked the unrest of early modern Switzerland, a fusion of ancient models and early modern social change.

The ancient and modern fused in the character of the Swiss Confederation itself. As Bernhard Stettler points out, a city-state like Zürich in the fourteenth and fifteenth centuries was itself a way-station between two worlds, growing steadily more different. To the north it belonged to the network of states and cities increasingly controlled by the Empire, by its princes and nobility, by prosperous imperial cities. This was the world of Cranach and Dürer, of Gutenberg and his press, of the chancellery, the office, the written word. To the Alpine south Zürich touched the world of peasant communities, not organised in states. There things went on in the archaic traditional way, without officials, regulated by the extended family, by informal arrangement among neighbours or communal corporations. Everything was discussed openly at political assemblies and hence nobody needed writing. The entire bureaucracy of Schwyz was a part-time scribe well into the fifteenth century.[43]

Yet these two worlds belonged to the same political confeder-ation, just as Germany and Greece both belong to the European Union today. Unity among such disparate communities was always fragile. It is hardly surprising that the legend of William Tell makes its appearance in the period. The first full account of the story in the famous *White Book of Sarnen* dates from 1474 and the first William Tell *Lieder* were composed during the last decades of the fifteenth century. It is also not chance that 1470 is the date of an equally remarkable document. Thüring Frickart's *Twingherrenstreit*, an eye-witness account of the social conflict between *Twingherren*, those who held traditional, feudal rights in the countryside around Bern, and the increasingly powerful and self-conscious urban authorities represented in the master butcher and Lord Mayor of Bern, Peter Kistler. The *Twingherren* demanded a return to the rights guaranteed in the 'alten Grechtigkeiten, Briefen und Siglen' (the old rights, letters and seals).[44] The language and tone of the Tell story, and that of Frickart's *Twingherrenstreit*, have a good

Plate 5 The west portal of the Minster, Bern

deal in common. The image of Tell rapidly came to stand for the Swissness of things, for those 'old laws, rights and seals', which the new ruling classes of the fifteenth and sixteenth centuries threatened. Eventually, it came to define the official Swiss attitude to their own past. The hardy mountaineer, who defies the Habsburgs and by his skill as a bowman thwarts their designs, who will not do obeisance to anybody, became for the Swiss and for others what the Confederation meant. The actual authenticity of the story is not the issue. The story of William Tell is not false, even if there never was a man of that name and he never shot an apple off his son's head. Its truth is the truth of a communal tradition by which the Swiss defined and made precise their public values. It was justification by history just as the protesting *Twingherren* of the 1470s, or the peasant revolutionaries of the 1650s and the citizens of Lugano of the 1790s, justified themselves historically. Swiss liberty became associated with William Tell and the faded symbolism lingers on today. Hence when revisionist historians in the 1980s and 1990s write William Tell out of their histories, they threaten an historic Swiss sense of self. They dissolve the bonds which tie disparate Swiss worlds together. For ultimately Switzerland is justified and sanctioned not, as in America, by an 'ism' like 'Americanism', but by its history. William Tell stands for a way of reading Swiss history which substitutes shared values for common identity.

Class conflict within Swiss communities had its roots in the sudden flood of new wealth. Much of it was simply booty seized from defeated enemies. The greatest haul was the huge collection of jewels, fine silks and money which the Swiss *soldateska* seized after they had defeated the Burgundians at the battles of Grandson, Morat and Nancy in 1476 and 1477. These victories, the most famous ever won by Swiss arms, were also historically the most important. Charles the Bold, one of the greatest feudal princes of the age, died at Nancy in 1477 and his territories passed to various heirs and disintegrated. In a sense, the Swiss indirectly helped to found the sixteenth-century French monarchy by eliminating its most dangerous rival.

The victories intoxicated the 'young men' of central Switzerland, as the documents call them, and they decided to use force to claim their spoils. In February 1477 they met, decided to act and hoisted a banner bearing a mace to show they meant business. Some 2,000 armed young men marched on the lowland cities which took fright and shut their gates. Illegal assemblies, so-called 'wilde Tagsatzungen', and autonomous soldiery frightened the authorities and led to conflict between urban and rural cantons as how to deal with the unrest. Legend has it that a saintly hermit Brother Klaus intervened to bring the warring brethren to sign a renewed oath of association known as the *Stanser Verkommnis* of 1481. As with William Tell, this event has also been 'stripped of its paintwork', as Peter Blickle puts it, and set into a wider European, less mythical context.[45] For our purposes it shows both the turbulence at the base of late medieval Swiss society and the capacity of very different communities to control it by common action.

Switzerland began the sixteenth century as one of the most formidable of European states. The temporary balance of power among Italian states after the Treaty of Lodi in 1451 created favourable conditions for Swiss expansion southward. Yet paradoxically, Swiss victories in the Burgundian Wars of the 1470s and the Swabian Wars of the 1490s undermined that late feudal Europe with its network of overlapping authority, which made Swiss greatness possible. The destruction of the great feudal house of Burgundy strengthened the French monarchy and it was that monarchy which invaded Italy in 1494. The decisive struggle for power in Italy began. As I said earlier in the chapter, the Swiss cantons had already become an Italian power by their conquests in the valley of the Ticino and on the shores of the lakes. Milan was a glittering prize only 60 kilometres away. The Swiss joined the Pope in coalitions against the French on the logical assumption that the weaker neighbour is always to be preferred to the stronger. They won spectacular victories. By 1512 Milan had become a Swiss protectorate and in June 1513 a Swiss army soundly defeated the French at Novara. This, the high point of Swiss power, proved also to be its end. Part of the subsequent collapse was military. In the 1490s, the *Landsknechtsorden* developed in Germany. *Landsknechte* were groups of foot-soldiers for hire, who used and mastered Swiss techniques. Unlike feudal knights, *Landsknechte* demanded to be paid in cash. The emergence of this new infantry and the expenses caused by innovations such as artillery priced the hire and fitting out of troops out of the small princely market. Only important princes with adequate sources of revenue could compete. The Swiss, whose strength had been diversity, now began to suffer from it. The thirteen cantons had different economic and international interests, and their only central institution was a Diet, the *Tagsatzung*, which was merely a formal assembly of ambassadors with no power to coerce its member states. Hence when the second round of the battle against the French began in 1515, the Swiss army fought without the support of the men of Bern, Fribourg, Solothurn and Biel. On 13 September 1515, Swiss troops suddenly burst from the gates of Milan to attack a surprised French army on the road to Marignano. A spectacular victory was just missed; the next day, the Swiss attack on prepared French positions was repulsed.

The defeat at the battle of Marignano was a startling event. The invincible Swiss had been defeated.[46] The Diet, when the news reached it, immediately ordered the assembly of another army, but by now it could no longer command the support of the western cantons and especially of Bern, by far the most powerful individual unit in the Confederation. Bern and the western cantons signed a separate treaty with France in November 1515, and in 1516 a Perpetual Peace was signed between France and the Swiss Confederation. The descent from great power to small neutral state after 1516 was sudden and is not easy to understand. Undoubtedly the scale of the defeat shocked the citizenry. Switzerland had been invincible and was now no longer. The cause of the defeat, internal disunity, was obvious; the remedy, to develop more powerful, central institutions, equally so, but none of the existing entities within the league, not even the powerful patrician republic of Bern, had the force to impose such a solution and none had the will. The internal equilibrium of the old Diet preserved the *status quo* but could not alter it. Moreover, from 1516 until 1792 the French were always ready with fat purses to persuade Swiss leaders of the wisdom of pursuing their wars under other people's banners. Solothurn became the residence of the French ambassadors and the strategic point from which French diplomacy operated to keep peace among the turbulent Swiss communities. The Protestant Reformation intruded only a few years after Marignano and divided the Swiss against each other in a new and more ominous way. Agreement between Catholic and Protestant cantons at the Diet was virtually impossible. If it had been hard to unite for gain, it was inconceivable for faith. Hence the Swiss Confederation sank into political torpor, gradually rotting away as an international force.

On 1 January 1519, Ulrich Zwingli, a thirty-five-year-old priest from the Toggenburg valley in eastern Switzerland, mounted the pulpit at the Grossmünster in Zürich to preach on the Gospel of St Matthew. For Zwingli the Word of God, not ecclesiastical tradition, was the sole religious authority, and with this revolutionary doctrine he attacked the entire apparatus of the medieval church and at the same time the degradation of standards in the Confederation. He condemned the sale of ecclesiastical office and also the sale of mercenary soldiers. Zwingli was an intensely political man. He rapidly gained a share of decision-making (never the control, as is sometimes argued)[47] in the city-state of Zürich. The reformed faith spread rapidly to towns like Basel, Schaffhausen and St Gallen but also into rural and mountainous areas like Glarus, Appenzell and Graubünden. The *Urschweiz*, the original Switzerland of the Forest Cantons, Luzern and Zug, remained Catholic, not least because they saw in the new faith merely a cloak for the old lust for expansion of Zürich, the cause of the fifteenth-century civil wars. As the Confederation began to disintegrate into religious camps, the old town–country fissure reopened, especially since after 1528 the Gracious Lords of Bern threw the patrician republic onto the Protestant side.

A new threat to the Confederation came from without. Not only did the two camps seek support among co-religionists outside the Confederation but both sides began to condemn as 'un-Christian' the policy of neutrality so painfully accepted after 1515. Zwingli urged the Confederation to grant asylum to the persecuted Protestants in 1524 and reacted furiously when the five central cantons not only refused but, in addition, banned the new faith in the *Gemeine Herrschaften*, the commonly administered territories. War broke out between Catholic and Protestant in 1529 and again in 1531. In the second of the two encounters, the Protestant forces were roundly defeated and Zwingli killed. In spite of the defeat the Reformation continued to make gains. In Geneva, independent but friendly to the Swiss Confederation, Calvin began his great work, transforming the city into the capital of a worldwide movement and its city administration into the 'new Jerusalem'. Aristocratic Neuchâtel became Protestant under Guillaume Farel; the southern valleys of the Bernese Jura and the Vaud joined the Reformed ranks. So throughout the Confederation communities shifted, split, regrouped and fought. Canton Appenzell split into a Protestant and a Catholic part, forming the basis of today's half-cantons. Solothurn and Fribourg remained Catholic, and the situation in the subject territories remained complicated.

On a much grander scale Europe armed for ultimate conflict. The revived Catholic church of the Counter-reformation, the new militancy of Calvinism, the grand struggles for empire among the European powers, the Dutch revolt, massacres of Huguenots in France, the emergence of England, all represented explosive matter which eventually burst out in a period of very nearly continuous warfare from 1600 to the mid-century. Central Europe was consumed. Germany, not for the last time, became a pile of rubble. No one knows for certain how much of her population died as a direct and indirect result of the war, but it may have been as high as a third of the whole.

The Swiss cantons found the fighting swirling around them. When the great Gustavus Adolphus of Sweden led his all-victorious Protestant army to the very borders of the Confederation, many Protestants yearned to join him. J. J. Breitinger, the head of the pro-Swedish faction in Zürich, condemned his fellow Swiss bitterly:

So do I condemn utterly our harmful and ridiculous temporising and damn the ugly, shameful and loathsome Monster of neutrality. May God spit out the lukewarm, that is, the neutralists who are neither warm nor cold seeing that the Lord Christ holds such for his enemies in bright clear words when he says that he who is not for him is against him.[48]

The lukewarm neutral is easy to attack. Religious passions were violent but, undoubtedly, and not for the last time, passion was assuaged by prosperity. Switzerland was an island of peace and an important food supply to a starving Europe. Even before the outbreak of war, the Venetian diplomat, Giovanni Battista Padavino, had observed: 'Travelling in Switzerland is very secure; one can travel the roads day or night without any danger and can halt in woods or mountains, and every class and family enjoys its own in profound peace and unbelievable security.'[49] Von Grimmelshausen described Switzerland in the war years as an earthly paradise which in comparison with other German lands seemed as strange as if he had been in China or Brazil. Three hundred years later William L. Shirer recorded in his *Berlin Diary* on 10 October 1939:

It was strange driving through Geneva town to see the blinding street-lights, the blazing store-windows, the full headlights on the cars – after six weeks in blacked-out Berlin. Strange and beautiful. In Basel this noon Demaree and I stuffed ourselves shamefully with food. We ordered a huge dish of butter just to look at it, and Russian eggs and an enormous steak and cheese and dessert and several litres of wine and then cognac and coffee – a feast! And no food cards to give in. All the way down in the train from Basel we felt good. The mountains, the chalets on the hillsides, even the sturdy Swiss looked like something out of paradise.[50]

That neutrality had its rewards was not lost on the Swiss either. Trade and living standards were never as good in the seventeenth century as they were during the Thirty Years War. The Swiss began to associate neutrality with profit, virtue and good sense. However they may have hated each other, they were better off living together as neutrals than dying apart as enemies. A natural feeling of superiority marked Swiss attitudes to the outside world. In a pious age it was easy to believe that God had willed them to prosper as a reward for their virtues. The attitude persisted and is not unknown today. In the midst of the first world war, the poet and novelist Carl Spitteler reminded his audience: 'Above all no superiority noises. No judgement!! That we as non-participants can see many things more clearly, weigh things more justly, than those caught in the passions of war is obvious. That is an advantage of our position, not an excellence of our souls.'[51] In 1647 the 'Defensionale of Wyl' created the first formal federal military command structure. In 1648, the mayor of Basel, Johann Rudolf Wettstein, as Swiss delegate to the European peace negotiations, managed to convince the powers that Switzerland was now independent, and no longer subject to the courts of the German Empire, a view incorporated in the Peace of Westphalia.[52] According to Edgar Bonjour, the leading authority on these matters, the Diet first formally announced its position as a neutral state in May 1674, but the practice had been increasingly accepted as the only way to hold the Confederation together.

The years immediately after 1648 brought trouble. As if the Swiss needed an external threat to remain one state, immediately it was removed they began to quarrel among themselves. An economic slump played a part. The artificial boom in agriculture sustained by the exhaustion of the countries around them came to an end.[53] The peasantry faced disaster. Class hostilities long submerged burst out. During 1653 in the Entlebuch valley in Canton Luzern a peasant protest against new taxation imposed by the canton turned into a full-scale rising, which eventually involved much of central Switzerland. Characteristically, the peasants organised themselves into *Landsgemeinden* and in the *Huttwiler Bund* repeated the entire ceremony of the Rütli oath of 1291, complete with the costumes and symbols of the legendary first *Eidgenossen*. The victory of the cantonal armies led to a large number of summary executions and the end of the *Bund*. Yet it could neither wholly erase the traditional freedoms which the peasants claimed nor could the individual cantonal authorities exploit the civil war to enforce the sort of absolutist regimes which were emerging in Brandenburg, Saxony and, above all, in France.

In his stimulating study of absolutism, the companion to his work on feudalism, the marxist historian Perry Anderson argues that absolutism may be seen as a transformation of rule by the feudal aristocracy. Their traditional economic status was eroded by the spread of the money economy and the end of serfdom in western Europe. Absolutism, according to Anderson, is a dual process. It 'conferred new and extraordinary powers on the monarchy [and] at the same time it emancipated from traditional restraints the estates of the nobility . . . Individual members of the aristocratic class who steadily lost political rights of representation in the new epoch, registered economic gains in ownership as the obverse of the same historical process.'[54]

Another feature of the change is the replacement of 'conditional' categories of property, which Anderson regards as characteristic of feudalism, by the revived Roman Law category of 'absolute' property.[55] By these criteria, Switzerland remained medieval until the end of the eighteenth century. Conditional property relationship and medieval parcelised authority never disappeared. Elements of absolutism obviously entered Swiss life. The city of Bern exacted ever stricter subservience from its rural subjects, and the mini-absolutism of the prince–abbot of St Gallen, complete with a fashionable rage for grandiose buildings, has a certain distant similarity to the political edifice of Frederick the Great's Prussia. But ultimately, the prince–abbot or a city-republic are by definition those feudal, oligarchical, contractual authorities which proper absolutism of the enlightened type must destroy. Absolutism in the Swiss cantons resembled the process of sawing off the branch on which one sits. If the 'absolutist' abbot of St Gallen tried to destroy the traditional rights of the 'free' Toggenburg valley, he would be destroying a part of his own rights, since both belonged to the same fabric of law and custom.

Religious wars continued in Switzerland later than elsewhere, which helped to make certain that no one absolute authority could emerge. The first and second Villmergen Wars (1656 and 1712) strained the Confederation to breaking point. The Catholic cantons began the dangerous game of alliance with foreign powers, a particularly perilous activity with Louis XIV on the throne of France. The Confederation became even more closely involved in French affairs when in 1685 Louis XIV revoked the Edict of Nantes, the religious compromise with his Protestant subjects which dated back to the previous century. Huguenot refugees poured into French-speaking Switzerland bringing their skills as goldsmiths, weavers and printers. It was a turbulent time in Swiss history, a time not unlike the present in its uncertainties. Europe was moving out of one age into another, and the Swiss were drawn out of the confessional conflict to face a new, secular international power system and a new intellectual climate of enlightened rationalism.

The Villmergen Wars were brought to an end in the Peace of Aarau of 1712. The Catholic party lost its commanding position in the Confederation and was forced to accept parity of faiths both in the commonly administered territories and in confederate tribunals. The French were furious, and the five original Swiss cantons, the Catholic Forest Cantons plus Luzern and Zug, made a secret treaty with France three years later in which the French promised armed support if the Confederation were again plunged into religious war. This treaty, the *Trücklibund* (from *Trückli*, the small box in which the treaty was concealed), would have meant the end of Switzerland, had it been carried out. Professor David Lasserre in his fascinating *Etapes du fédéralisme* points to the Peace of Aarau and the *Trücklibund* as one of the great crises of Swiss history along with the 'miracle of 1848' and the Labour Agreement of 1937.[56] I would add the General Strike of 1918 to the list but his point is surely right. Here was a group of defeated states, profoundly convinced of the God-given rightness of their cause, accustomed to think of themselves, and rightly, as the founders of the Confederation, and absolutely sure that the heretical beliefs preached by Reformed pastors brought death and damnation. In the wings, a powerful Catholic ally with inexhaustible funds stood ready to finance their crusade. A war of revenge seemed natural, inevitable and right.

No war took place. The Confederation survived. Another turning point passed at which nothing turned. The reasons for this go to the heart of the mystery of Swiss survival. Undoubtedly the experience of two centuries of religious war had bent the awareness of the most fanatical *Urschweizer* in the direction of union. As Benjamin Franklin once said in an equally perilous moment in the history of a different federal union, 'we must indeed all hang together or, most assuredly, we shall all hang separately'. In spite of its baroque palaces and patrician style, and its pre-eminence in the Confederation, what was Luzern in a world of great European powers without the whole of the union? The particularism of the tiny Alpine democracies, too, needed the protection of the whole Federation, and to get it one had to give. This is not an obvious truth and never easy to accept. Democratic forms often conceal undemocratic sentiments. The man who is right and knows it never enjoys the prospect of triumphant error. It is always tempting to force men to be free or virtuous or class-conscious or whatever. The Catholic cantons had to swallow the pill that they could not force their fellow confederates to be godly nor, much harder and bitterer, ought they to do so, if they could.

In the crisis of 1712, which I might add the Swiss themselves have long since forgotten, we see in precisely what sense Switzerland can be said to be a European exception. Switzerland had not been exempt from the trends of the times. When Europe fought religious wars, the Swiss had them too. When Europe had revolutions in 1830, 1848 or 1918, the Swiss had them too. What differentiates Swiss history from the European pattern is the outcome. Swiss communities built from the bottom up, growing out of free peasant or urban associations, are in a curious sense bottom-heavy, rather like those dolls which spring up no matter how often the child pushes them over. The weight is at the base. The communities have a deep equilibrium to which, as the point of rest, the social and political order tends to return.

As always no one explanation is adequate. Clearly the mercenary service played an important part. A very shrewd Englishman travelling in Switzerland at just this period put it well: 'If they did not continually drain their Country, by keeping troops in foreign service, they would soon be so much overstocked in proportion to the extent and fertility of it that in all probability they would break in on their neighbours in swarms, or go further to seek out new seats.'[57] Obviously the service of the Bourbon King of Naples was a better place to see a turbulent young Obwaldner than at the gates of Basel, and no doubt the acceptance of compromise owes much to the export of the uncompromising. Yet compromise was in a way less galling because one tasted it rarely. Since the Confederation had long since abandoned collective enforcement of anything, Catholic Uri stayed as blackly orthodox as the dour temper of the mountain folk could wish. What the heretics and sinners did in Protestant Schaffhausen was as remote to the men of Uri as what the Protestants did in Scotland. Common affairs caused trouble, and any federal intervention might bring an explosion, but, in the daily round, the Peace of Aarau changed little save, perhaps, the subjects of conversation in the local tavern.

Because Swiss communities are bottom-heavy, they are stable and slow. Most general developments follow in the Helvetic Confederation after a discreet time-lag and no doubt when the end of the world comes it will be two days late in Altdorf and Schwyz. Hence the changing circumstances of European culture, its growing secularism and the emergence of new ideas about man and the community, began to affect public opinion in Switzerland in the decades after the Peace of Aarau for the first time. The unenfranchised citizenry, the peoples in the *Gemeine Herrschaften*, the non-voting burghers of old towns, the poorer peasants began to stir politically. In 1721 in Glarus, 1723 in Lausanne under the leadership of a Vaudois patriot Major Davel, in 1749 in Bern, in 1755 in Ticino and more or less continuously from the 1760s on in Geneva there were risings.[58] These revolts under various banners and for various causes were accompanied by continuous struggle among the governing elites for control in places like Luzern, Zug and Schwyz.

The sheer variety of Swiss legal authorities prevented uniform control by elites in any of the cantons, which in its turn permitted an explosion of 'proto-industrial activity' in the least likely places. As Rudolf Braun shows in his study of the end of the *ancien régime* in Switzerland, the poorest districts reacted most quickly to the 'putting out' system of manufacture. Indian dyeing, watch-making, cotton-spinning, linen-weaving, fanned out into districts which, precisely because they were poorer, less integrated and less stable than the richer valleys, adopted the new working habits most

Plate 6a Line of pack animals, Hospenthal, *c.* 1790

easily.[59] In central Switzerland, the urban patricians began to buy up Alps and the traditional herdsmen began to accumulate capital. The world turned upside down and new wealth and new poverty appeared as if by some wizardry. As the capitalists pushed for greater gains from their holdings, they forced further rational-isation and reform programmes into rural areas, which in turn undermined the patriarchal relations of old Switzerland. Every-where oligarchies closed ranks and limited access to their closed circles.[60]

As Walter Bodmer has shown, the prices of corn, butter and feed, which had been tolerable for the first six decades of the eighteenth century, began to shoot up after 1770. Central Switzerland had ceased to be self-sufficient in corn by the seventeenth century. By the eighteenth century, urban populations could be plunged to starvation levels overnight. The years 1770–1 were 'hunger years'.[61] In addition, proto-industrialisation had spread with the rapidity of a bush fire. By 1780 the whole of eastern Switzerland had become a giant factory. By 1780, Georg Thürer reckons that there were 100,000 peasant weavers and spinners at work serving the

Plate 6b The cattle market, Lugano, 1799

specialised muslin, cotton and embroidery businesses of the towns, especially St Gallen.[62] A kind of micro-capitalism emerged, which I shall consider in Chapter 5. Here it is only necessary to note that the combination of peasant small-holding and organised production in individual, peasant dwellings made parts of Switzerland at once among the most densely populated rural areas in Europe but potentially the most prosperous. The peasant way of life and the social structure survived the great economic changes of the eighteenth century better in Switzerland than elsewhere in central or western Europe.

The old Confederation in its last decades was a marvellous thing, a patchwork of overlapping jurisdictions, ancient customs, worm-eaten privileges and ceremonies, irregularities of custom, law, weights and measures. On the shores of Lake Luzern, the independent republic of Gersau flourished with all of 2,000 inhabitants and enjoyed much prestige among political theorists of the time as the smallest free state in Europe. The famous Göttingen Professor Friedrich Christoph Schlosser seriously toyed with the idea of writing a multi-volume history of the Republic under 'a universal–

historical' aspect as a microcosm of all of European history. The pre-1798 Canton Zug was a kind of mini-confederation of a city-state (Zug itself with its subject territories) and three entirely 'free' peasant communes with equality of rights, Baar, Aegeri and Menzingen. Only if all four entities agreed could the canton act on anything. The government of Geneva depended on a quarter of the citizenry, themselves divided between Burgher and Citizen class, and represented in a complex of large and small councils very like the flywheels of a gear box.[63] The Act of 1738, guaranteed by the cantons of Zürich and Bern and the Kingdom of France, gave the Genevese a government of five 'orders': the four Syndics, the Small or Executive Council of Twenty-Five; the Council of Sixty; the Council of Two Hundred; and the General Council. Professor Robert Palmer explains its workings:

The General Council met once a year and elected the four Syndics from a list of candidates containing double the number of names, submitted to it by the Small Council. The Act of 1738 specified that all candidates for the office of Syndic must be members of the Small Council, whose members in turn had to belong to the Two Hundred. The Two Hundred, conversely, were named by the Small Council. In short, the Two Hundred (on which far fewer than two hundred families sat) were the ruling aristocracy at Geneva.[64]

Geneva was undoubtedly one of the most interesting and most turbulent representatives of this sort of oligarchy, but systems not unlike it existed elsewhere in the Confederation and, as always, elsewhere in Europe. The influence of Jean-Jacques Rousseau, the most brilliant Genevese of his age, and the constant attention of enlightened Frenchmen from across the frontiers, provided ideas and slogans for the Genevese revolutionaries. In Bern a splendid, slow-moving aristocracy of gentlemen ruled a peasant republic. In Zürich the city government was complicated by ancient guild survivals.

It was this set of rotting structures which the French pushed over in 1798 and which Napoleon reformed in 1803. When the Napoleonic Empire collapsed in 1814, the allied powers had the whole of Europe to put together, not just Switzerland. The old patricians and oligarchs demanded all their former rights and received some of them. Not all were lucky. The republic of Gersau, in spite of its illustrious history, was not revived, but it continues to exist as a separate administrative district within the modern Canton Schwyz.

Plate 7 The mayoral throne, Bern – a symbol of the *ancien régime*

Similarly, the cloister-state of Engelberg disappeared for ever but remains a separate entity within the canton of Obwalden. The attentive traveller in Switzerland will notice everywhere the evidences of the survivals of the older political units as distinct presences within the structures of the new. The number of the cantons was enlarged by the inclusion of Valais, Neuchâtel (still a Prussian possession in spite of its new membership of the Confederation) and Geneva. The Confederation was given a much looser framework, closer to the old Diet than to Napoleon's version. Each canton now had equal voting rights regardless of size. War and peace and treaties required a three-quarter majority of the cantons, and the cantons were allowed some freedom to conduct foreign affairs individually. The one important restriction on cantonal sovereignty was the provision forbidding internal alliances between individual cantons. There was no central government but a sort of travelling secretariat which moved every two years to the *Vorort*, one of the three Director-cantons, Zürich, Bern and Luzern. The apparatus of government, including the two permanent officials, the Chancellor and Secretary, could travel in one coach, and there was a day when the whole Swiss central government was stuck in the snow by the Reuss bridge near Mellingen. The system has a pleasingly antique quality and was, of course, cheap.

Considering that they had been 'collaborators' with Napoleon, the Swiss could think themselves very fortunate in the treatment they received at Vienna. Their delegate, the deft Pictet de Rochemont of Geneva, proved to be fully the equal as a negotiator of the very distinguished members of the Swiss Committee of the Vienna Congress: Freiherr vom Stein, Lord Castlereagh, Capo D'Istria and Stratford Canning. The biggest prize that he came home with was the agreement of the 'puissances à reconnaître et à faire reconnaître la neutralité perpétuelle du corps helvétique'. The external boundaries of Switzerland, under an international guarantee, were not seriously threatened until the 1930s.

If the international status of Switzerland now enjoyed wide acceptance, the domestic scene was unsettled. The attempt to turn the clock back proved unsuccessful and led to a series of revolutions. The oddest of these in my view was the attempt by French-speaking aristocrats in Canton Fribourg to restore German as the official language of the canton because in the period to 1798 it had always been so. In the wake of the revolution of 1830 in Paris, there were revolutions in Thurgau, St Gallen, Zürich, Luzern, Solothurn, Schaffhausen, Aargau and Vaud, all of which brought liberals to power and radical, democratic constitutions to the cantons. In 1831 the Bern aristocrats with becoming elegance surrendered their ancient powers to the massed peasantry of the country districts, and the less becoming patricians of Basel let the countryside split away to form a new canton rather than surrender one jot of theirs. The conservative European powers were not pleased to be so rewarded for their previous kindnesses, and watched with the irritation which can be found in the remarks of Metternich cited in Chapter 1. The new regimes tended to give asylum to outrageous persons such as Louis Napoléon or Mazzini. Above all, they were not pleased when enthusiastic liberals began to install the free public school and attack the powers of the churches. Liberalism in nineteenth-century Europe was often no more than intense anti-clericalism. In the 1830s and 1840s, liberalism and religion clashed openly all over Europe. In 1841 in Switzerland Augustin Keller, a Catholic turned radical, stirred the Protestant canton of Aargau to revoke the constitutional equality of the two religions and to close all religious houses in the canton. In May 1841 in reaction to the Aargau 'outrages', the former radical Constantin Siegwart-Müller and the charismatic peasant leader Josef Leu von Ebersol won a great victory in Luzern, abrogated the liberal constitution and challenged the radicals in the neighbouring canton to a conflict. As scuffles and threats increased the temperature, Josef Leu von Ebersol convinced the Luzern parliament to invite the Jesuit Order to take over the schools in Luzern, the most provocative possible gesture. For liberals and radicals education was the battlefield between modernity and medievalism. Free, scientific, rational, progressive education was now handed to the arch-enemy, the representatives of 'blackest superstition and enforced ignorance'.[65]

Gangs of radical volunteers attacked Luzern in 1841 and 1845. The conservative and Catholic cantons organised concerted resistance and formed the *Sonderbund*, composed of Luzern, Uri, Schwyz, Ob- and Nidwalden, Zug, Fribourg and Valais. The league was secret and had to be so, since it was illegal under the Federal Pact of 1815. As *Schultheiss* of Luzern, Constantin Siegwart-Müller opened secret talks with Metternich and plans were worked out to reorganise the boundaries of the cantons and thus to drive a wedge between the radical cantons of eastern and western Switzerland.

Plate 8 Popular assembly, 1830

When the existence of the *Sonderbund* became known, the radical cantons pressed to have it abolished. During 1846 and 1847 more and more cantons fell into the hands of the radicals, and when in the spring of 1847 St Gallen elected a radical government in a hotly disputed election, there was an absolute majority of radical cantons in the federal Diet. The Diet declared the *Sonderbund* dissolved, demanded the expulsion of the Jesuits from all Swiss territory, and the promulgation of a new democratic federal constitution.

Switzerland stood on the brink of civil war and everybody knew it. The *Sonderbund* chose the Protestant aristocrat from Graubünden, Johann Ulrich von Salis-Soglio, as its military commander and appealed for help from abroad. In October 1847, the two sides met for the last time in Bern, the *Vorort* of that year. Passions were high. The issue of the Jesuits alone was almost a cause of war: here is Burckhardt writing in a relatively moderate vein by the standards of the time.

We have never deceived ourselves nor our readers about the true nature of the Order nor its character. For two decades they have insinuated themselves ever more deeply into the affairs of Switzerland. The Jesuits are a curse on all those lands and individuals who fall into their hands.[66]

The issues were equally clear on the other side. Here is Landammann Abyberg addressing the *Landsgemeinde* in Schwyz:

What is demanded of us is nothing less than the sacrifice of our freedom in church and state. We are not supposed to educate our children as we see fit, order our own house as we choose and – listen to this, you brave and solid men – if you try to save your own skins, then they say, you are breaking the law.[67]

The president of the Confederation, and hence presiding officer of the Diet, was Ulrich Ochsenbein, a leader of the Free Corps who had invaded Luzern, and a notorious radical. Under his direction the Diet voted to dissolve the *Sonderbund* by force. The representatives of the *Sonderbund* cantons rose and left the hall in absolute silence. The roll of the drums as the Guard of Honour saluted the departing deputies could be heard inside the hushed chamber.

The federal commander-in-chief, a shrewd, conservative Genevese, General Henri Dufour, saw that only a lightning strike at the heart of the *Sonderbund* could save the Confederation. If the war lasted for any length of time, the Austrians, the Prussians or the French might be tempted to intervene and the bitterness

Plate 9a The radicals' revolt, Lugano, 1839

between the two sides would deepen beyond the point of reconciliation. Dufour saw too that the *Sonderbund* would have great
geographical difficulties in concentrating its forces; by seizing
Fribourg early on 14 November and then Zug, he drove a wedge
between the western and central cantons. His next objective was
the city of Luzern which he took nine days later. The brilliant
twenty-six-day campaign cut the core out of the *Sonderbund* and the
outlying cantons surrendered. The Federals had lost about 100 men
and the *Sonderbund* rather fewer. Bismarck dismissed the affair
contemptuously as a *Hasenschiessen* (a hare shoot).[68]

The Swiss civil war may have been relatively bloodless, but, as
in the case of the Peace of Aarau in 1712, the Confederation stood at
a turning point. For twenty years unrest, guerrilla warfare, revolution and religious passion had turned Switzerland into one of the
most turbulent countries in Europe. Yet within a matter of months
a new federal constitution had been worked out which became the
basis of modern Swiss government. An era of almost unbroken
domestic tranquillity began which lasted until the 1914–18 war.
Quick reconciliations are not common in human history. Most civil

Plate 9b The Carabinieri arrive at Lugano to quell the revolt, 1839

wars leave legacies of bitterness and recrimination which poison
the reunited community for generations. Yet even more remarkable is the stability of the post-war arrangements. A quick glance at
the other political settlements of the year 1848 is instructive. The
second French republic lasted three years and gave way to a
dictatorship and eventually to the Empire of Napoleon III. The
united Germany of the Frankfurt Parliament lasted a few months.
The Habsburg monarchy changed its constitution several times
between 1848 and 1851 without arriving at a permanent equilibrium. There were three Austrian constitutions during 1860–1 alone.
Yet the Swiss Confederation or, more accurately, some twenty-
three leading figures in it, drafted a document so suited to the
conditions that the Switzerland of 1849 and that of 1847 seem to
belong to different eras. J. H. Plumb has written about stability:

There is a general folk-belief, derived largely from Burke and the nineteenth century historians, that political stability is of slow coral-like
growth: the result of time, circumstances, prudence, experience, wisdom,
slowly building up over the centuries. Nothing is, I think, further from
the truth. True, there are, of course, deep social causes of which

contemporaries are usually unaware making for the *possibility* of political stability. But stability becomes actual through the actions and decisions of men, as does revolution. Political stability, when it comes, often happens to a society quite quickly, as suddenly as water becomes ice.[69]

The Swiss example fits Professor Plumb's hypothesis very neatly. Stability was achieved by political decisions; in this case decisions taken initially by the twenty-three delegates of the Diet who drafted the new federal constitution but ultimately by the entire people. The basic issue, and the one which had caused the war, lay between two different visions of the Swiss Confederation. A Luzern politician, Philipp Anton von Segesser, put one side well: 'For me Switzerland is only of interest as long as the canton of Luzern – this is my fatherland – is in it. If Canton Luzern no longer exists as a free, sovereign member of the Helvetic Confederation, then Switzerland is as irrelevant to me as the lesser or greater Tartary.'[70] This stubborn parochialism expressed in the Swiss phrase *Kantönligeist* ('little cantonal spirit') or the Italian *campanilismo* is the heritage of centuries of narrow, often petty sovereignty. The other side, the protagonists of a 'new' Switzerland, wanted a more centralised, parliamentary, progressive or even radical union.

The conflict between the two views met in the basic dilemma of all federalism: how to divide sovereignty between the centre and the autonomous or independent units which created the union in the first place. One historic answer has been to divide it by assigning parts of the system to each side and so to balance the two structures. In the Swiss case, as in the United States of America, state or cantonal equality expresses itself in an upper house (the US Senate; the Swiss *Ständerat, Conseil des Etats, Consiglio degli Stati*) in which the states or cantons have equal representation regardless of size, while popular sovereignty rests in a parliament based on population (the US House of Representatives; the Swiss *Nationalrat, Conseil national, Consiglio nazionale*). The two views of federalism, the centralist versus the federalist, are then built into the actual structure of representation, but neither is superior to the other. In the constitution of Switzerland of 1848, Article 89 reads: 'Federal law and federal decrees require the consent of both houses.' The constitution is silent on what would happen if that consent were refused and, as in most federal systems, there is a grey area of uncertainty where federal and state powers overlap. The solution

of the civil war rested in part on this compromise between centralism and particularism, a compromise which in retrospect looks
natural and almost inevitable. There were precedents in the
successful union of states in the United States constitution,
although the auspices there, a successful collective war against
Britain, had been more favourable than the aftermath of a civil
war in the Swiss case. There was the long historical experience of
consultation among cantons on matters of joint concern. During
the bitterest religious divisions of the Reformation, neither
Catholic nor Protestant cantons had seriously interrupted or
denied the rights of their religious opponents to cooperate in
running the *Gemeine Herrschaften*. The new constitution merely put
into modern form what had always been an established grey area of
Swiss practice, an area in which negotiation had to occur. Having
said all that, I am still impressed by the willingness of passionately
committed nineteenth-century liberals, who had just won a short,
glorious war, to share the victory with what they must have seen as
bigoted, backward Catholic communities. As in the Peace of Aarau
the drafters of the new constitution returned to an essential feature
of all Swiss life – that the identity and survival of the one is a
function of cooperation with the many. While they were at work in
the early months of 1848, revolutions broke out all over Europe, and
the frightening news of rebellious masses surging through German,
French and Austrian towns must have concentrated their attention
on the task in hand. If the civil war were not tidied up, much nastier
difficulties might arise.

The constitution was ratified by popular vote, and here too the
continued existence of an ancient form of popular voting known
as the referendum played an important part. Since the old
Confederation had no powers of its own, the delegates to it were
said to be *ad audiendum et referendum*, to listen and to report back. In
the mountain cantons with *Landsgemeinden*, the sovereign body of
citizens had the ultimate right to accept or reject confederal
decisions. In Graubünden before the French revolution the government had been of 'the most marvellous complexity', as A. L. Lowell
put it. Here were leagues of sovereign communes or districts united
in a central diet which, in turn, referred back to the over two
hundred 'sovereign villages' almost everything of substance. The
village community remained the repository of legal sovereignty.[71]
The Valais had a similar 'microscopic' organisation. Consulting the

people had traditional roots and, covered with modern representative theory, the drafters of 1848 and the Diet adopted the new
constitution as the basic law of the new Swiss Confederation.[72]

Ratification by majority vote would never of itself have brought
stability to Switzerland after 1848. Northern Ireland or Bosnia,
where resentful minorities nurse the memory of historic defeats
with vengeful intensity, suggest that historic losers rarely accept
their fate peacefully. Swiss Catholics, many in exile, all embittered,
shared those feelings. The transformation of religious hatred into
religious accommodation owes a great deal to the institutions which
1848 established and, in particular, to two: federalism and semi-
direct democracy. It also owes a great deal to a man whom most
Swiss have forgotten, the Luzern patrician Philipp Anton von
Segesser (1817–88). Segesser belonged to one of the old *regiments-
fähigen* families of Luzern, that is, the ruling patrician caste. His
ancestors served in Imperial and French armies, as office-holders in
the cantonal government, and as comfortable incumbents of
baroque church livings. Philipp Anton entered politics as naturally
as certain old Etonians become Tory MPs and, like some of the
'wetter' among them, he incorporated the paradox of the aristocrat
as democrat. Late in life he described his long career as representative of his class, church and canton in these words:

I spoke and voted in this chamber, as everywhere in my public life, as a
democrat, as a federalist, as a Catholic. These three concepts determined
my actions.[73]

The existence of representative institutions on local and
cantonal level after 1848 gave the minority Catholic community a
weapon to use against the Protestant, anti-clerical majority. The
Catholic conservatives had discovered a deep truth about democracy, known to the Greeks but obscured in the English-speaking
world by the fusion of the terms 'liberal–democratic', that democracy can be turned to entirely reactionary ends if the sovereign
people wills them. As Segesser wrote in 1866,

My firm conviction is that we of the conservative camp must put ourselves
entirely onto a democratic basis. After the collapse of the old conditions
nothing else can provide us with a future and a justification except pure
democracy. Even if democracy has its dark side it is preferable to the
quasi-bureaucratic aristocracy of the representative system.[74]

The gradual transformation of violent confrontation into

political obstruction changed the terms of Catholic–Protestant hostility. They loved each other no better but found ways to get along. Segesser's tactics allowed Swiss Catholics to survive the ferocity of the *Kulturkampf* of the 1870s better than their German cousins. Bismarck's liberal, half-constitutionalism gave the embattled Catholics of the Rhine, Ruhr and Danube the options of surrender or siege. The German church chose siege and drew the faithful into a closed Catholic 'milieu', a kind of sectarian ghetto, from which the state could be excluded. This left the German Catholic community, as Thomas Gauly has written, with a *Bildungsrückstand* – an educational and cultural deficit – even as late as the 1960s.[75] Swiss Catholics also retreated into what the Swiss historian Urs Altermatt has called their 'ghetto' but they counter-attacked with referenda, initiatives and constitutional reforms. As Altermatt argues, the loose network of Catholic societies, singing, yodelling and hiking clubs, the charitable, devotional and educational societies gave conservatives like Segesser the perfect weapon against the liberal, bourgeois, Protestant and capitalist majority:

In numerous referenda they organised oppositional voting alliances, which slowed or halted the radical law-making machinery. In this way the Catholic–conservative opposition, excluded from executive authority in the government, found a compensation for its powerlessness in parliament.[76]

By the end of the 1880s radical majorities began to seek compromises with conservative minorities. It is not a coincidence that 1891 saw simultaneously the establishment of the 1st of August as the Swiss national holiday; the celebration of 600 years of Swiss history held in the Catholic canton of Schwyz; the election of the first Catholic member of the national executive, Federal Councillor Joseph Zemp; the great papal encyclical on the 'social' question, Leo XIII's *Rerum novarum*; and the adoption by the German social democrats of the marxist definition of revolution in their Erfurt programme. The depression of the early 1890s frightened liberals and Catholics out of their sectarian trenches. The rise of an industrial proletariat and the spread of slums threatened them both.

Swiss national identity developed slowly and painfully as a process of conflict resolution. In the nineteenth century the very idea of a 'Swiss' identity was controversial. The radicals, who made the Swiss constitution of 1848 and 1874, who fought the fight for 'progress' against what they saw as Catholic superstition and reaction, saw a world in which secularism, moderate Protestantism, liberalism and capitalism would reinforce and invigorate each other. Their vision of Switzerland included a strong and increasingly centralised government, the *Bund*, embodied in Victorian statues of Helvetia, armed and watchful, standing guard before the banks and bourses of the new age. The reaction to that came from people like von Segesser:

> I shall be either a free man or a subject. If as a Luzerner I cannot be a free man, I should rather be a subject of the King of France or the Emperor of Austria or even the Sultan himself than of some Swiss republican diet.[77]

Federalism is more than simply a form of government which the Swiss happen to have chosen; it embodies the painful experience of conflict and its resolution. Federalism allowed the two sides in the religious trenches to lay down their arms. The constitution of 29 May 1874 states the premise in Article 3:

> The cantons are sovereign, in so far as their sovereignty is not limited by the federal constitution, and exercise all those rights, which have not been transferred to federal power.[78]

If the institutions of federalism and democracy allowed the Swiss to resolve the religious issue, the changes in the outside world pushed for reconciliation. No sooner had the struggle between church and state begun to ease with the 1891 gestures of reconciliation, than a new ideology emerged to threaten Switzerland along different fault lines. Religion united French-speaking and German-speaking Swiss; nationalism divided them. The doctrines of race, of nationality, of social darwinism, of biologistic popular science eroded the historical category 'Swiss' by elevating the 'organic' ideas of nation, *Volk* and blood. To be Swiss was by definition to assert a political, historically determined, notion of citizenship against the seductive, 'modern', 'scientific' conceptions of national self-determination. It was also to choose dull reality and not romance. The fading image of William Tell could not compare with the heroic reality of Garibaldi and his thousand red-shirted young poets, scientists, artists and professional men. Even Cavour with some distaste had to admit that the unification of Italy was being widely regarded as 'the most poetic fact of the century'.[79] The brilliant revival of French culture and art under the Third Republic and the achievements of the new German Empire with its scientific prowess, its immense military prestige, its flourishing economy, its advanced social welfare systems (Germany introduced the first compulsory insurance schemes against accident, old age and sickness in the 1880s) and its cultural landmarks, exerted a powerful attraction in advanced circles in both French- and German-speaking Switzerland.

Intelligent Swiss Germans warmed themselves vicariously in the glow from the Reich. German triumphs were their triumphs, German literature and language theirs too. In French Switzerland the movement called *helvétisme* attracted the interest of young Swiss intellectuals like Gonzague de Reynold, Robert de Traz and J.-B. Bouvier. They drew inspiration from the elitist ideas of the Frenchmen Maurras and Barrès. As one critic saw it at the time,

If one takes the trouble to dissect a little bit of this *helvétisme*, one realises quickly that it is simply vulgar plagiarism, covered in Swiss sauces, of the ideas of *L'Action française*. We find there, in fact, the same haughty disdain for democracy and parliamentary government, the same aspirations to become a separate, privileged caste, destined to govern.[80]

Foreign cultural influences spread. That there was no 'Swiss' culture to resist it reflected the extreme particularism of Swiss life. The poet Carl Spitteler suffered from it:

The direct literary commerce from city to city and canton to canton is virtually nil . . . Under such circumstances the main stream of literary life flows from one of these small places into the far distance, here toward Germany and there toward France and only then does it find its way back to the other Swiss towns.[81]

What was Swiss anyway? In the overheated, fetid climate of extreme nationalism, the crab-like defensiveness of Swiss authorities toward foreign influences seemed absurd. The Swiss Italian philologist Carlo Salvioni mocked them in 1914: 'Every schoolboy becomes used to saying "we" for the Helvetii but not Julius Caesar, to call "his" writers whose language he cannot understand, to claim Rousseau, Bodmer and Keller but to consider as foreign Dante and Manzoni.'[82] Yet if the cultural boundaries disappeared completely, the language groups would be sucked into the larger cultural worlds of their neighbours, and Swiss identity would disappear. The intoxicating ideas of race and nationality were sliding the Confederation toward a crisis as real (if less apparent) as the religious divisions had been.

The central institutions of the state, especially the higher commands of the army, had been thoroughly Prussianised. The chief of the General Staff, Colonel-Corps Commander Theophil Sprecher von Bernegg, had agreed with the German General Staff in 1910 that his staff would provide the Germans with secret military information. Many Swiss officers, blinded by their Prussian sympathies, expected gross violations of their neutrality to come from the French side only. When the war broke out, the exchange of intelligence began, as the German minister in Bern reported on 29 September 1914:

> From the very first day since the outbreak of war Switzerland has discreetly placed at our disposal her entire secret military intelligence service. They give us information about intercepted cables, which might be useful, and more important news from their overseas representatives.[83]

For leading German Swiss, it was obvious which side to support, as the head of the Military Department of Canton Bern, Karl Scheurer, wrote in his diary in August 1914: 'On general cultural grounds as well as political I believe that a German victory is desirable.'[84] A deep fissure, which came to be known as the trench or the *Graben*, opened between French and German Switzerland. Scheurer noticed how meetings of the federal parliament were poisoned by the division. The long period of general mobilisation began to take its toll. To maintain an army of 250,000 in varying degrees of readiness out of a total population of about 3 million required immense effort. The economic situation was parlous; surrounded by belligerents, Switzerland had to depend on the goodwill of neighbouring countries. Writing in his diary on 15 June 1915 Scheurer expressed his despair:

> Our situation is getting worse. Externally things are not too bad, and even the entry of Italy does not seem to threaten us too much. At home, on the other hand, things are nasty. The conflict between German and French gets worse rather than better as does the struggle between town and country over food prices.[85]

As the war dragged on, relations between French and German Switzerland became entangled with the issue of neutrality. General Ulrich Wille came under increasing criticism for his pro-German bias, and when two of his staff officers were caught and tried for passing secrets to the Germans and Austrians, the demand for his resignation grew. The most spectacular violation of neutrality, however, occurred at the very top of the political hierarchy. Federal Councillor Arthur Hoffmann, head of the Political Department (the Swiss foreign office), had to resign in 1917, a very rare event in Swiss politics, when his secret attempt to bring about a separate peace between Germany and the new revolutionary regime in Russia became known. He had used the Swiss socialist Robert Grimm, who knew all the leading Bolshevik and Menshevik leaders, to act as his agent in the promotion of a peace without annexations. Hoffmann had to submit to a formal inquiry during which he defended himself by arguing that 'it was definitely in the interests of Switzerland that peace be concluded before either France or Germany had been definitively beaten'.[86] This proposition was based on a reading of Swiss history which had a lot to be said for it. Swiss neutrality had always been safest when Europe was in an international equilibrium and most threatened when one European great power achieved a position of hegemony. This was clearly true during the Napoleonic era and was to be demonstrated again under Hitler in the second world war. Hoffmann was not wrong about ends but about means. Swiss neutrality forbids the conduct of an active foreign policy of any sort. By trying to serve Swiss neutrality, Hoffmann had dangerously compromised it. The line between what a Swiss foreign minister may or may not do is unusually delicate.

A different crisis began to erupt during 1918. During the war the conditions of Swiss working men deteriorated. Long, poorly paid periods of military service left many of them destitute at the very moment that the peasants seemed to be squeezing the last centime out of the town dweller. The traditional Swiss custom of asylum had opened the doors to a distinguished collection of dangerous men, including Lenin, Trotsky, Zinoviev, Axelrod and Martov among the leading Russian revolutionaries as well as exiles from Germany and France. Between 5 and 8 September 1915 at Zimmerwald in Canton Bern, and from 20 to 24 April 1916 at Kiental, two conferences were held which made Switzerland the revolutionary capital of the world. The influence of these powerful presences on Swiss socialists was great. Swiss social democracy began to develop an extreme revolutionary wing.

The progress of the war made a revolutionary socialist interpretation of events very plausible. Lenin believed that the first world

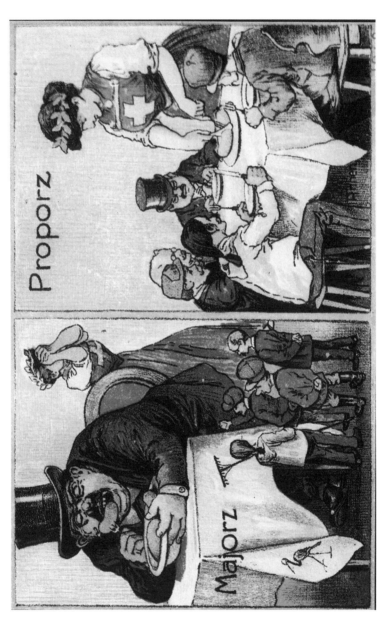

Plate 10 Majority and proportional representation, 1910

war represented a final stage, a kind of Armageddon of capitalism. What else could account for the prolonged slaughter? The bourgeois governments of all European societies were financing the war at the expense of the poor, and Switzerland was no exception. Between 1914 and 1918, the cost of living index had gone up from 100 to 229, while mobilisation and the resulting short-time working had reduced wages by an average of 6%.[87] The Swiss government had, in addition, reneged on a long-standing promise to permit a referendum on proportional representation. The Socialist Party of Switzerland knew well what the reasons were. In the elections of 1914 based on a single member and majority vote system, the ruling Radical Party, the party of bourgeois liberalism and capitalism, had 111 of the 189 seats, while the Socialists had 19. For every 34,000 votes in the elections of 1908 the Radicals had picked up eight seats in the federal parliament, while the Socialists required the same number to win two. In fact, when proportional representation finally began in 1919 in national elections, the Socialist Party jumped from 19 to 41 and the Radicals fell to 60.[88] Hence the sense of being disenfranchised added to the grievances of daily life and the demands of ideology.

The leaders of the radical wing of the Swiss Socialist Party and trade union movement began to look to the General Strike as the weapon to use. The notion of the political mass strike had a distinguished, if untested, pedigree in socialist theory and seemed to offer a compromise between the armed seizure of power, Bolshevik style, and ordinary 'reformist' political tactics. Robert Grimm, the most influential left-wing socialist, had seen the Russian Revolution at first hand on his secret mission for Federal Councillor Hoffmann and had worked closely with Lenin earlier in the war. After the Bolshevik seizure of power, he decided to act. He formed an action committee of party and union leaders, the Olten Action Committee, which met for the first time in February 1918. It served as the revolutionary equivalent of the federal executive during the preparation and conduct of the General Strike of 1918.

Swiss realities and revolutionary illusions met head-on during that year. Among the realities were the characteristics of industrial history in Switzerland which I shall discuss in Chapter 5. The growth of industry had mainly taken the form of small-scale, high-quality production (watches and precision machinery in the Jura and the textile industry of central and eastern Switzerland). There were no natural resources, but there was water power. The free, relatively well educated population and highly developed mercantile communities were an additional strength of the Swiss economy. As a result, industry fanned out in small units of production along the rushing streams. 'White coal' left none of the filthy marks of black coal on the environment so the Swiss escaped the most degrading stages of the industrial revolution. Textile units flourished in the deepest rural peace. The workers were part-timers who never lost contact with the soil, the harvest and the peasant communalism of their village. A self-conscious working class emerged slowly where it appeared at all. Cities developed less violently and slums less gruesomely than in Britain or Germany. In 1910, of the total Swiss population of 3,750,000 only 25% lived in towns of over 10,000. England and Wales by comparison had reached that level of urbanisation by the late 1840s.[89] Moreover the union movement was small compared to other advanced countries. In 1914 the nineteen unions in the *Schweizerischer Gewerkschaftsbund* counted 65,177 members, and even today (figures from 1993) union membership stands at 431,052 out of just over two million workers classified as industrial.[90] Now that unionisation has declined in most developed countries, the Swiss figures look less anomalous than they did even twenty years ago. In 1918 the Swiss working class was different and that difference weakened it.

The peasantry remained a powerful economic and political force in Swiss life. The bottom-heavy features of Swiss society and politics, the existence of an upper parliamentary chamber based on cantons rather than population, and a certain amount of gerrymandering assured the peasantry a disproportionate role in politics. Ernst Laur, the 'king of the peasants', was a leader who knew how to exploit it. Laur used his close friendship with the director of the Economic Department, the powerful Federal Councillor Schulthess, to solve many a small problem. While the war accelerated industrialisation and union membership tripled, it also gave the peasants unusual economic leverage. Cut off from the outside world, Switzerland might starve unless the peasantry cooperated. Many socialist leaders such as Otto Lang saw these realities and in the Central Committee of the Socialist Party he pleaded against the call for a General Strike: 'Look at the facts. We have worked ourselves into deep hostility to the peasants. Look at our import and export figures, our 8,000 factories and 25 cantons.

No Russian illusions can help that . . . Radicalism is no temperature measure of the rightness of a principle.'[91] In spite of such warnings the General Strike went ahead in November 1918 and for three days the country was paralysed. The Federal Council, having first negotiated, hesitated and then turned hard. The army was called out. By November troops had begun to take controlling positions in Bern and Zürich, the main centres of radicalism. By the 14th the army controlled the country and had even begun to make use of the railway rolling stock. The strike collapsed. The Olten Action Committee capitulated and ordered a general return to work.

The General Strike of 1918 was no joke. A little more heat here, a little more intransigence there, and a bloody civil war would have occurred.[92] Again the Swiss managed to escape the worst. The wounds healed, not so quickly as in the case of 1848, but in good time. The citizenry showed its remarkable political canniness by voting for the referendum on proportional representation by 19½ to 2½ cantons and by 298,550 to 149,035, even though they were, in effect, rewarding the Socialists for having brought the country to the edge of civil war.[93] The Federal Council, for its part, having finally settled on a firm line, met the Olten Action Committee face to face for concrete negotiations. The fact that Grimm and eight other Olten Committee members were also parliamentarians helped to save face on both sides, but the Federal Council deserves credit for recognising the need. The civil prosecutor and army leaders were shrewd enough not to press home their triumph. General Wille forbade any sort of parading in Zürich or Bern to celebrate the collapse of the strike, and the treatment of the accused at the trial of the members of the Action Committee was matter of fact and sensible. As the right to strike existed, the accused were only charged with having undermined military and civil authority by urging soldiers and civil servants to refuse to obey. The penalties inflicted on the four found guilty were as near the minimum as the court could give: six months' imprisonment and an eighth of the cost in three cases and four weeks plus 50 francs for another.

In the subsequent years both sides gradually moved toward a reconciliation. The Federal Council took up many of the Olten Committee's demands and by 1 January 1920 had introduced the forty-eight-hour week as law. In 1919 work began on the extension of the social security system and the introduction of laws on worker participation, still an issue today in Swiss industrial life. The trade union and socialist movements gradually abandoned class war and intransigence, not least because of the split between the communist and socialist parties which took place everywhere in the Western world in these years. As Charles Naine, a delegate to the Socialist Party congress in 1920, put it, 'You have rejected dictatorship of the proletariat with tartar sauce, now we have to see if you accept it with western sauce or with Bernese sauce.'[94] That Swiss socialists preferred their ideology *à la sauce bernoise* became clear almost at once. The members of the Olten Action Committee returned to public life and many, like Grimm, served in parliament for years.

Two further developments hastened the move from class war to social partnership: the impact of economic crises and the rise of fascism. For reasons which I shall discuss in Chapter 5, the depression hit the specialised Swiss manufacturing industries (watches and embroidered textiles) with unusual severity. The collapse of whole industries and regions occurred. One St Gallen manufacturer offered to sell his entire textile company for one franc to anyone who could keep his employees in work for one year.[95] There were no takers. The capitulation of the marxist parties before triumphant fascism in Italy in the 1920s and Germany after 1933 had a sobering effect on the Swiss left. It became clear that the Swiss proletariat had a homeland after all, one very much worth fighting for. The transition was aided by the remarkable openness of Swiss democracy, which enabled both Swiss socialism and communism to find expression in the prevailing order, no matter how bloodthirsty their rhetoric. Between 1925 and 1939 there was always at least one Communist representing Basel-Stadt in the national parliament. Zürich's Communists were represented in the 1920s and 1930s on local, cantonal and national level. Walther Bringolf led a Popular Front government in Schaffhausen as an ex-Communist and Léon Nicole led one in Geneva, gaining over 40% of the votes in the 1935 elections.[96] By 1935 with fifty seats the Socialist Party was the largest party in the *Nationalrat*.[97] In 1943 the Radicals gave up one of their 'reserved' seats on the Federal Council to the Socialists. It was a considerable sacrifice. For the first time in the hundred years of the modern federation the Radicals did not have an absolute majority of the seven seats on the Federal Council. Here too one of those curiously Swiss arrangements had been made by which those with power surrender it not always cheerfully, but usually smoothly, to those who might otherwise claim it by force.[98]

In 1937 Konrad Ilg, president of the Swiss Metalworkers' and Watchmakers' Union, signed an agreement with Ernst Dübi, the president of the Federation of Metal and Machine Industry Employers, which effectively ruled out the strike as a weapon of collective bargaining. The so-called *Arbeitsfrieden* of 1937 is an astonishing achievement. It was initially accepted for two years but has been renewed at five-year intervals ever since.[99] Other industries followed the engineering and metal-working branches and have made their own arrangements. In 1956 the *Nationalrat* passed a law making such agreements 'generally binding' (*allgemeinverbindlich*) across an entire industry whenever the parties who have signed the agreement constitute more than half of the employers and employees of a given branch (Article 2, Section 3). Hence a labour peace treaty can be made to extend to firms and workers not party to the original agreement. Built into the new law is the principle of arbitration from without (Article 6) in the case of disagreement, but in the new law as in the original 'Pact' the basic principle is of self-regulation within an industry by its own members. The employers and unions accepted each others' claims to recognition 'in loyalty and good faith' and shortly thereafter the strike virtually disappeared from the Swiss industrial scene.[100]

It is tempting to see in this uniquely Swiss institution another of those special turning points which I have underlined so heavily. The parallel with, say, 1481 or the Peace of Aarau is real. If 1481 marked the acceptance of a political compromise between urban and rural states, and 1712 peace between the confessions, then 19 July 1937 can be called 'peace between the classes'. Giuseppe Motta, perhaps the most distinguished of the inter-war members of the Federal Council, called it just that, 'the *Stanser Verkommnis* of the machine industry', an obvious play on the intervention of Brother Klaus between the feuding cantons in 1481. Konrad Ilg, the union boss who signed for the workers, had, after all, been an active figure in the Olten Action Committee, and remained both a militant trade unionist and committed socialist. He saw perfectly well that the *Arbeitsfrieden* supported the *status quo* and put off the advent of socialism. Ernst Dübi for the employers had to surrender the entire arsenal of lockout, 'black-leg', non-recognition and so on, which a very conservative group of employers were loath to drop. Yet they did it, and the example spread. Characteristically all such agreements follow the original model and have a prologue. The law now required (Article 357 OR) that when such agreements are 'unlimited', a prologue is obligatory. The prologue has the features of a state treaty and very much reflects the traditional Swiss desire to keep the control of internal affairs in the hands of those inside. Sometimes, as in the original case, caution money must be laid down by both parties as a pledge of good behaviour. Is it far-fetched to see this treaty of arbitration in the same context as the Treaty of Alliance of 1291 or the other compromises of Swiss history?

It was also helpful, and very characteristic of Swiss politics, that Konrad Ilg not only led the Swiss Metalworkers but was also a member of the Bern City Council, of the cantonal parliament, the *Grosser Rat*, and a Socialist deputy in the federal parliament. The overlapping of political, economic and social functions in modern Switzerland makes what has been called 'bargaining democracy' much easier. There are circles within and across circles, and many points of contact exist on many levels. As Professor Gruner remarked, 'In Switzerland one is always in a minority by comparison with somebody.'

The threat of class war at home reflected the threat of international war abroad. As the country struggled to come to terms with the emergence of revolutionary socialism on the streets of Swiss cities, it took the first steps out of its traditional neutrality. On 19 July 1919 Felix Calonder, head of the Political Department, the equivalent of the Swiss foreign ministry, told a press conference in Bern that Switzerland had a 'moral duty' to join the League of Nations.[101] Against the strong objections of the army, which argued for traditional absolute neutrality, the Federal Council, convinced by the experience of the first world war, concluded that strict neutrality was no longer possible.[102] On 16 May 1920, the 'Sovereign' (the people) voted to join the League by 416,870 votes to 323,719 in popular voting and by 11½ to 10½ among the cantons.[103]

Swiss membership of the League brought certain advantages. Geneva became its headquarters and attracted all sorts of organisations and institutes which needed to be near it. Geneva became for a brief period, in effect, a kind of world capital, a position which it never entirely surrendered even after the death of the League. Yet League membership posed a dilemma for Swiss foreign policy which grew more vexing as world tension increased. If the League took its mandate to keep the peace seriously, it might have to call on its members to execute League decisions, to set up military or economic blockades. In such cases, Switzerland might find itself obliged to abandon neutrality in order to do so. The military problem never became acute because the Swiss had negotiated an exclusion when they joined the League, but collective economic action could not be evaded, when in 1935 the League punished fascist Italy for aggression in Abyssinia by imposing sanctions. By that time Giuseppe Motta, a conservative Swiss Italian, had succeeded Calonder as foreign minister. Motta, who had some sympathy with Mussolini's aims, balked at the imposition of sanctions and then had to square the circle by getting Switzerland out of its 'moral duty' to the League while not losing the League's business in Geneva. On 22 December 1937 Motta announced in parliament an end to *neutralité différentielle* and a return to its traditional absolute neutrality. In May of 1938, the League reluctantly allowed Switzerland to renege on its obligations.[104] So ended the experiment in foreign policy as 'moral duty'.

1937 and 1938 were bad years for Europe and for Switzerland. Democracy was in retreat everywhere. Franco was winning the civil war in Spain, and Italy establishing its *Impero* in Abyssinia. The League of Nations, powerless and divided, disintegrated. As Italy and Germany drew closer together, Nazi Germany annexed Austria. A steel wall of totalitarian hostility threatened Switzerland's borders, while streams of Jewish refugees begged to be let in. Swiss relations with Nazi Germany became increasingly strained. Although Hitler had assured former Federal Councillor Edmund Schulthess on 23 February 1937, that Switzerland was a 'European necessity', a year later he showed that independent Austria was not. Schulthess had gone out of his way to assure the Führer that the Swiss press had not become *verjudet* and that 'Jewish influences' were contained.[105] Antisemitism, official policy in Hitler's *Reich* and after 1938 in Mussolini's *Impero*, tainted Swiss reactions as well. When in December 1938 Federal police chief Heinrich Rothmund replied to a deputy who had accused him in parliament of antisemitism, he scarcely bothered to deny it: 'Certainly every Swiss, from worker to intellectual, feels that the Jew in general is a foreign element. He hardly takes him into his circle of friends.'[106] Rothmund's policy, supported in similar terms by the Federal Council, made certain that, as the consul in Venice called them, 'these poor, hunted people'[107] would be kept out. Yet, as in the League issue, the Swiss had to keep them out without damage to tourism or Switzerland's reputation. The solution arrived at was a compromise. Rothmund wanted to impose visas on all German passport holders, but at a conference on 28 September 1938 in Berlin with SS Brigade-Führer Dr Werner Best of the Gestapo, Rothmund agreed to the introduction of the infamous 'J' in all 'non-aryan' German passports.[108] Officials like the St Gallen police commander, Paul Grüninger, who continued to let Austrian and German Jews into Switzerland on humanitarian grounds, were dismissed and punished.[109] As Federal Councillor Kaspar Villiger put it to parliament in May 1995, 'there is for me no doubt that our policy toward persecuted Jews burdened us with guilt. The introduction of the so-called "Judenstempel" in passports was a German response to Swiss wishes.'[110]

In 1934, Mussolini, addressing factory workers in Milan, made threatening noises about the *Italianità* of Canton Ticino. An active Nazi network had begun to work in Switzerland, and a native Swiss 'National Front' movement was stirring. Its membership was small but Nazi Germany knew how to use such tiny cells of sympathisers as pretexts for invading peaceful small countries. Relations with the Soviet Union were dreadful. Motta, a deeply conservative Catholic politician, wielded his prestige at the League of Nations to delay Soviet membership and personally prevented any improvement in relations between Bern and Moscow. After Munich and especially after the Nazi invasion of Czechoslovakia in March 1939, the Swiss realised that they were diplomatically isolated, and, when war broke out in September, they were in fact physically isolated from the outside world. In 1939 an international system which had preserved Switzerland since 1815 collapsed. As the deputy chief of staff put it after Hitler occupied Czechoslovakia in March 1939, 'now we know that the thieves who rule these two states [Germany and Italy – JS] will not shrink from any lie or trick'.[111]

War meant mobilisation of the entire Swiss army, as it had in 1914. On 30 August 1939, Colonel Henri Guisan was elected general by 202 of the 229 votes of upper and lower houses of the parliament. Guisan made a marked contrast to the Prussian ponderousness of General Wille, the general during the first world war. Guisan, a Vaudois, had the right democratic image. Edgar Bonjour describes him approvingly as an 'affable, open, hearty, natural man from the countryside'.[112] His superior at the Military Department, Rudolf Minger, represented the Peasants' Party in the Federal Council and rural doggedness in his person. These men embodied the values which the Swiss demanded and still expect of their politicians. The ideal is simplicity of manner and a direct humanity of heart. In the darkest days of early 1940, Giuseppe Motta died after more than twenty years as a Federal Councillor. The eulogy read over Radio della Svizzera italiana sums up perfectly the portrait of the ideal Swiss statesman:

> He was a man of exemplary simplicity. For nearly thirty years the citizens of Bern saw him leave for his office on foot, wait for the bus to go home for lunch and back to the office and then return home on foot in the evening after a day of work guiding the destiny of our country . . . Patiently, serenely, cordially, he replied to everyone; he answered, he wrote letters, sometimes only a single line but always in his own hand, sometimes only a single word added to an official letter above his signature but in his own hand. It was enough. People said, 'he answered me, he remembered me, he understood me'.[113]

The tone may be a little cloying for our tastes, but against the background of Hitler's 'new order' the democratic virtues of a Minger or a Motta were more precious than they seem today.

The country mobilised rapidly. With pride Guisan reported to the Federal Council on 7 September: 'On Sunday, 3 September 1939, when at 12.10 Central European time, Great Britain declared war on Germany, our entire army had been in its operational positions for ten minutes.'[114] The American journalist William Shirer, travelling through Switzerland in October 1939, was very impressed:

> Swiss train full of soldiers. The country has one tenth of its population under arms; more than any other country in the world. It's not their war. But they're ready to fight to defend their way of life. I asked a fat businessman in my compartment whether he wouldn't prefer peace at any price (business is ruined in a Switzerland completely surrounded by belligerents and with every able-bodied man in the army) so that he could make money again. 'Not the kind of peace that Hitler offers', he said. 'Or the kind of peace we've been having the last five years.'[115]

It would be pleasing to be able to say that this Churchillian doggedness was universal and permanent. Certainly the first months of the war showed the Swiss united and resolute, more so than at any time in the twentieth century, but conditions in 1940 began to erode that cohesion.

On 9 April 1940 German armies invaded Denmark and Norway and on 10 May they marched into Holland, Belgium and Luxemburg. By 15 May the Dutch had capitulated and by 28 May the Belgians. General mobilisation was again declared in Switzerland; the entire army manned the frontiers. By the end of May, the defeat of France was certain and on 14 June 1940 a German army entered Paris. By this time almost no British troops were left on the continent of Europe and Hitler stood where only Napoleon once had, but more powerful and threatening.

The conduct of foreign policy lay in the hands of Federal Councillor Marcel Pilet-Golaz, a French Swiss who lacked the democratic virtues, as Professor Bonjour describes him: 'With his overly sharp expressions, his snobbish elegance and glittering personality, he got nowhere with the ordinary citizen. His often thoughtless jokes were taken too heavily and too seriously . . . '[116] It is not clear which of these grave defects most harmed Pilet. I suspect that making jokes may have been the worst of his sins; the Swiss demand high seriousness of their leaders. In any case, he lacked the common touch and the collegial habits of a good Swiss politician. On 25 June 1940, after a brief consultation with some of the other members of the Federal Council, he made a famous radio speech in which he announced partial demobilisation and in extremely obscure phrases warned the Swiss that they must be prepared to play a part in a Europe 'très différente de l'ancienne . . . et qui so fondera sur d'autres bases'. Ominous references to 'redressement', to 'décisions majeures' and to the breaking of 'd'habitudes anciennes' dotted the misty prose.[117] One such habit was shooting down German planes violating Swiss air space. Swiss fighter pilots had begun to run up a respectable score on that front, and Pilet-Golaz wanted them to stop. He knew, which the public did not, that Germans had uncovered compromising documents in French headquarters at La Charité-sur-Loire.[118] The German advance had been so spectacular that French intelligence officers had not had time to destroy their papers, among which were the terms of a secret agreement on the exchange of military information between the Swiss and French intelligence staffs. The Nazi regime had used much flimsier pretexts than that in their other aggressions.

Pilet's speech had a mixed reception. Several leading parliamentarians noted with dismay that he had not said a word about democracy. His choice of words had a sinister similarity to the language of the new Vichy regime in France. A group of young army officers was so alarmed that they began to make preparations for a possible *putsch* if the Federal Council showed any further signs of weakness.[119] The commander-in-chief then took a dramatic step, one so risky that only a grave crisis could have justified it. On the morning of 25 July 1940 the entire senior officer corps, over five hundred men, boarded a steamer in Luzern to cross the lake to the famous meadow of Rütli, the legendary birth-place of the Confederation. General Guisan described it:

Toward noon of a very fine day I had nearly all my senior officers before me. On the Rütli meadow, where the flag of the Uri Battalion 87 fluttered, the officers formed a large semi-circle looking out over the lake. The Army corps commanders in the first row, behind them in rows the divisional commanders, the brigadiers, regimental officers, battalion and section chiefs.[120]

The general took a few notes from his pocket and spoke, in German, for half an hour. According to the official communiqué the general issued an order of the day: 'The will to resist any attack from without and all dangers on the home front, such as sloth or defeatism; Faith in the value of resistance.'[121] It was a grand and significant moment in Swiss history. Guisan saw that the symbolic renewal of the Rütli oath a mere month after the questionable radio talk of Pilet would be a pledge of good faith. The risk in putting the entire army command in one lake steamer was the token of his seriousness. The staging was perfect, and the gesture worked. The radical young officers were calmed. Guisan was then able to make precisely the same compromises, including extremely questionable dealings with SS General Walter Schellenberg, that Pilet knew had to be accepted.[122]

Guisan also altered the defensive posture of the Swiss army. He saw that the German victory in France had created an extraordinary situation. From Geneva to Sargans there was one enemy who might attack at any point. The army's mobilisation, hitherto based on the defence of the frontier against any aggressor, could hardly be sustained against Hitler's Germany. In July 1940 the army was withdrawn from the frontiers and took up positions in the

massive chain of the Alps. By the spring of 1941 all the field divisions
had taken up Alpine positions, in some cases as in that of Division
4 on the Pilatus mountain near Luzern, in almost impassable
terrain. Over 900 million francs were spent on fortifications, and
the Swiss army settled into its *réduit*. It was an uncomfortable nest
for modern officers schooled in the tactics of Guderian and
Rommel, but it had, as had the Rütli Order of the Day, the highest
possible symbolic significance. General Guisan declared openly by
this strategy that the Swiss army would fight to the end. It would
watch Zürich, Basel, Bern, Lausanne, Geneva, Biel, the entire
lowlands, fall to the Germans but it would not surrender. As the
chief of the General Staff, Jakob Huber, put it in reply to attacks on
the idea of the *réduit national*: 'In our situation there can only be one
aim, to resist as long as possible . . . We want to go down fighting,
leaving the aggressor only a totally devastated country without
material or human resources of any kind.'[123]

There is now a good deal of evidence to support the view that the
Germans seriously considered dealing with Switzerland, once and
for all, in the summer of 1940. The chief of the German General
Staff, Franz Halder, said: 'I was constantly hearing of outbursts of
Hitler's fury against Switzerland, which, given his mentality, might
have led at any minute to military activities for the army.'
'Operation Tannenbaum', the German code name for the invasion
of Switzerland, was prepared for just the sort of eventuality that
Halder feared.[124] We shall never know how far Hitler was deterred
by the spectacle of hardy mountaineers defending their crags
and how much dissuaded by other considerations. In the German
Foreign Office, Secretary von Weizsäcker thought Switzerland 'an
indigestible lump' and not worth swallowing.[125] After all, neutral
(on the whole, cooperative) Switzerland had its uses in Hitler's
plans. It is probable that the obvious determination of the Swiss to
defend the Alpine passes, even at the sacrifice of the lowlands, had
some effect, but, even if it did not, it is certainly no hyperbole to call
1940–5 one of Switzerland's 'finest hours'.

The trouble with 'finest hours' is that less fine ones follow them.
From July 1940 to August 1944 Switzerland sat in the centre of
Hitler's 'New Order' surrounded on every border by his forces. The
entire Swiss economy depended on raw materials from outside its
borders, but Hitler needed the Swiss railways, the Alpine passes
and the resources in engineering, watch-making and precision

machine tools, which Switzerland provided. The Allies watched these relations with distaste and contempt. In 1943 the Swiss government prepared a lengthy report on its economic relations with Nazi Germany for the British and American governments in which there was an instructive balance of trade in goods between 15 September 1939 and 31 August 1943:

Swiss imports from Germany	Sfr 2,258,000,000
Swiss exports to Germany	Sfr 1,972,000,000
Balance	Sfr 286,000,000

Net 'invisible' items – banking services, insurances, freight, licence fees and tourism (traditional Swiss specialities) – amounted to roughly Sfr 200 million per annum. If these sums were added, Switzerland had, in fact, ended up with a small negative balance of trade with Nazi Germany.[126] It was embarrassing but a fact that Switzerland had made money during the war. Nor was that all. From 1940 on the German Reichsbank made regular and substantial deposits of gold with the Swiss National Bank. The figures showed that between 1 September 1939 and the end of the war, the Reichsbank deposited Sfr 1,638,000,000.[127] Here too Switzerland, by acting as a reserve bank for the Germans, had done very handsomely out of the war.

The Allies had already taken action against Switzerland by establishing a black list of Swiss firms who had traded enthusiastically with the Axis. The Swiss were unpleasantly surprised to find that the British government had no intention of lifting the sanctions on such companies just because the war had ended. As Lord Lovatt wrote to the Swiss ambassador in June 1945:

Your memorandum referred to Swiss firms listed on account of their exports to the Axis. These firms contributed, in many cases by production of direct military requirements, to the equipment of the German war machine and thereby to the loss of Allied soldiers, sailors and airmen in battle, and to the aerial attacks on this country, and they certainly deserve their place on the Statutory List. I should emphatically disagree with any suggestion that their offence was of a minor character.

Besides, as Lord Lovatt pointed out, there was no reason to give companies who had made money trading with the Axis during the war a chance to profit from 'a strong competitive position' in the post-war world.[128]

The humanitarian role of Switzerland left a great deal to be desired. The full official story awaits the publication of the relevant volume in the series *Documents diplomatiques suisses* but Jean-Claude Favez, using the archives of the International Red Cross in Geneva, has shown that in the autumn of 1942 the ICRC received direct and incontrovertible evidence of the systematic murder of the Jews of Europe. On 14 October 1942, the governing committee of the Red Cross met in Geneva to consider the launch of an appeal against Nazi genocide. Under the influence of the Swiss government, the committee decided to remain silent.[129] Meanwhile on Swiss borders Jews committed suicide, as a Swiss report of 1957 confesses, 'often at the feet of Swiss soldiers rather than fall into the hands of the Germans'. 'The lifeboat', said Federal Councillor von Steiger, 'is full'.[130]

This dark side of Swiss neutrality was not widely known, some of it not even suspected. For most Swiss the war had been a triumph of national will. The heroic years in the *réduit national* not only left a legacy of patriotic rhetoric (NB: the Swiss did not actually win the war; they just stayed out of it) but also some unfortunate illusions about the real degree of unity. The cohesiveness of the years between the 1930s and the late 1950s had been artificial. For roughly thirty years, international fascism and the ensuing cold war threatened the Confederation externally. As in the years 1618 to 1648, an entire Swiss generation had been hermetically sealed off from the general trends of European development, and in both post-war periods, the sudden reappearance of strife, rapid change and innovation was a shock.

Another important legacy of the war years was the special position of the Swiss economy, which I shall discuss more fully in Chapter 5. In a Europe covered in rubble, the Swiss offered an island of fiscal stability and industrial capacity. For nearly twenty years, artificial boom followed artificial boom. Hundreds of small and not wildly efficient firms made money. Rationalisation was put off as hordes of foreign workers flooded the labour market. Huge reserves of capital, much of it foreign, stood behind the economic activity. This too came to seem normal, inevitable, right. The Swiss government looked with benevolent disinterest on the early stirrings of European unity. It postponed its infrastructure investments and public works for the rainy day which it gloomily expected to occur at any moment. The late 1960s brought a rude awakening. Growth had outstripped the powers of federal, cantonal or communal government. The precious Swiss environment was threatened in all sorts of ways: pollution, the sale of land to foreigners, the destruction of unspoilt nature for roads, hotels, ski lifts or army manoeuvres.

A final consequence of the *réduit* era is that, as so often in the past, Switzerland managed to carry into a new age the structures and habits of the old. Everywhere else in continental Europe, the Nazi occupation, the disruption of battle and the flow of refugees provoked vast upheavals. The old order was frequently swept away or much transformed. In Switzerland things stayed put. The cramped defensive posture of the *réduit* made change very difficult.

During the 1950s Switzerland began to be 'quaint'. There, in comfort, and for a fee, the modern German or Italian could enjoy a bit of the 'old' Europe, with its pretty dresses and antique folkways. Swiss habits changed slowly. The generation who had known privation in the 1930s and isolation in the 1940s saved their new money, and went on living as they had before. During the 1960s spending and consumption habits changed sharply. Not only had a younger generation reached the age at which pop culture and its tastes made an impact on spending habits, but the older groups began to consume as well. Washing machines appeared in peasant houses which had always washed by hand, and in the evening the family gathered before the television, which by the 1970s had been exchanged for a colour set. The once frugal governments at federal, cantonal and local level also began to spend lavishly. Switzerland had a backlog of autobahns, old-age and pension systems, schools, new jet fighters, sewage plants and atomic power generating equipment, which suddenly seemed urgently necessary. Total spending by all three levels of Swiss government tripled in money terms between 1959 and the middle of the 1970s.

Changes of every kind seemed to cascade onto the country like one of its disastrous spring avalanches, and as the unity and simplicities of the *réduit* era receded into the distance, many Swiss grew very nervous. Reactionary movements to preserve the Fatherland sprang up. The political peace was broken by protest from right and left, and the 'Helvetic *malaise*' spread.

The return to the mainstream of European development has

strained the traditional Swiss political machinery. It is possible that the historical inheritance of Switzerland has finally been spent. The next four chapters will attempt to assess the cohesive elements in the political, linguistic, economic and religious structures of past and present Switzerland. In Chapter 7, I take up the question of the survival of a distinctive Swiss identity under the pressures of the 1990s. It is one thing to show why there was a Switzerland in the past, a very different one to answer 'Why Switzerland?' now.

CHAPTER 3

Politics

The Swiss are justly famous for their political institutions and practices: the ancient assembly of free citizens in the *Landsgemeinde*, the elaborate devices for direct participation by the citizen in the process of decision through referenda and initiatives, the variety and precision of the federal system, the refinements of voting practice and proportional representation, the thriving local and cantonal governments, the evolution of the uniquely Swiss collective executive bodies on local, cantonal and federal level, the overlapping office-holding which enables a person to be simultaneously an elected officer of township, canton and federal parliaments, the instrumental attitude to constitutions which enables easy revision and extension to what elsewhere would be legislative activity, the astonishing stability of Swiss voting habits which have held the four main parties in very nearly perfect equilibrium since 1919 and the late entry of women into politics. The simple enumeration of Switzerland's 'peculiar institutions' adds up to an impressive statement of the uniqueness of Switzerland in the European context. Other societies have some but none has all these channels of direct and semi-direct democracy. The net of politics seems to stretch farther in Switzerland than elsewhere. Activities thought of as technical or administrative in other countries tend to be made elective and political in Switzerland. The ground rules of politics, that unspoken agreement about what is or is not 'done', and the unwritten provisions of Swiss constitutionalism make up a further middle area of values and habits which profoundly affect the workings of the machinery. For example, the Swiss prefer to see the executive at federal, cantonal and local level vested in a committee rather than a president and that committee must be elected. Yet candidates are rarely defeated and thrown from office; it is simply not 'done'.

Describing how all these things work is hard enough, and most of this chapter will do little else. Understanding their significance is much more difficult. How do all these elaborate bits and pieces of machinery fit the economic, social, linguistic, historical and legal aspects of Swiss life? The 'national character' is frequently deployed to help in this difficulty. The Swiss are famous for their *Feinmechanik* and they themselves often mock their own perfectionism, so it is not too far-fetched to compare the delicate machinery of a watch with the intricacies of Swiss proportional representation. In a general, very general, sense, these comparisons are legitimate. A society in which the work ethos is so highly developed and in which precision is valued will certainly seek the same attributes in politics. But why have these attitudes and values established themselves across linguistic and historical boundaries? Why is a Swiss French as likely to rise at dawn as a Swiss German or a Swiss Italian? 'National character' ends up in circularity: the Swiss behave like Swiss because they are Swiss. Another objection is that looking at the machinery of politics distracts one from the 'real' sources of power, which are economic.

It is certainly true that today tiny cantonal sovereignties are dwarfed by the international corporations whose headquarters they are. Giant firms have turnover figures many times larger than cantonal or even federal budgets, and the three biggest banks have balance sheets whose collective totals almost add up to the amount of the Swiss gross national product. The disparity between corporate and conventional political power is wider in Switzerland than in any other European country, but this does not make the political machinery and its functioning irrelevant. Big Swiss firms depend on the government to manage currency, to pass laws, to administer taxes and to cope with social conflict as do any other groups in society. Ciba-Geigy of Basel, one of the biggest chemical and pharmaceutical companies in the world, has an annual turnover of more than Sfr 20 billion (£12 billion) but, as Dr Albert Bodmer, former vice-chairman of the board of Ciba-Geigy, explained to me, the owners of the equity capital remain overwhelmingly Swiss, and the corporate culture is pure 'Basel'. At company headquarters the directors take the tram to work. They rent a Mercedes of the right grandeur, he said, 'when the Germans come'. If they were in Zürich, he assured me, they would all be driven about in Rolls.[1]

This is not 'politics' in the obvious institutional sense but part of a Swiss way of doing things, which links the corporate board room and the local town council. The Swiss way of doing things, for want of a better description, moulds behaviour in churches and charities, in brass bands and sporting clubs, in the factory and on the farm. It unites the Swiss across language, economic, religious and geographical divisions. Social scientists describe this interaction of political institutions, attitudes and behaviour by the term 'political culture'. Swiss political culture goes well beyond the limits of politics in the strict sense and comes close to being a surrogate for conventional national identity. As Clive Church has shrewdly observed, 'the Swiss have – rather like the Americans – been bound together by their political process'.[2]

Unwritten rules and assumptions about how things ought to be done express themselves in quite specific political institutions and mechanisms. The Swiss prefer proportional representation to majority systems. Their institutions reflect their desire for what they call 'concordance' and their dislike of conflict. Whereas the British and American systems produce winners, the Swiss prefer to protect the losers. Where other systems strive to generate a powerful majority which can govern, the Swiss opt for complex formulae that produce coalitions. All political machinery in Switzerland has a provisional quality because the 'Sovereign', 'the people', is really sovereign and may exercise its power to change this or that instrument of its will.

The most striking single manifestation of that sovereignty is the intricacy of voting. The Swiss have instruments for measuring popular will of such delicacy that, as Christopher Hughes shows, sometimes even official publications get things wrong. Take one case which Professor Hughes cites: the workings of the d'Hondt system of proportional representation. He quotes an official handout at the Swiss Embassy: 'If ten National Councillors are to be elected in a canton, and of the 60,000 voters, 36,000 vote for List A, 12,000 for List B, 6,000 for List C, 5,000 for List D, and 1,000 for List E, the distribution of seats will be 6:2:1:1:0.' As he points out, this seems common sense. 'The interesting point about it is that it is wrong. List A, surprisingly, would elect 7 members and List D none.' The reason is that under the d'Hondt system the seats are based on a 'Final Quotient', that is, the number which can be divided into each party's total of votes to give the right number of seats. In the particular example, it would work as follows:

Divide the total vote (60,000) by the number of seats *plus* one (11). The result is called the Provisional Quotient (5,454). In our example, it gives the provisional result of 6:2:1:0:0. But this only adds up to 9, and there are ten seats to be allocated. The second sum seeks the Final Quotient. This is obtained by dividing each party's votes by the provisional number of seats it obtains, *plus* one. Thus List A (36,000) is divided by 7 (6 plus 1) and gives the result 5,142. This sum is repeated for each seat in turn, and the highest of the results is the Final Quotient; in our example, 5,142 is the highest. It is the number which when divided among each result in turn gives the right number of seats.[3]

Those of you who have just put aside your pencils will know that it works. The rest will have to take it on faith. In both groups sympathy must be growing with the ordinary Swiss citizen in the face of such intricacy. The system is also opaque. It is impossible to tell without pencil and paper what difference to the final outcome a shift of, say, 1,000 votes from List B to List C might have. Swiss politicians call the curious permutations and combinations which occur *Proporzpech* and *Proporzglück*, 'proportional bad luck' and 'proportional good luck'. Since the citizen has the right to alter the party lists by voting twice for the same candidate (*cumulation*) or by striking a name on, say, List A and replacing it with a name from another list (*panachage*), devices which are frequently used both by the party in preparing its official list and by the citizen in editing the list, the game of voting becomes more and more complicated and hard to see through. In the Appendix there are some concrete examples taken from the official guide to these procedures prepared by the Federal Chancellery.

To make matters worse, the complicated electoral system tends to reproduce itself not only on the national but also on the cantonal and local level. A resident of the city of Zürich, for example, has the privilege (or burden) of electing the *Nationalräte* (deputies to the lower house of the national parliament) from Canton Zürich, two members to represent the canton in the *Ständerat* (the upper house of the national parliament), the members of the cantonal parliament, the members of the city parliament of Zürich city, the members of the city executive council, district councillors, district magistrates, district prosecutors, members of the district school board, members of the area school board, arbitration magistrates, a notary public, who is both agent in bankruptcy and keeper of the property records, secondary and primary school teachers and so on.

He or she may also have to vote on matters of substance, for in Switzerland the citizen has powers which are known as 'semi-direct democracy' and which take the form of votes on referenda and initiatives at all three levels of government. Although participation by the 'people' in decision-making has an ancient lineage in Switzerland, the elements of direct democracy came relatively late to the federal level – the referendum in 1874 and the initiative in 1891. Today citizens go to the polls on federal issues four times a year to vote on everything from unemployment insurance to the abolition of the army.[4]

The second layer of Swiss politics is that of the cantons. There are twenty-six cantons, or more accurately twenty full cantons and six 'half-cantons' (the two Appenzells, Basel-Stadt and Basel-Land, Obwalden and Nidwalden). The present division between cantons and federal authority grew out of the crisis of the civil war, as I showed in the previous chapter. It led to a compromise and to a bicameral legislature where the sovereignty of the canton is protected in an upper house, the *Ständerat* or *Conseil des Etats*, in which each canton has, like the American senate on which it is modelled, two representatives (half-cantons have one) regardless of its population. The constitution of 1874 emphasises the status of cantons, as we have seen, in Article 3:

The cantons are sovereign, in so far as their sovereignty is not limited by the federal constitution, and exercise all those rights, which have not been transferred to federal power.

In this respect the Swiss federal system seems to be very much like the American. The Tenth Amendment of the US Constitution makes the same claims as Article 3 of the Swiss. Here is the American version:

The powers not delegated to the United States by the Constitution, nor prohibited by it to the States, are reserved to the States respectively or to the people.

Cantons make up essential pieces of the Swiss political machine. They vary hugely in size and significance. Canton Zürich has well over a million inhabitants and as a political unit is both richer and more populous than independent states like Estonia or Slovenia. The tiny Appenzell half-cantons with 50,000 and 13,000 would not merit more than district councils in English local government. Yet

the Appenzells and Zürich share the same attributes of sovereignty
and form part of the same federal state. Their politics reflect
certain general features of Swiss political reality and need to be
understood. Although every imaginable activity is, as the Swiss
ruefully admit, 'different from canton to canton', they are more
alike than different and a look at one will serve to illuminate how
they all work.

Canton Zug with its 239 square kilometres and population of
about 85,000 people is very small. Even among Swiss cantons it
ranks near the bottom in area and population; yet it is number one
in national income per head. Its sovereign status allows it to enact
a very relaxed taxation system which has encouraged companies to
register their head offices in its capital town.[5] Canton Zug has its
own constitution, dated 31 January 1894. Like all Swiss constitutions
it was ratified by popular referendum and has been amended more
than thirty times over the past century. Swiss constitutions are not
sacrosanct pieces of ancient parchment but a form of running
record of the decisions of the voters.

The first article proclaims that Canton Zug is 'a democratic free
state'.[6] Like the twenty-five other Swiss cantons and half-cantons
Zug has all the attributes of sovereignty – constitution, executive,
legislative and judiciary, its own system of laws and practices, a flag
and coat of arms. It has a proper parliament with eighty members
elected by proportional representation for four-year terms.[7]

The basic unit of Swiss politics, and the key to understanding
them, is the *Gemeinde* or *commune*. There is no suitable English
translation of *Gemeinde* because there was no parallel development
in the English-speaking world. The nearest equivalent is, perhaps,
the self-governing New England town, where the citizenry
assembled in the town meeting constitute the ultimate legislative
authority. In certain parts of Switzerland, the community of
citizens has always been understood to be 'sovereign' and in Swiss
political parlance today, the citizenry as a whole, as we have seen, is
still 'the sovereign'. Politicians 'consult the sovereign' or 'fear the
reaction of the sovereign' as the case may be. Nowhere is that
sovereignty more obvious and direct than in the *Gemeinde*, the
essential and uniquely Swiss unit of communal activity.

Communes enjoy the same sort of semi-sovereignty within the
canton that the canton enjoys within the federation. A typical
definition of the powers of the communes is that in Article 2 of

Canton Zug's *Gemeindegesetz* (communal law) of 4 September 1980 which recognises and regulates the status of communes in phrases very like those of the federal constitution's Article 3:

The tasks of the communes can be all affairs which affect the well-being of the commune, which are not exclusively tasks of the Federation or the Canton.

Within that framework the *Gemeindegesetz* regulates the election, powers and rights of communes. The *Einwohnergemeinde* or residential commune is the primary political unit of cantonal politics. Article 59 of the *Gemeindegesetz* lists the powers of the residential communes: conduct of elections and other referenda or initiatives; security of essential needs; law and order; primary schooling; social and welfare services; promotion of culture and health; civil defence; local planning; public transport; police and fire services; civil registration office and maintenance of cemeteries.[8] Article 64 states that

the highest organ of the commune are those persons entitled to vote, who exercise their rights at the ballot box or in the general communal assembly.

Communes are substantial enterprises and levy taxes to defray their costs. The citizens often pay more direct taxes to the commune than to the canton. In 1994 official statistics show that of Sfr 98,207,000,000 in national revenues, communes raised Sfr 36,200,000,000 or 36.9% while the federal government raised Sfr 34,417,000,000 or 35.1%.[9] The executive of a commune is the elected *Gemeinderat* (communal council) which according to Article 83 of the *Gemeindegesetz* in Canton Zug must be composed of five members plus the elected *Gemeindeschreiber* (communal clerk). This form of executive repeats itself at every level of Swiss politics from tiny communes with a few hundred citizens to the Federal Council in Bern. The number of members in the council may vary but the formula is constant, a number of elected councillors plus an elected chief civil servant. At federal level the chief civil servant is the Federal Chancellor elected by the Federal Assembly; at cantonal level in Zug there is the *Landschreiber* elected by the cantonal parliament and at local level, as we have seen, the *Gemeindeschreiber* elected by the people of the commune.

Communes confer citizenship, a power which reflects the rooted, 'bottom-up' quality of Swiss life. As Herr Josef Geisseler, the *Gemeindeschreiber* of Malters, explained it to me, they do so by vote. The prospective citizens present themselves to the local political parties, show competence in the local dialect and then offer themselves as potential citizens on the ballot. There is normally a picture of the prospective candidate as well, which allows the citizens to see the race of candidates without having explicitly to ask.[10] A fee is charged which varies from commune to commune and in a recent case in Zug even varied from candidate to candidate. The children of a local immigrant family discovered that the commune in which they had been born intended to charge them a higher fee for citizenship than a recently settled surgeon. Their complaint, supported by the cantonal executive in Zug, resulted in litigation before the Federal Court in Lausanne.[11] A very large number of immigrant children, born in Switzerland, raised and schooled there, entirely at home in local dialect, are not Swiss citizens. Since, according to the census of 1990, foreigners make up 18.1% of the resident Swiss population,[12] a substantial number of Swiss residents suffer the consequences of democracy, Swiss style. In June 1994, a government-sponsored referendum to ease the restrictions on citizenship for foreigners between the ages of 18 and 24 who had spent at least five years in Swiss schools received 52.9% of the popular vote but failed to get that majority of cantons which constitutional amendments require.[13] If Swiss democracy has some ugly features, it shows them to its foreigners.

In addition to the residential commune, there is the commune of origin, so-called *Bürgerort*, the place where one is, as Swiss say, *heimatberechtigt* (entitled to be at home), written large. This communal citizenship remains within the family and its descendants even if they have been living elsewhere for several generations. Most Swiss will instinctively answer the question 'where are you from?' with the *Bürgerort*, even though they may never have set foot in the place. The home commune today has less significance than it used to, since only about a third of the population now actually live in the *Gemeinde* where they have rights. Nevertheless there are rights of last resort to be claimed. The commune of origin, not the commune of domicile, must support its citizens if they fall on hard times. Commune of origin plays a role in the election of members of the *Bundesrat*, since locality is one of the many elements to be balanced among the members of the seven-member executive. The commune of origin may be one with ancient collective holdings or, in some cases, collective obligations. There may be profits to be collected or dues to be paid. It says something about the rootedness of Swiss identity that this curious yet important, fictional yet very real, form of citizenship should be so instinctively accepted.

In addition to the *Einwohnergemeinde* and the *Bürgergemeinde*, there are other corporate bodies in which the Swiss exercise their rights. There is the *Kirchgemeinde*, which administers the local church according to the particular cantonal legislation and raises a church tax, the *Kirchensteuer*, which covers the cost of parochial salaries and church maintenance. This structure, which can also be found in other European countries, has certain, peculiarly Swiss, features which will be discussed in the chapter on religion later in this book. Then there are various pre-modern corporate bodies, the so-called *Korporationen*, whose rights to woods, pasturage or water may go back for centuries, or corporations to build and maintain roads in mountainous areas which present features of a political community mixed with those of a joint-stock company.

One of the oddest features of this corporate, collective politics is how important political parties are in making it function. Let us take a single commune in a single canton and put it under the microscope. There are 107 *Gemeinden* in Canton Luzern. Several of these have intense party political activity, activity which stretches into areas wholly outside 'politics' in the Anglo-American under-standing of the word. The town of Malters lies in the pretty river valley of the Kleine Emme about 20 kilometres west of the city of Luzern. There are about 4,000 persons on the electoral roll, yet organised party interference is strong. The two main parties, the Liberals and the Christian Democratic People's Party (Christlich-demokratische Volkspartei) known as CVP, are powerfully represented in the commune, and constitute an additional, extra-constitutional arm of government. The party balance has remained unusually stable over the years since the second world war. Until the elections of 1991, when the CVP gained a seat and the presi-dency of the *Gemeinderat*, elections, no matter how hotly contested, always produced three Liberals and two CVP members. The *Gemeindeschreiber*, Herr Josef Geisseler, has been in office for over four decades, and, although a Liberal, was re-elected in 1991 by the CVP majority. The unwritten rules of Swiss political life ensure that servants of the commune, canton or federal government, who are formally party political candidates, in fact get re-elected automatically as civil servants and are expected to be beyond partisanship.

Although the Liberals dominate Malters, the CVP is the largest party in the canton with, in recent years, between 70 and 85 seats in the *Grossrat*, the cantonal parliament of 180 members.[14] Invisible partitions separate party members in a community like Malters. Everybody knows who belongs to which party, and party membership frequently determines who gets which jobs. In nearby Willisau, divided for historical reasons into Willisau-Stadt, controlled by the Liberals, and Willisau-Land, controlled by the CVP, there are separate Liberal and CVP pubs, clubs and hotels. An architect from Willisau-Land – a CVP member – told me that in seventeen years in practice he had only received one contract from a Liberal, who happened to be a cousin.[15]

Malters has to have drains and a water supply. There are two firms in town which could carry out the work, but they are not chosen by competitive bidding for each contract as would be the case elsewhere. Instead, the *Brunnenmeister* (the master of the fountains) is elected by the *Gemeinderat* on a party vote. In 1971 I met the then *Brunnenmeister* who had been recently elected by the Liberal majority on the *Gemeinderat* and who had invested substantially in new equipment to carry out the work. The competition, a CVP plumbing contractor, was sharpening its spanners in the hope of a CVP victory. In reply to my amazed question as to whether his firm was at least technically the better of the two, he smiled modestly and replied 'I wouldn't say that.' I recall from the same period a conversation with a Young Liberal activist in a pub in the mountains, who looked round conspiratorially and, seeing a group of young men at a nearby table, began to whisper, observing 'we are not all Liberals here'.

Here too, as in other elements of Swiss life, the ancient identities have begun to crumble. The automatic allegiance to a party, as a kind of familial inheritance, has eroded. Young and old agree that party labels no longer bind as they once did, not least because the end of the twentieth century has seen the erosion of ideology everywhere. The 'C' in Christian Democracy, the 'L' in the Liberal Party of Luzern and the 'S' in the Socialist Party have been drained of real content. Partisan politics continue as habit rather than conviction and even in rural, central Switzerland,

European matters have broken traditional ties. In the referendum on membership of the European Economic Area on 6 December 1992, both the CVP and the Liberals officially backed membership. Malters voted emphatically 'No' by over two to one in a turnout of 85.6% of those entitled to vote and in April 1995, in elections for the Luzern cantonal parliament, the two dominant, historic parties, the Liberals and the CVP, dropped to a mere 70.3% of the vote. The surprise winner was a party which said 'No' to Europe and 'No' to change of any kind. The traditional Bernese and largely Protestant party of the lower middle classes, the Swiss People's Party (Schweizerische Volkspartei or SVP), which had never been represented in Catholic Luzern, took 8.86% of the vote in Malters and 8.10% in the canton of Luzern as a whole.[16]

If party allegiance is now weakening, its previous ferocity still presents a puzzle. Why were the divisions so deep and bitter? When I asked an activist in 1971, he found it hard to explain. He had to confess that there were few matters of principle that separated CVP and Liberals. As a leftish Young Liberal, he thought the CVP social policy rather better and more progressive than the Liberal. Of course he had CVP friends, though rather fewer than Liberal ones. Yes, his family were solidly Liberal on both sides and always had been. He tried to put into words the differences between the parties and retreated into emotional expressions of a rather vague kind. Liberals were in some way more open-minded, not less Roman Catholic than the CVP, but less clerical, more attached to free enterprise and less attracted to 'étatist' solutions. Malters Liberals feel an affinity with the Liberal Party of Luzern city, a certain cosmopolitanism, radicalism even, combativeness. Finally, he urged me not to confuse the Luzern Liberals with the Zürich *Freisinnige* or the Basel Radicals. They were, he said with some contempt, the parties of big business, not a popular people's party like the Liberals in Luzern.

Party history in Canton Luzern is in a curious way a shorthand for social and economic history. The CVP of today is still in many ways the old *Katholisch–Konservativ*, the 'KK' of yesterday, entrenched in certain country districts in Canton Luzern and in the *Waldstätte* (the 'Forest Cantons' of Uri, Schwyz and Unterwalden), Valais and Fribourg. Its new 'Christian Democratic' image is an attempt to get out of the Catholic ghetto by following the example of the German Christian Democratic Union; what was a confessional must become a mass party. In Canton Luzern the key to party politics lies buried in the centuries of estrangement between the patrician, cosmopolitan oligarchy who ran the elegant little city of Luzern and the more backward, democratic, conservative, clerical peasantry of the valleys. In Luzern, unlike the position in Bern, the aristocracy were among the leaders of the Liberal regeneration of the 1830s. The content of Luzern liberalism, its elitism and its 'Josefine' view that the state must control the church, pushed it into a head-on collision with the mystical, violent, peasant-born Joseph Leu von Ebersol, whose democratic, conservative and Catholic *coup* of 1841 began the process leading up to the civil war, the *Sonderbundskrieg*. Again it was the Liberal, rationalist, anti-Vatican, patrician leadership who regained power after the defeat of the *Sonderbund* and who maintained it in distant alliance with the very different sort of liberalism represented in the victorious Protestant cantons until the 1870s. These conflicts, the struggle between city and country, between enlightened, rationalist cosmopolitanism and clerical, pious, democratic conservatism, live on in the shimmering, almost invisible mental structures of the attitude of the Young Liberal in Malters. The continuity of history in Switzerland reproduces these attitudes from generation to generation until both origin and ideological content seem lost in a haze. I have no idea what permutations of historic circumstance, settlement or local condition gave Malters a predominantly Liberal character. Each community will have its own version of the history of the whole, long, complicated and difficult to assess. What strikes the eye here is the rootedness in the past of even the election of the president of the communal council in one small Swiss *Gemeinde*. As Johannes von Müller, the great Swiss historian of the eighteenth century, said, 'above all, nothing is either large or small, because it looks to be so on the map; it all depends on the spirit'.

The spirit of a community like Grenchen in Canton Solothurn is obviously going to be different. Grenchen, known as the most 'proletarian' city in Switzerland, produces 70% of the internal parts for watches made in Switzerland and contains the headquarters of several of the most famous Swiss watch companies, as well as the administrative centre of Ebauches SA with its central computer controlling the operation of its subsidiary companies. There are many other large and small firms in the watch and allied industries. Its population of 17,000 spreads out over the flat basin of the River

Aare and along both sides of the motorway from Biel to Solothurn. Yet it too is a *Gemeinde* and has all the forms of communal government which Malters has. Grenchen has 11,000 voters compared to 4,000 and an annual expenditure of about Sfr 80 million compared to Sfr 23 million in Malters.[17] As an industrial town, where a high percentage of the population have settled in the last twenty-five years, politics lack the personal intensity of a face-to-face community such as Malters. The scale of Grenchen is larger. The *Gemeinderat* in Grenchen has thirty members. In the 1993 elections the Socialists had twelve members, the *Freisinnige* (Radicals, the sister party of Luzern's Liberals) had ten, the CVP four, the Greens two and the Freedom Party two, a distribution of votes that, with the exception of the rise and fall of fringe parties, had hardly changed for years.[18] As in Malters, so in Grenchen Swiss voters prefer continuity to change. Although 11,000 persons are entitled to vote in the commune, the city still operates through a town meeting system of *Gemeindeversammlung*. As Stadtschreiber Herr Rolf Enggist explained to me, this means that only a small fraction of the population actually exercises its right to vote. A normal turnout might be anything from 150 to 500 citizens. Even on controversial matters, when a thousand might appear, the active citizenry will still be less than a tenth of those eligible.

In Grenchen, as elsewhere, the old communalism has become a fiction. The natural alternative to the *Gemeindeversammlung* is the postal ballot, which, its advocates argue, would yield a higher and more democratic participation in civic affairs. Busy, professional people simply lack the time to attend the *Gemeindeversammlung*. Oddly enough Malters, though much smaller, no longer has a *Gemeindeversammlung* and is one of the two communes of 107 in Luzern to use postal ballots exclusively for all communal voting, although the *Gemeindeversammlung* was abolished in Malters because it was too partisan, not because it was unrepresentative. Grenchen and many other urban communes resist the change. Grenchen has, at least, recognised realities by adding to the unwieldy and unusually large *Gemeinderat* of thirty an executive committee of seven members, which actually takes decisions and has really for practical purposes become the *Gemeinderat*.[19] In some Swiss communities failure to participate in democratic life has now become chronic. Geneva is notorious for low turnout but other cities are not much better.

The city of Zürich poses these problems in their most acute form. Until the late nineteenth century, the city had a comfortable population of about 28,000, while the eleven communes around it had grown rapidly. The depression of the 1890s hit them hard and bankruptcy forced a fusion of Zürich city and the surrounding communes on 1 January 1893. At a stroke Zürich's population passed the 100,000 mark and the city's area was twenty-eight times larger.[20] Today with a population of 355,297, of whom 89,284 are foreigners, Zürich city is more than twice as large as any other Swiss city. The canton of Zürich with its 1,176,983 residents represents one in six of the entire Swiss population. The city of Zürich had an annual expenditure in 1993 of Sfr 5,680,400,000, which was larger than the total outlay of the six eastern Swiss cantons of St Gallen, Thurgau, Graubünden, Schaffhausen and the two Appenzells put together.[21] Its *Gemeinderat* is, in effect, an urban parliament with 125 members, for which in the 1994 elections 1,488 candidates, distributed among nineteen parties, competed. The results concern us less than the trends in voter participation. Since 1928 the share of those entitled to vote who actually exercise their rights has fallen steadily from 90.6% in 1928 to the 1990s when only 49.0% (1990) and 48.6% (1994) bothered to turn out.[22] Exactly what the trend means has been the subject of debate in Switzerland for more than a generation without yielding any agreement.

Yet even in the anonymity of a great modern city, the Swiss 'way of doing things' persists and shapes political behaviour. As in little Malters, so in Zürich the voters rarely eject anybody from office. Arthur Gilgen continued as education minister of Canton Zürich for twenty-four years even though he had long severed connections with the party that put him there.[23] The late Emil Landholt served on the city council of Zürich equally as long and for seventeen of those years was the mayor. He chose to step down at the age of seventy-one; nobody would have forced him to go. In a long obituary, Alfred Cattani summed up Emil Landholt's virtues, those essential qualities that made him the perfect *Stapi*, a dialect and rather affectionate abbreviation for *Stadtpräsident*:

Emil Landholt gave to Zürich during his term of office the charm and familiarity of a village. He knew, or so it seemed, each and everybody, and used the familiar 'Du' with many of them. If one invited him to something, he would come, and if you met him on the way to one of his countless receptions, he would spontaneously invite you, whether it was a grand official occasion or a private party . . . His 'be nice to each other' [in dialect, of course, 'sind lieb miteinand' – JS] was directed at those whom he wished to tie into the personal and political consensus.[24]

Landholt embodied every virtue the Swiss value in politics. He was not grand, nor abrasive. He put consensus and community above ideology, even though he became the first 'bourgeois' mayor after a long period of 'Red' dominance. He said 'Du' to people, spoke dialect and made Zürich seem like a village, not a megalopolis. Like the directors of Ciba-Geigy who take the tram to work, the *Stapi* was *volksnah*, near to the people, an essential attribute of political success in Switzerland.

Swiss political structures all strive to be *volksnah* and to respond to the wishes of the citizen. By dividing power equally among three levels of government, Swiss federalism spreads a denser net of political institutions over the body politic than any other system in Europe. The fact that the communes spend as much tax money as the cantonal and federal governments gives local politics a direction and impact not found in other systems, which praise devolution but do not practise it. The system operates as it does because higher authorities leave lower ones alone. It is an unwritten rule of Swiss federalism that cantonal governments leave communes to get on with their affairs as they see fit. When Canton Zug took up the case of the immigrant family whose commune had charged too much for citizenship, it did so unwillingly even though higher principles, such as natural justice and the constitutional guarantees of equality before the law, were involved. It took much persuasion by the *Landschreiber*, as chief professional advisor to the canton's government, to convince members of the government that they had no choice but to act.[25]

Swiss federalism rests on structures with replaceable parts. Since cantons are the result of complex historical aggregation, with bits and pieces added and taken away over time, they can, if necessary, be divided or adjusted, as long as the 'sovereign people' gives its consent to such changes. Division of political units often eases a conflict. During the 1830 revolution the aristocrats in Basel city, threatened by rebellious peasants demanding greater rights in government, preserved their regime by allowing the peasants to secede. They accepted a division into two half-cantons, a city-state called 'Basel-Stadt' and a country canton called 'Basel-Land', which in spite of reunification efforts remain half-cantons to this day.

The jigsaw puzzle of communal sovereignty produces jagged and irregular cantonal boundaries and in some cases results in bits of territory not contiguous with the cantonal borders. Such bits and pieces are called 'enclaves' or 'exclaves'. Canton Schaffhausen, which is on the right bank of the Rhine, contains several bits of German territory. Kleinlützel and Mariastein belong to Canton Solothurn although they are on the other side of the Birs river and have no contiguous borders with their nominal authority, and a piece of Italian territory, Campione d'Italia, sits on Lago di Lugano surrounded by Swiss territory. Splitting political units in this way acts to reduce friction or, at least, to contain it in the smallest element of tolerable dissatisfaction. Swiss federalism is both absolute and relative at the same time. The system works because the parts are moveable. The parts are moveable if the 'sovereign' says they are.

None of this overlapping and irregular jurisdiction would have seemed odd to anybody who knew Europe before the French Revolution. Enclaves and exclaves occurred all over the map and especially among the three thousand sovereignties which belonged to the Holy Roman Empire of the German Nation. The French with their obsession with uniformity, equality and centralisation impressed their ideals on modern consciousness so that it seems strange now to imagine a political authority without integrated territorial cohesion. Swiss politics combines in a unique, historic amalgam the surviving bits of the old Empire infused with modern practices of popular sovereignty from below. Switzerland represents a model of a Europe that might have evolved if the French Revolution had not succeeded in transforming the European state. It is for this reason that each canton resembles a set of Chinese boxes, or, perhaps better, a beehive into which history has built dozens of smaller boxes, the *Gemeinden*. They in turn are often subdivided into ethnic, religious or cultural sub-units which, while not formally recognised, give the commune its characteristic colour or tone. This cellular political system allows ethnic and other particularisms to flourish side by side. It gives to Swiss political life a marvellous mosaic surface. The residents of the communes 'sous les roches' may be Catholic and anti-Bernese while those 'sur les roches' may be the opposite, but as long as the walls between compartments have been drawn adequately and the larger cantonal box has room for both, no troubles arise.

Yet even in Switzerland, as we have seen, troubles can and do arise. For thirty years Swiss politics was troubled by a separatist movement of the residents of the Swiss Jura. The problem of separatism and incompatible communities refusing to live together is alas too common; the Swiss solution is unique. Describing how the Swiss 'peace process' worked not only illuminates the essential character of Swiss federalism but may offer some useful reflections applicable to other areas where similar territorial battles rage. The Jura crisis was small in scale but large in significance, like so much in Swiss history.

The origins of today's troubles can be seen in the debris left by Napoleon's new order. Before 1789 the Jura districts had belonged to the prince–bishop of Basel. Exiled by the Reformation, the prince–bishop had established his see in the pretty Lilliputian residence of Arlesheim, from which he ruled the poor, remote valleys of the eastern Jura for more than two centuries. In the name of reason and revolution, the French republic put an end to the secular domain of the prince–bishop as it was to do to so many other mini-principalities and tiny kingdoms. For a while the Jura became part of the republican French 'Département du Mont Terrible' only to be reassigned several times during the Napoleonic era. The conservative statesmen who tried to put Europe together again in 1814 and 1815 knew that turning back the clocks would not work, though rulers like the Elector of Hesse–Cassel and the King of Savoy tried to do that by demoting all those promoted and abrogating all decrees sanctioned under Napoleon. The Gracious Lords of Bern wanted their subject territories back, especially the lovely and prosperous Vaudois lands along Lac Léman, but the Swiss Committee of the Vienna Congress considered that too risky. Napoleon's nineteen cantons were sanctioned and the Bernese were compensated for the loss of the Vaud by being given the miscellaneous possessions of the former prince–bishop of Basel. It was a poor deal. 'They have taken our wine cellar and corn chamber', said a contemporary Bernese wag, 'and left us the garret'. As the inset to Map 2 on p. 95 shows, the image is well chosen. The northern districts of Porrentruy, Delémont and Saignelégier, are very like the Swiss garret, remote, self-contained and very hard to reach even by today's means of transport. The formal decision of the Vienna Congress could, of course, not be refused and so Canton Bern was notified that it had been agreed 'to procure for it and to guarantee to it Bienne with its territory, Erguel, Moutier and the Porrentruy'.[26] The formal union of the city of Biel–Bienne and the francophone districts along the lake, the Bieler See, was, on the other hand, a real gain. The residents of the southern districts of the Jura were content for they were largely Protestant and welcomed the union with a large, comfortable Protestant state like Canton Bern. The residents of the northern territories were Roman Catholic, poor and discontented.

The nineteenth century saw the religious and geographical divisions harden. By the twentieth century, better economic conditions had eroded the coolness of the north Jura towards Bern but had also complicated the situation by bringing German-speaking immigrants into hitherto purely French territories. In the census of 1880, the whole Jura contained 24% German-speakers while in some of the southern districts it was over 30%. The first world war revived separatism, but as the Protestant Synod noted with deep suspicion in 1917: 'All members of the separatist committee are Catholic; not a single Protestant has taken part. Are we not justified, we Jurassien Protestants, in seeing in the separatist movement clericalism at work in one of its most audacious enterprises?'[27] French-speaking Jurassien radicals were convinced of it and even welcomed German immigration on the grounds that every Protestant vote was a vote against clericalism. During the 1920s and 1930s the Jura as a whole was so hard hit by the depression that separatism as an issue and the Catholic–Protestant division tended to fade out.

The rebirth of the separatist movement can be dated: 20 September 1947. Bern was one of the few cantons left in which the *Regierungsrat* (Executive Council) was still elected within the *Grosser Rat* (the cantonal parliament) and not directly by the people. On that day a member from the Jura was refused election to the executive because he spoke French. The language question temporarily united both Protestant and Catholic, north and south, in the Comité de Moutier. The committee's efforts eventually led to amendments to the constitution of Canton Bern recognising the identity of the Jura in practical and symbolic ways. During the 1950s a new movement, the Rassemblement jurassien (RJ) gained ground in the north and began a popular initiative for a separate canton.

The leaders of the separatist movement managed to get 24,000 signatures on the petition calling for a referendum among the Jura people about separation. This amounted to 55% of those eligible to vote. The separatists hoped to demonstrate in the ensuing ballot that the Jura was solid. They knew they would be heavily outvoted by the rest of Canton Bern, but a big 'Yes' vote in the Jura would create a splash. When the votes had been counted not only had the whole canton said 'no' to opening the separation question but so had the Jura by a small margin('Yes': 15,163; 'No': 16,354). The division was geographical and religious. The three Roman Catholic northern districts (Porrentruy, Delémont and Saignelégier) voted two to one in favour, while the three Protestant southern districts (Moutier, Courtelary and La Neuveville) voted three to one against. The confessional line was particularly sharp in the Vallon de St Imier where the old Catholic communes 'sous les roches' which had once belonged to the bishopric of Basel voted overwhelmingly 'Yes', while the villages 'sur les roches', which had never been part of the bishopric and were Protestant, voted equally overwhelmingly 'No'. Another attempt at the direct democratic instrument, an initiative of May 1962, was an even more embarrassing failure for the separatists.

The dilemma for the residents of the northern Jura seemed complete. Direct democracy must defeat them. They were a minority of the total population of the canton and even of the historic territories which they claimed. They made up a smaller proportion of the population of Bern in the 1960s than they had in 1900. On the other hand, they refused to abandon their claim to all of the Jura even though the southern Jura resolutely opposed separation. They felt their frustrations and nursed their very real sense of grievance. The slogan of the anti-separatists in 1959 – 'Votez non, et on n'en parlera plus!' – proved as false as the hopes of the separatists. Almost inevitably, the Rassemblement jurassien moved toward direct action and violence. In 1962, the youth wing of the movement was formed. They called themselves *les Béliers* after the medieval battering rams which became their symbol. Bernard Varrin, their leader, summed up their position: 'We use provocation because we believe that it is the only language that the Swiss understand.' After the early 1960s direct action and political moves were linked in a counterpoint of unrest utterly familiar to those who know Northern Ireland.

In 1965 the Jura members of the Bern parliament placed before it a seventeen-point programme for an autonomy statute, and after the cantonal elections of 1966 the new *Regierungsrat* worked out plans for both a constitutional revision and a statute of autonomy. In March 1970 the voters of Canton Bern approved an amendment to the constitution according to which a petition signed by 5,000 eligible Jura voters could demand a vote on separation. Only Jurassiens were eligible to vote on the matter. If separation were accepted, individual communes might vote in a second ballot on whether they wished to remain in Canton Bern. The *Regierungsrat* gave itself the right to make this provision operative as soon as an autonomy statute had been passed by the cantonal parliament. Unfortunately the deadlock remained. The separatists, knowing that on those terms they would lose a plebiscite, rejected the constitutional amendment on the grounds that only 'genuine' Jurassiens should have the right to vote. They demanded that all non-resident Jurassiens living elsewhere in Switzerland be included and all 'non-genuine' Jurassiens, in practice, German-speaking residents, be excluded. No democratic regime could possibly agree to a 'cooked' electoral roll of that kind and, knowing that, the separatists refused to look at any solution short of 'Canton Jura' but more autonomous than the existing arrangements. The Union des Patriotes jurassiens founded in opposition to separatism rejected both the initiative or plebiscite and the idea of a new statute of autonomy. The 'Third Force', the Mouvement pour l'Unité du Jura founded in 1969, wanted an autonomy statute, which would make the Jura a separate electoral unit for national and cantonal elections, the creation of a Jura regional council and the establishment of a regional capital.

In June 1973, the separatist spokesman in the *Nationalrat* M. Jean Wilhelm (CVP), the editor of the Porrentruy newspaper *Le Pays*, moved a resolution urging the *Bundesrat* (Federal Council) 'to intervene decisively in the Jura problem, to find a way out of the dilemma and to seek a genuine solution'. He argued that Canton Bern by its own devices could never achieve one. By this stage, the *Béliers* had a membership of about 2,000, organised now in tightly knit paramilitary units. During the previous five years they had concentrated their activities on making the cantonal authorities look silly and in popularising their slogan 'Jura libre'. In 1968 they celebrated Swiss National Day on April Fool's day instead of the first of August. They had dressed as chimney sweeps to demonstrate against the visit of the president of the *Regierungsrat*, the cantonal executive, in Porrentruy. They occupied a police station in Delémont in June 1968, the Swiss Embassy in Paris in 1972 and in a flashy double action occupied the Belgian Embassy in Bern and the Swiss Embassy in Brussels at the same time to show international solidarity with Walloon extremists. Other actions were directed at the army, the national parliament and the city of Bern. They attacked four times in 1972 in acts of provocative violence, pouring tar in the tracks of Bern's trams, trying to nail the door shut to the City Hall and burning old tyres in the public squares.

During the autumn of 1973, the crisis seemed to deepen. The debate in the Bern cantonal parliament inflamed sentiments in all the communities. The Volkspartei (SVP) deputies, representatives of the German-speaking Bernese peasants who set the tone of cantonal politics, enraged the French minority with their complacency. Canton Bern, they argued, had made great concessions in limiting the referendum to the Jura districts and in accepting such provisions in its constitution. On 18 December 1973, the *Regierungsrat* announced that it had decided to put into effect the provisions of the amendment of 1970 and set 23 June 1974 as the date for a referendum on separation.

Once again, the melancholy lesson of the past fifteen years had been confirmed. Violence had worked. The RJ had put themselves on the map in a big way but with the slightly ironical result that the party could only succeed by sacrificing its previous principles. If it accepted the plebiscite as legitimate, it conceded that 'Canton Jura', a united francophone canton including Biel–Bienne and the southern districts, would never be realised. By participating in the plebiscite it also surrendered the principle that only 'genuine' Jurassiens be allowed to vote. At first the RJ stuck to its old line. Roland Béguelin, the General Secretary of the RJ, a gifted and charismatic figure (and incidentally a Protestant from the southern Jurassien commune of Tramelan) gave a long, exclusive interview to the left-wing *National-Zeitung* in which he predicted that there would have to be casualties before a solution was reached. Violence was the only way. Gradually opinion shifted, and when the party met in May 1974, delegates voted overwhelmingly to take part in the plebiscite. On 23 June 1974, the RJ duly went to the polls along with over 90% of those entitled to vote. 36,802 voted for separation and

34,507 against, an overall majority of 2,745. The story made the front pages of foreign papers like *The Times* and *Le Figaro* and was universally hailed as another example of Swiss good sense; *Sonderfall Schweiz* had again set an example to the world.

Violence is, however, not so easily laid to rest. What one side starts, another may finish. The 23 June vote shook the southern communities very profoundly. Ancient hostilities revived. Fears of Catholic plots could not be allayed by soothing promises that the RJ would accept the separate identities of the southern districts and that it would be prepared to give them cantonal status as a half-canton like the two Appenzells. The active southerners wanted no part of the new canton. In Map 2 (excluding the inset) the reader can see how the Jura districts voted on 23 June 1974. Those areas cross-hatched and dotted in grey voted for separation; those in white opposed it. Nine communes indicated by horizontal lines in the Moutier district voted for separation while five northern communes (vertical lines) opposed the separatist trend of their neighbours. In Bonfoi on the French border there was a tie.

In the six months after the plebiscite, an anti-separatist youth movement sprang into life. Its membership grew to 5,000 by the end of 1974. The *Sangliers*, the wild boars, promised to meet the *Béliers* head-on and in language too tragically familiar in Northern Ireland Jean-Paul Gehler, their leader, warned his opponents that while the *Sangliers* would not strike first, they would retaliate. The remaining elements of the so-called 'Third Force' (Mouvement pour l'Unité du Jura) found themselves ground down between increasingly intransigent separatist and anti-separatist movements. Anti-separatists began to take a violent line, and talk of *Irlandisation* became common on both sides of the deepening divide. After some confusion, anti-separatists in the three southern districts launched a petition calling for a second plebiscite in which the three southern districts could vote to detach themselves from the north. Extremely complicated legal battles began, as the RJ desperately tried to contest the legality of the initiative. At that point, as tempers were becoming very heated, the *Bundesrat* intervened and appointed three of its members as a mediation group. In January 1975 Dr Furgler, one of the three members, went as far as to meet Béguelin secretly, a meeting discovered only by a chance indiscretion. Petitions, counter-petitions, court judgements and governmental pronouncements on federal and cantonal level

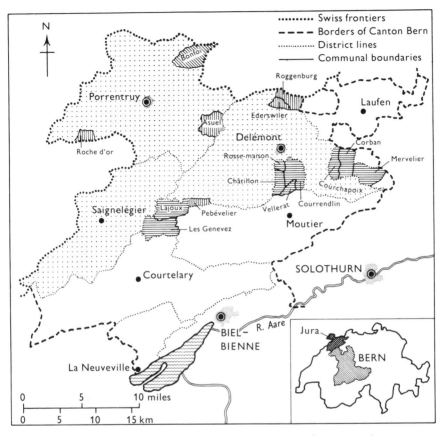

Map 2 Voting patterns in the Jura, 23 June 1974 (see page 97)

gradually began to focus on the issue of the second plebiscite. Attempts to contest the provisions of the amendment of 1970 failed. The Bern government stuck to its right to hold a plebiscite once the petitions by the requisite number of citizens had been duly accredited and verified. Hence on 16 March 1975 a second plebiscite in the three southern districts took place on the issue of remaining within Canton Bern. Table 3.1 shows the results of the voting (the figures in brackets are those of the plebiscite of 23 June 1974).

The vote clarified some but not all of the issues. The narrowness of the outcome in the town of Moutier provoked protests, and in April 1975 the RJ wrote formally to the *Bundesrat* demanding that the results in the district of Moutier be set aside on the grounds that the outcome had been 'manipulated' by the Bernese authorities. During the night of 24 April, a demonstration of *Béliers* in Moutier got out of hand. Eight hundred demonstrators fought a six-hour battle with police in the worst violence of the entire crisis. Militant separatists threw petrol bombs, rocks, paving stones, iron bars and bicycle chains, and ten policemen were seriously injured.

The next stage of the process involved plebiscites on 7 and 14 September 1975 in each of the fifteen communes which voted differently from the majority of their district in the plebiscite of 16 March 1975. These communes, as a result of the vote, were now either to be made into Bernese enclaves within the new Canton Jura or vice versa. The result in Moutier was about as close on 7 September 1975 as on 16 March 1975 (2,151 for and 2,540 against joining the new canton) and was followed by the worst rioting in the recent history of Switzerland. Six hundred police were in action against hundreds of separatist demonstrators rampaging through the town. The cantonal police chief Herr Robert Bauder described the incident as 'not mere clashes but an attack on the constitutional order'. Roland Béguelin promised his supporters in a speech in Delémont on 14 September 1975 to fight on until the whole Jura had been 'liberated'.

By the end of 1975, the three plebiscites had determined that there would be a new twenty-sixth Swiss canton, Canton Jura (23 June 1974), that the other districts of the Bernese Jura, though French-speaking, would remain Bernese (16 March 1975) and that the German-speaking but Catholic Laufenthal could choose its cantonal allegiance, i.e. move its political membership from Bern to another canton. Béguelin's threats turned out to be empty. A constituent assembly, elected in the new Canton Jura, met in 1976 and by 1978 had drafted a new constitution and on 1 January 1979, La République et Canton du Jura, its cantonal coat of arms the episcopal mitre of the historic Bishopric of Basel, began its existence. As Bernard Prongué observes, Jura soon accepted a 'politique consensuelle bien helvétique'.[28] On 12 November 1989, the Laufenthal voted by 4,650 to 4,343 to join Canton Basel-Land, which was confirmed by the Bernese parliament by 95 to 20 on 25 June 1991. A joint commission was established to assess and transfer cantonal assets from Bern to Basel-Land which completed the transfer on 1 January 1994. All of these moves had to be further ratified by additional referenda at cantonal and national level. The

Table 3.1. *Results of plebiscite of 16 March 1975 (in parenthesis results of plebiscite of 23 June 1974)*

	For Bern		For Jura	
Moutier	9,947	(9,330)	7,749	(7,069)
Courtelary	10,802	(10,260)	3,268	(3,123)
La Neuveville	1,927	(1,776)	997	(931)
Total	22,676	(21,366)	12,014	(11,123)
Town of Moutier	2,524	(2,194)	2,238	(2,124)

whole process came to an end when the tiny commune of Vellerat with seventy voters opted in June of 1995 to leave Bern and join Jura, subject, of course, to a final national referendum on the issue.

Over thirty years passed before the Jura crisis could be resolved, but it was resolved ultimately without violence. The fact that in the 1970s the world-wide depression and the particular crisis of the Swiss watch industry hit the whole Jura region unusually hard concentrated minds on more immediate issues than 'Jura libre' but the speed and smoothness of the adaptation still needs further thought. Three general features of Swiss political reality stand out. The first is the way the cellular structure of politics acts to focus issues into ever smaller and more precise geographical units. The adjustment of a unit as tiny as Vellerat illustrates the point. The second has to do with identity. If Porrentruy or Delémont had really been 'French', as some extremists wanted, they would never have become important. They would sleep the deep slumber reserved by the extreme centralisation of the French state for small, remote, market towns. There is an irony here. These two little towns make domestic and international news because, and only because, they are Swiss. The essence of Swiss identity is the preservation of even the smallest ethnic, linguistic and cultural units. The circle comes round. By granting the Jurassiens their wishes, the Swiss assert the most important characteristic of 'Swissness', the equality of all human communities before the bar of history.

A third feature of the Jura crisis is the peculiar flexibility of Swiss constitutions. The ultimate solution to the Jura crisis, if it is the ultimate solution, was made possible by an amendment to the Bern constitution accepted by the voters in 1970, but Bern is not unique in this. All cantons have constitutions like the federal one. The constitution of Canton Solothurn of 1887, which in its turn had wholly replaced the constitution of 1867, had been revised twenty-three times by 1963, and the process of revision continues merrily. Swiss constitutions are pedestrian, practical and detailed. Constitutions are merely substitutes for the sovereignty of the people and can easily be altered if the 'sovereign people' change their opinions.

Underlying the provisions of a Swiss constitution is the assumption that ultimately the ideal state is the direct democracy or the *Landsgemeinde*, the assembly of all free citizens in the historic Ring. This, the pure form, not the clauses of a constitution or its preamble, is the truly venerable element in Swiss political life. The institutions of collective, communal self-government are very old. Reasonably firm evidence exists for the existence of *Landsgemeinden* as early as the 1230s in Canton Uri. The first *Landsgemeinden* seem to have taken place in Zug in 1376, Appenzell in 1378 and Glarus in 1387. Schwyz, Obwalden, Nidwalden and Uri have had regular *Landsgemeinden* since the early fourteenth century and Ob- and Nidwalden have them today, along with the two Appenzells and Glarus. Similar evidence from neighbouring Graubünden indicates that the first loose alliance or league of free valley communes, the League of the House of God (*Gotteshausbund*), had begun to operate by the latter part of the 1360s. Gradually the independent valley communities united, in the Swiss case in a set of federal treaties, in the case of Graubünden in three loose-knit leagues, but in both associations, sovereignty remained firmly placed at the base. Until the outbreak of the French Revolution, the Republic of the Three Leagues, today's Canton of Graubünden, represented the most extreme form of communal sovereignty. The Republic was made up of three leagues, twenty-six higher juris-dictions, forty-nine jurisdictional communes and 227 autonomous neighbourhoods 'with competitive, overlapping frequently incompatible claims', or as an eighteenth-century traveller put it, 'each village of Raetia, each parish and each neighbourhood already constituted a tiny republic'.[29] The union of these tiny republics was accomplished by a system of referenda in which the village community, not the voter, was the sovereign body. Tiny Bündner villages were consulted on everything from a state treaty with the Habsburgs to the repair of certain barrels and vats in Maienfeld; the equivalent in *Landsgemeinde* regions was frequent and lengthy meetings. Twenty-four took place in Canton Schwyz in 1765. Benjamin Barber believes that these historic circumstances still mould Swiss political attitudes:

To this day, the Swiss seem less interested in the power of offices and the personality of officeholders than the citizens of other less direct democracies. The collegial federal executive with its anonymous rotating presidency continues to embody this predilection of direct democracy for treating the citizenry as the real government and the elected government as powerless attendants.[30]

It is certainly true that representative, parliamentary governments never really took root. There were no Edmund Burkes nor James Madisons in Swiss history. When the ultra-modern liberals of the 1840s tried to impose representative parliamentary structures, they were not entirely successful. The traditions of direct democracy were so deeply rooted that borrowing from the US constitution could not transform the new *Bundesstaat* into a Western, representative republic. In the end, the men of 1848 were Swiss too, sharing certain instinctive assumptions about the 'sovereign people'. They submitted their draft to the people for ratification by referendum, as if that were the most natural thing in the world. They put in clauses making a referendum on revision of the federal constitution obligatory and allowing popular initiative for a 'total revision' of the constitution. It is, I think, equally significant that in the same year, 1848, Schwyz and Zug, two of the oldest cantons, gave up the *Landsgemeinde*, and Schwyz immediately adopted the referendum as a substitute.

1848 turned out not to be the last word on the subject of constitutions. It began a process which has not yet ended, the reflection of a constant tension between Swiss governments and the 'sovereign people'. In the years after 1848 the as yet unfulfilled aspirations for popular participation in government bubbled up in cantonal politics first. A typical manifestation of that urge found expression in the *Landsgemeinde* of 15 December 1867, to press for more democracy in Canton Zürich. The proclamation declared:

It is an irrevocable right of free men to meet under open skies in public assemblies to discuss affairs of the country and to decide them in principle . . . thousands of us today make use of that right to demand a revision of our cantonal constitution.[31]

The democrats in other cantons pushed for similar changes and in the early 1870s the movement gathered momentum on federal level. After a first attempt to ratify a completely revised constitution in 1872 failed, a second attempt in 1874 succeeded. 340,199 citizens and 14½ cantons voted 'Yes' to the new constitution to 198,013 and 7½ cantons who said 'No'. The new constitution contained a provision for *fakultative*, that is, optional, referenda on parliamentary legislation, if 30,000 citizens demanded one within three months. In 1977 that number was raised to 50,000. In 1891 the right of initiative for individual, as opposed to total, revision of the constitution was added. Under the amended provision 50,000 voters (also raised in 1977 to 100,000) have the right, as Article 121 states, to offer such amendments either 'in general form' or 'as written drafts'. Between 1874 and 1977, 6.8% of federal pieces of legislation had been subjected to referendum, of which about two out of three had been rejected.[32]

The great Swiss novelist, Gottfried Keller, who served in cantonal government, greeted these changes of the 1870s with suitable pragmatism. 'A constitution is not a stylish examination performance . . . but a great big sieve, through which the final, secure and clear legal majority must be strained . . . common responsibility helps to bear the consequences.'[33] The constitution turns into the minute book of popular decisions. At the back of the official document entitled *Bundesverfassung der Schweizerischen Eidgenossenschaft* (Federal Constitution of the Helvetic Confederation) there are nineteen printed pages for the 130 amendments adopted between 1874 and 1994 and a further seventeen pages to list the 133 rejected amendments. Successful amendments cover topics as different as equality of rights for men and women (14 June 1981), which is clearly a 'constitutional' issue in the normal sense of the word, and the schedule of licence fees for lorries over 3.5 tonnes (referendum of 26 February 1984) which quite clearly is not. The Swiss Constitution could not be more different from the hallowed parchment housed in the United States National Archives, which a reverent citizenry may see each day in the Rotunda behind its thick glass protection. The US Constitution of 1787 would certainly qualify in Keller's terms as 'a stylish examination performance'. The Swiss would not. As Wolfgang Linder has written about the Swiss Constitution, 'the image of the stablest government in the world is in contrast with the most unstable constitution'.[34]

The growth of pressure groups and the spread of mass communications make it easier to mobilise small bodies of voters to arrive at either 50,000 or 100,000 signatures. The number of constitutional amendments brought to a vote has doubled every twenty years since 1930 but with one unexpected and baneful consequence. The equality of cantons (the federal principle) demands that revisions be approved by a majority of cantons as well as a majority of individual votes cast (the democratic principle of one person, one vote). Federalism and democracy clash head on over the votes on referenda and initiatives. As the population leaves the rural areas, voting power paradoxically increases in the cantons losing people. Since a majority in more than half the cantons must ratify a popular vote, the votes of just 9% of the whole population in the under-populated rural cantons, if distributed in the right way, can block an important amendment or treaty voted by a majority in the urban and densely settled areas. Whereas in 1848 a vote in Appenzell-Innerrhoden equalled that of eleven people in Zürich, today it has risen to thirty-eight.[35]

The Federal Constitution resembles a sheet on which history has scribbled changes, crossed out certain sentences and forgotten others. Pieces of constitution embody today in fossil form conflicts of early periods such as regulations on bridal dowries, emigration agencies and child work in factories. There is something unsatisfactory and undignified about the details of heavy goods vehicles being enshrined in a constitutional framework. For thirty years the federal government and parliament have been moving, crab-like, towards a 'total revision' of the federal constitution of 1874. Finally in June 1995, the Federal Council presented a proposal for a step-by-step rewriting of the constitution to be submitted to the people in 1998 on the 150th anniversary of the modern federal state and the constitution of 1848. The process which the Federal Council has likened to a series of military advances (*Nachführung*) will regroup provisions, scrap obsolete ones and introduce specific rights and protections which have become in fact the unwritten law of the land, like the new Article 10, 'Protection of Private and Family Life', which forbids telephone tapping or bugging and guarantees protection against misuse of computerised data.[36]

In the area of popular rights the new draft reorganises and defines the existing referenda and initiatives. There will be a new general initiative which will permit 100,000 registered voters to introduce, repeal or amend both constitutional and legislative provisions. The *fakultative* or optional referendum will be extended to all state treaties, not just those which must be embedded in national legislation, and finally a new category of referendum will be created. If a third of both houses of parliament so vote, certain important substantive or financial measures, such as the approval of a major investment, may be submitted to popular approval. At the same time the draft raises the barriers from 50,000 to 100,000 signatures for existing *fakultative* referenda and from 100,000 to 200,000 for the existing constitutional initiatives.[37]

The existence of cantons acts today as it did in the nineteenth century as a laboratory of experimental politics. In the thirty years between 1965 and 1995 in which federal authorities have inched towards a total revision of the federal constitution, twelve cantons have adopted completely new constitutions and another eight are still in the process of revising.[38] Our specimen canton, Canton Zug, belongs to the minority of cantons which have not revised their constitutions. The Zug constitution of 1 January 1894 has been amended more than thirty times over the past century. It too provides for a variety of obligatory and optional referenda. It may help the dazed reader if we look at the position in graphic form. Figure 1 illustrates how laws are passed in Canton Zug and which ones require popular participation.[39]

Another form of popular participation in politics requires corporate bodies to be consulted, not just individual voters. This procedure, known as *Anhörung* (listening to) or *Vernehmlassung* (permitting communication), has roots in constitutional practice. The Federal Constitution requires the federal government to 'listen to' cantonal governments before it exercises powers conferred on it. Laws or decrees which affect federal rights to control water resources, to provide public housing, to regulate gymnastic organisations and sport instruction, to alter the rights of Swiss citizens abroad, to subsidise Swiss films, or which affect federal–state relations in other ways, must be submitted to the cantons so that their opinions can be heard. In addition both federal and cantonal governments have formalised consultative procedures which lay down precisely which bodies, boards or agencies have the right to be, and which may be, consulted in the evolution of particular legislation. Any Swiss bill goes through a tortuous process of consultation long before the executive submits a draft

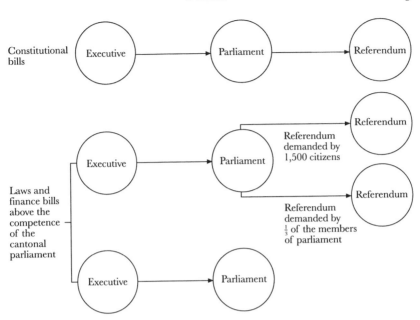

Figure 1 The passage of a law in Canton Zug

to the legislature. If the legislature eventually passes the bill, a negative outcome of a referendum may bury the project anyway.

The Swiss system aims to integrate diverse interests and to lock them into the negotiation of compromises. Government becomes a system of administration, adjustment, aggregation and consultation. The outcomes emerge slowly, if at all, from such processes. Urs Altermatt believes that as a result of the integration and reintegration of interests, groups and parties, the interlocking of political, economic and social pressure groups, the Swiss system has become 'blocked', and can no longer respond quickly enough to challenges.[40] This sense of frustration has eroded popular satisfaction with all the levels of Swiss government. Even the very institutions of direct democracy have become unsettled and uncertain.

Direct democracy in Switzerland has profound effects on political life, but they are not easy to summarise. Their study has occupied a number of distinguished political scientists and political sociologists for nearly a century. In 1896 A. Lawrence Lowell gave the referendum good marks: 'it has certainly been a success in the sense that it produced the result for which it was established. It seems, on the whole, to have brought out the real opinion of the people.' The initiative on the other hand seemed to him 'bold' in conception but 'not likely to be of any great use to mankind; if, indeed, it does not prove to be merely a happy hunting-ground for extremists and fanatics'.[41] Denis de Rougemont cites the case of a referendum in 1961, when the people rejected a law raising the tax on petrol by 7 centimes but allowed an amended one raising it by 5 to pass. My reaction is to think of this incident as a '2 centime' folly, but de Rougemont argues that the referendum 'obliges the authorities to justify in public their intentions, the press to discuss the text, the electorate to reflect on it and to inform itself, and all that keeps up and animates civic life'.[42]

It would be nice to believe that, but the evidence hardly supports the claim. The provisions for an obligatory and optional referendum have an honourable democratic pedigree but lay great burdens on officialdom. In the mid-1970s the *Staatsschreiber* of Canton Solothurn, the rough equivalent of the chancellor on federal level, very kindly showed me the books on these matters in his office. A cantonal referendum in March 1972 cost the taxpayers Sfr 83,019. Since there had been thirty-one such ballots in the ten years from 1962 to 1972, the citizenry were paying out at the rate of a quarter of a million francs per annum to allow an average of 40% of their number to say 'Yea' or 'Nay' to propositions such as the following:

The cantonal Constitution of 25 October 1887 will be amended by the following clause: Article 19*bis*: By means of legislative action and for the protection of the population in the event of catastrophes or warlike events measures may be taken which grant the *Regierungsrat* or the Cantonal Parliament for a limited period powers which deviate from the regulations governing the competence of such authorities in the Constitution.

In the past twenty years referenda have not got cheaper nor less numerous. Official statistics for 1992–4 show that between 6 June 1993 and 12 June 1994 the Swiss were called to the polls five times to vote on twenty-one federal initiatives and referenda with an average turnout of 45.6% of those entitled to vote. As we have seen in voting for city elections in Zürich, participation in referenda

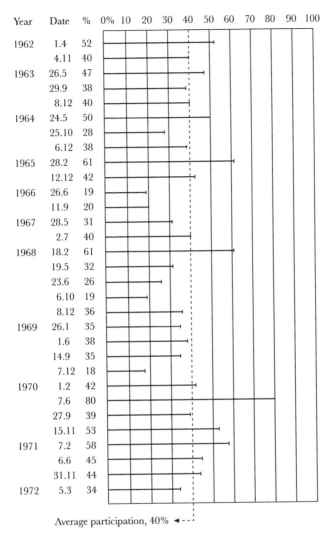

Year	Date	%
1962	1.4	52
	4.11	40
1963	26.5	47
	29.9	38
	8.12	40
1964	24.5	50
	25.10	28
	6.12	38
1965	28.2	61
	12.12	42
1966	26.6	19
	11.9	20
1967	28.5	31
	2.7	40
1968	18.2	61
	19.5	32
	23.6	26
	6.10	19
	8.12	36
1969	26.1	35
	1.6	38
	14.9	35
	7.12	18
1970	1.2	42
	7.6	80
	27.9	39
	15.11	53
1971	7.2	58
	6.6	45
	31.11	44
1972	5.3	34

Average participation, 40% ◀--

Figure 2 Participation of voters

at all three levels of Swiss politics has declined, though not so catastrophically as pessimists predicted.[43] Two prominent Swiss observers, René Rhinow, a *Ständerat* (Senator) from Basel-Land, and Annemarie Huber-Hotz, general secretary of the Swiss parliament, have pointed out that since registered voters make up only 60% of the inhabitants of Switzerland and that of those only 40% go out to vote on referenda and initiatives, about 12% of the population will make up the majority in national matters. They also point out that referenda, introduced by progressives to achieve majorities for change, have instead given opposition groups a blocking leverage on Swiss legislation and in the end forced majorities to co-opt stubborn minorities into the consensus.[44] What is also clear is that the number of popular initiatives continues to rise on both federal and cantonal level and suggests to Rhinow and Huber-Hotz a 'destabilisation of the system'.[45]

The referendum and initiative exercise an influence even if the voters never get to the polls at all. Every piece of legislation in a cantonal or federal parliament undergoes subtle alterations because a referendum might be the consequence of a given clause, a process which Jürg Steiner has called *Referendumsdrohung* – the referendum threat.[46] The elaborate process which the civil service goes through before drafts of bills even get to parliament is also overshadowed by the moods of the 'sovereign'. Various political scientists have examined the legislative process in detail and others have looked at the consultative machinery, the *Vernehmlassung* procedures, to see where and in what ways the possible rejection of a bill has influenced its development. The results seem to be inconclusive. No one doubts that semi-direct democracy influences both consultation and legislation. Nobody, on the other hand, can establish exactly when or how it does so.

There is one exception: the obligation to hold referenda on state treaties which are without time limits or involve membership in international organisations or organisations dedicated to collective security. This amendment to the Constitution, adopted itself by referendum like all constitutional amendments, received over-whelming popular approval on 13 March 1977. Today critics like the Lausanne political scientist, Raimund E. Germann, consider it a form of 'foreign political mutilation' and the Basel economist Silvio Borner considers it 'the most serious failure in constitutional construction of the post-war era'.[47] These strong views arise because foreign politics today increasingly involves membership of international organisations, membership of collective security groupings and assent to world trade agreements. The weight of foreign affairs burdens Swiss politics but in a wholly new way.

'Europe' has forced the Swiss to confront their identity problems again and again. Whereas the threats of nationalism, fascism, nazism or communism strengthened the determination of the Swiss to remain apart, the threat of Europe works to weaken it. The Helvetic Confederation developed its institutions to confront external enemies. From 1 January 1995, for the first time in its history, Switzerland is surrounded by 'friends'. Germany, France, Italy and Austria are peaceful, capitalist, bourgeois republics, and all are members of the European Union. The European Union, because it is multinational and confederal, calls into question, at least as the Swiss now feel it, the need for their special case to survive.

The role of direct democracy in Switzerland's European crisis cannot be overestimated. A classic case was the sad fate of the so-called European Economic Area at the hands of the Swiss 'sovereign' in 1992. The story illustrates vividly how direct democracy limits Swiss foreign policy. On 17 January 1989 Jacques Delors offered an apparent solution to the Swiss identity crisis. He proposed in a speech to the European parliament in Strasbourg a 'structured partnership with common decision-making and administrative institutions' for the members of the European Free Trade Area (EFTA).[48] The Swiss as members of EFTA began to negotiate a new status of partial membership. As State Secretary Franz Blankart, the Swiss negotiator, put it to me, they were hoping for European Union membership 'extra muros'[49] because, it was generally believed, the 'sovereign' would say 'No' to direct membership.

When negotiations began, the EFTA members found it more difficult than they had anticipated. Delors got cold feet after the Berlin Wall fell in November 1989 and a unified Germany added to its weight in the European Union. It seemed more urgent to contain the German giant than to extend privileges to outsiders, which might weaken the containing wall. Brussels demanded that EFTA negotiate as a bloc and accept as a pre-condition the so-called *acquis communautaire*, around 11,000 pages of legislation derived from over 1,400 directives and regulations.[50] The Swiss are not accustomed, as we have seen, to accepting legislation 'from above' and certainly not from abroad. The rights of the Swiss 'sovereign' to vote on every aspect of his or her life collided with the centralising traditions of French bureaucracy. The European Union said to EFTA: 'take it or leave it, but don't expect to haggle'. The promise of common decision-making and administrative institutions disappeared during the course of the negotiations and the EFTA partners began to divide. The European Union offered EFTA the so-called four freedoms – free movement of goods, services, persons, and capital – but at a high price. Sweden, Austria and ultimately Finland decided to join the European Union and Switzerland was left isolated and weakened. On 20 May 1992 Switzerland applied formally for membership of the European Union.[51]

The referendum set for 6 December 1992 on Switzerland's membership of the European Economic Area had been planned long before the Swiss application for full membership. The referendum on the issue took place under inauspicious circumstances. Many Swiss voters could not – quite understandably – separate the EEA from the EU and voted against the latter rather than the former. There was an exceptionally vigorous 'No' campaign and in the event the voters did, narrowly, say 'No' by a margin of 23,195 out of over three and a half million voters. Turnout at 78.3% was unusually high for Swiss referenda, but even more striking was the distribution of 'Yes' and 'No' votes. In French-speaking Switzerland more than 70% of the population voted 'Yes', while in the German part of the country 56% voted against.[52]

This division of sentiment frightened many Swiss. It called to mind those perilous moments in the Swiss past, which we recorded in the previous chapter, when German and French Swiss had divided on 'national' issues, taking the sides of Germany and France in the Franco-Prussian or the first world war. For a moment it looked as if the so-called *Graben* (trench) had once again divided the two groups. Subsequent and calmer analysis showed a more differentiated picture. In March 1993 the Federal Statistical Office published a study of voting in the 1992 referendum, carried out by the Forschungszentrum für Politik of the University of Bern, which showed that the divisions ran just as sharply between city and country voters or between higher- and lower-income groups as between language communities. The urban middle classes voted for Europe while German- or Italian-speaking workers in the towns and peasants and lower middle classes in the Alpine areas tended to vote 'No'. Certainly French Switzerland was more solidly pro-European than German but language was only part of the story. After all, the half-cantons of Basel, both German-speaking, had also voted 'Yes'.[53]

The voters have continued to make things hard for their government. A striking case in point has been the series of measures on European issues, which the government has introduced to make Switzerland 'Euro-compatible' as a kind of half-way stage to membership. With the exception of the vote to accept Value Added Tax, 28 November 1993, which, with a 45.4% turnout, was accepted by a two-to-one majority, the citizenry has said 'No' to measures to make it easier for young resident foreigners to gain Swiss citizenship and 'No' in June 1995 to a measure to liberalise the 'Lex Friedrich', which limits the acquisition of Swiss property by foreigners. In addition, the last two years have seen the rise of a demagogic right, composed of the Zürich branch of the SVP under the businessman Christoph Blocher, the League of the Ticinese led by the former professional football player Giuliano Bignasca and the Swiss Democrats, all of whom say 'No' to Europe and 'No' to their own government.

Herr Blocher's style of politics may be assessed from the SVP electoral poster (Plate 11) which appeared in many Zürich newspapers (other than the *Neue Zürcher Zeitung* which refused to print it). Both the Nazi jackboot and the imputation that those who favour European Union membership are either left-wing or 'tired of the fatherland' made the other parties furious, but Blocher's tactics work. He hammered away at the 'sell-out' of the homeland, at the hordes of foreigners who would buy up the homes of honest Swiss folk and at the motives of those who wished to lift the restrictions. On 25 June 1995 the citizens rejected the amendment by 959,794 to 832,324 with a turnout of 39.6% of the vote. In sophisticated Zürich city, Blocher's forces mobilised 50,727 'No' voters to 40,813 'Yes' voters. Equally alarming was the regional split among the voters. Not one German-speaking canton voted for the liberalisation, whereas all the French-speaking cantons and the Italian-speaking Canton Ticino did.[54]

Max Frenkel, a senior editor of the *Neue Zürcher Zeitung*, took stock of the débâcle:

Historians of the next generation will probably describe the conflicts of the 1990s as the *battle between two virtual realities*. For each side moves in its own world which has little to do with reality . . . A part of the leading classes in this country in politics, the economy and the media are caught still in the illusion that it is all only a question of enlightening the people, 'anchoring' foreign policy in domestic politics and showing some leadership. The real challenge consists in taking seriously the ever shriller and sharper cry of those made uncertain by their anxieties.[55]

That diagnosis certainly commands respect but it evades what to an outsider seems the obvious clash of principle. Switzerland, as it now is, cannot accept an *acquis communautaire*, the command economy from Brussels or rule by higher civil servants, because the very essence of Swiss identity lies in self-determination from the bottom up. A top-down government confronts a bottom-up one and they are simply incompatible. The logic of the two approaches to government dictates that the Swiss either give up their national identity or stay out of the European Union.

The real world exists, of course, somewhere between these two poles. A less doctrinaire European Union may eventually be persuaded to tolerate Swiss eccentricities and to offer it an improved European Economic Area treaty but even there the question of the ultimate jurisdiction of the European Court in Luxemburg is not negotiable. The Swiss may have to swallow the presence of 'foreign judges in our valleys' as the price of access to the European Union's privileges. For in the long run the Swiss cannot exist as an off-shore island in a European sea. They will not tolerate standing in queues for hours among the 'others', while their fellow Europeans enter EU countries without passport control, and all the other indignities that united Europe imposes on its visitors.

Yet if the choice comes to 'Yes' or 'No' the Swiss will, I think, continue to say 'No' to the European Union if it means the end of democratic rights and practices. Nor should those members of the elite groups who have grown impatient with direct democracy forget its importance as legitimation of their rule. In a fascinating study, the sociologists Marliss Buchmann and Stefan Sacchi have shown that Switzerland presents the following paradox: it has the greatest degree of inequality in income distribution in Europe but the least popular dissatisfaction with these inequalities:

We have explained this striking difference between perceived inequality and low level of conflict by looking at the political system in Switzerland and its tendency to relocate conflict. The system of direct democracy and the political culture support policies orientated towards compromise and prevent the articulation of conflict.[56]

Popular rights, in effect, support the system. They are not pieces

Plate 11 SVP poster opposing the liberalisation of land acquisition in Switzerland by foreigners, 1995

of machinery that can be dismantled and stored in the junk yard of historical anachronisms. Direct democracy constitutes an essential element of Swiss self-definition and will not be surrendered without cost.

The instruments of semi-direct democracy also affect the role of parliament and the activities of political parties. In his fascinating study of political parties in Switzerland, Professor Erich Gruner argues that the referendum is responsible for one of the most striking peculiarities of Swiss parties, their lack of powerful central organisations:

> The referendum conceals the solution to the puzzle. It permits the party strategists to get the masses of the people under way easily and quickly without the need for a great party apparatus nor a disciplined group of followers. This rapid mobilisation is only possible because the staff and workers – in contrast to the masses – do not fall back into lethargy. They keep party passions among the closed circle of prominent members cooking over a low flame. In this respect the Swiss party system is a just reflection of our militia system in the army.[57]

By using referenda and initiatives, a party can be in the odd position of being government and opposition at the same time. This practice has become particularly popular with the Socialist Party (SPS) since it tends to soothe the irritation of left-wingers who feel that the SPS ought not serve in bourgeois governments. The SVP practises the same double game when the leader of its Zürich party, Christoph Blocher, leads the anti-European opposition against the pro-European government in Bern which his fellow SVP member, Adolf Ogi, serves. The very frequent resort to referenda and initiatives, especially on dramatic issues, sucks much of the life out of parliamentary politics. If the great debate will be outside the walls anyway, why listen to what is said inside? If the parties spring to life on issues, the issues capture the public imagination and not the political parties themselves. A paradox emerges. The total politicisation of Swiss life leads to its opposite, a lifelessness in daily politics and indifference to it.

There are certainly reasons for the paleness of Swiss politics other than those which arise from direct democracy. The careers of a Blocher or a Duttweiler, the retailing eccentric who built both the Migros chain and his own political party to go with it, show that charismatic politics are indeed possible. One cause lies in multiplicity. There are twenty-six different political units, called cantons, and each has its own political party system. François Masnata, who has studied the Social Democratic Party in Switzerland, undoubtedly the most centralised of all Swiss parties, concludes: 'Each cantonal party has the tendency to consider itself the whole and not as a part of an ensemble.'[58] The party which appears in parliament tends to resemble a patchwork quilt rather than a seamless cloth. Since the cantonal party was itself a federation of local parties, the national party turns into a federation of federations. There is, secondly, the tendency to accumulate overlapping offices at various levels and on the same level across various interest groups. The alert member of a Swiss trade federation or craft union or employers' organisation will be well informed by central office as to the doings of 'his or her' representatives in cantonal and national parliaments; 'his or her' understood as the representative of an interest group. Since Article 32 of the Constitution makes it obligatory that 'the economic groups concerned shall be consulted during the drafting of the laws' the representative of the interests will get his or her say one way or the other. The work in committee, or even before the committee stage in the civil service commissions of 'experts', will be more useful, if less dramatic, than a speech in parliament.

No great careers are to be made in the English or American sense of the word in a cantonal or national parliament. The rise of a Disraeli or an F. E. Smith, a Lyndon Johnson or a Daniel Webster, is not conceivable under the Swiss arrangements. There is no place for grand confrontations and fiery speeches. Proceedings in a Swiss parliament normally resemble a board meeting.

Another feature of Swiss politics at all levels is longevity. It is considered a great insult in most communes, cantons and federal authorities to fail to re-elect a member of an executive. On the level of *Gemeinde* this frequently means that the members stay on until they drop. The Swiss voters have to have unusual provocation to let a sitting member of the executive fall from grace. Periods of service in *Gemeinde*, canton and federal executive of ten or even twenty years are not unknown. The famous Professor Albert Gobat served as *Regierungsrat* (member of the executive) in Canton Bern for thirty years. It was, his junior colleague Karl Scheurer confided to his diary, a good omen that the executive 'was able to bear so difficult a colleague for so many years'.[59] The long service produces an amiable but rather anonymous atmosphere at the centre of Swiss politics, especially on cantonal level.

The political virtues the Swiss prize most tend to be worthy and unexciting. Christopher Hughes argues that everywhere in Switzerland a predominance of *Sachlichkeit*, 'the executive frame of mind', 'the virtues of the good civil servant' are accorded too much prestige. 'The weakness of the practice of *Sachlichkeit* is that it assumes as best something which is in fact only second best, namely uncontroversial administration.'[60] *Sachlichkeit* is a hard word to convey. 'Impartiality', 'objectivity', 'practicality' all catch a bit of the flavour which arises from the root of the word *Sache*, or 'thing'. Work is the key element in this quality. The good Swiss politician is earnest, high-minded, works a seven-day week and leaves his desk spick-and-span each night. Here too the virtue is real but not exciting.

Language is another problem for the Swiss politician of the German area. Debates in most cantonal parliaments and in the federal parliament tend to be in the 'written language', the Swiss version of High German. As Max Frisch's hero puts it in *Mein Name sei Gantenbein*: 'I decide that it's better to take on my role in High German. I always have a feeling of role-playing when I speak High German, and so fewer reservations.'[61] Speaking High German tends to have a similar effect on politicians. They too adopt roles and employ a wooden, pompous idiom known as *Grossratsdeutsch*, the German of the Grand Council chamber.

A final element which makes Swiss politics on the national level less exciting than in many other European countries is the astonishing stability of voting patterns. Table 3.2 illustrates the point remarkably. Over the entire period since 1919, when proportional representation was introduced, the hallmark of Swiss politics has been great stability among the main parties. The Radicals/Liberals lost ground early in the period but since 1971 have achieved an almost unchanged share of the poll. The CVP has dropped slightly since 1971 and the Socialists lost a chunk of their electorate, almost certainly to the Greens, which they have not recovered.

On federal and cantonal level this stability has made possible what amounts to permanent deals to share power. Since 1959, the main parties on federal level have operated according to a 'magic formula' by which CVP (Christian), FDP (Radical) and SPS

(Socialist) have two places and the SVP (People) one on the Federal Council (the *Bundesrat*) (Table 3.3). Since no significant shift of opinion has occurred in the general elections since that year, the formula works tolerably well.

The *Bundesrat* is quite unlike any other executive branch of government in the world, and Lowell quite rightly saw it as 'the most thoroughly native and original'[62] of all federal institutions. Each Federal Councillor (*Bundesrat*) is head (*Vorsteher* or *Chef du département*) of one of the seven main departments of state. They are all elected at the same time by each new parliament at its first session for a term of four years. Both houses – *Nationalrat* and *Ständerat* – vote together in the so-called Federal Assembly or *Bundesversammlung* and each seat is filled in turn; that is, seven separate elections are held on the same day. The members of the *Bundesrat* benefit from that unwillingness to turn out incumbents which we have already noted. In this, as in many other ways, they resemble the executive of a small commune or *Gemeinde*. Normally those members of the *Bundesrat* who wish to go on are allowed to do so, although there have been cases in which, as Professor Hughes points out, persons not likely to be re-elected have prudently chosen not to stand. 'The admirable use made of the power, which election by the assembly gives to party leaders and fellow Federal Councillors, to "take their colleague by the arm" and to call to mind the pleasures of retirement, is a chief justification for parliamentary (rather than popular) election.'[63] Occasionally, as in 1917 or 1953, a member of the *Bundesrat* will resign, and there have been other cases of premature retirement because of a defeat suffered either in the Assembly or in the public performance of duty.

Since neither the distribution of seats on the Federal Council among the parties, 'the magic formula', is likely to change nor are the actual incumbents in danger of defeat, the elections of members of the *Bundesrat* at the beginning of most four-year sessions of parliament have a certain formal quality, but they offer a discreet indication of how members of the two houses see each Federal Councillor. Since each must be re-elected in turn, attention focuses on the number of votes he or she gets. The *Bundesversammlung*, which elects the Federal Councillors, consists of the upper and lower houses voting together, so there are a total of 246 votes to be gained (200 lower house and 46 upper house). A result under 150 comes as near as anything can in Swiss parliamentary

Table 3.2. *Party strength in the* Nationalrat

(a) Party strength by seats since 1919

Party groupings	1919	1922	1925	1928	1931	1935	1939	1943	1947	1951	1955	1959	1963	1967	1971	1975	1979	1983	1987	1991	1995
FDP/PRD	60	60	60	58	52	48	47	47	52	51	50	51	51	49	49	47	51	54	51	44	45
CVP/PDC	41	44	42	46	44	42	43	43	44	48	47	47	48	45	44	46	44	42	42	36	34
SPS/PSS	41	43	49	50	49	50	45	56	48	49	53	51	53	50	46	55	51	47	41	41	54
SVP/UDC	30	34	30	31	30	21	22	22	21	23	22	23	22	21	23	21	23	23	25	25	29
Dem/Dém.	4	4	5	3	2	3	7	5	5	4	4	4	4	3	–	–	–	–	–	–	–
LPS/PLS	9	10	7	6	6	6	6	8	7	5	5	5	6	6	6	6	8	8	9	10	7
LdU/AdI	–	–	–	–	–	7	9	7	8	10	10	10	10	16	13	11	8	8	8	5	3
EVP/PEP	1	1	1	1	1	1	0	1	1	1	1	2	2	3	3	3	3	3	3	3	2
PdA/PST	–	2	3	2	2	2	4	–	7	5	4	3	4	5	5	4	3	1	1	2	3
DACH/ASV	–	–	–	–	–	–	–	–	–	–	–	–	–	–	5	0	2	3	4	1	–
GPS/PES	–	–	–	–	–	–	–	–	–	–	–	–	–	–	–	0	1	3	9	14	9
SD, Rep/DS, Rép.	–	–	–	–	–	–	–	–	–	–	–	–	–	1	11	6	3	5	3	5	3
AP/PA	–	–	–	–	–	–	–	–	–	–	–	–	–	–	–	–	–	–	2	8	7
Others	3	0	1	1	1	7	4	5	1	0	0	0	0	1	0	1	3	3	2	6	4
Total	189	198	198	198	187	187	187	194	194	196	196	196	200	200	200	200	200	200	200	200	200

(b) Party strength by percentage of the vote since 1971

Parties	1971	1975	1979	1983	1987	1991	1995
FDP/PRD	21.7	22.2	24.1	23.3	22.9	21.0	20.2
CVP/PDC	20.5	20.6	21.5	20.2	19.7	18.3	17.0
SPS/PSS	22.9	24.6	24.4	22.8	18.4	18.5	21.8
SVP/UDC	11.1	9.9	11.6	11.1	11.0	11.9	14.9
LPS/PLS	2.2	2.4	2.8	2.8	2.7	3.0	2.7
LdU/AdI	7.6	6.1	4.1	4.0	4.2	2.8	1.8
EVP/PEP	2.1	2.0	2.2	2.1	1.9	1.9	1.8
CSP/PCS	*	*	–	*	*	*	*
PdA/PST	2.6	2.4	2.1	*	*	*	*
PSU	*	*	*	*	*	*	*
DACH/ASV	*	1.0	1.9	3.3	3.7	1.5	*
GPS/PES	–	*	*	1.9	4.9	6.1	5.0
Rep./Rép.	4.3	3.0	*	*	*	*	*
SD/DS	3.2	2.5	1.3	2.9	2.5	3.3	3.1
EDU/UDF	–	*	*	*	*	1.0	*
AP/PA	–	–	–	–	2.6	5.1	4.0
Lega	–	–	–	–	–	1.4	*
Others	1.2	2.6	1.6	2.5	2.5	2.5	*
Total	100	100	100	100	100	100	100

* = less than 1%

Abbreviations: AP/PA = Auto Party; CSP/PCS = Christian Social Party; CVP/PDC = Christian Democratic People's Party; DACH/ASV = umbrella organisation of left-wing 'Progressive Organisations of Switzerland' (POCH); Dem./Dém. = Democrats; EDU/UDF = Federal Democratic Union; EVP/PEP = Evangelical People's Party; FDP/PRD = Radical Party; GPS/PES = Green Party of Switzerland; LdU/AdI = National Ring of Independents (Migros); Lega = League of the Ticino People; LPS/PLS = Liberal Party of Switzerland; PdA/PST = Party of Work (Communist); PSU = Socialist Unity Party; Rep./Rép. = Republicans; SD/DS = Swiss Democrats; SPS/PSS = Socialist Party of Switzerland; SVP/UDC = Swiss People's Party.

Source: Statistisches Jahrbuch der Schweiz 1995, Tables 17.3 and 17.4, pp. 368–9.

practice to a vote of no confidence. Insiders and incumbents note carefully whose stock has risen and whose fallen over the four years since the last election to the Federal Council.

One of the members of the *Bundesrat* is elected president and one vice-president of the *Bundesrat* at the same election at which they all stand for re-election. The president of the *Bundesrat* is also president of Switzerland. The term of office is one year and rotates among the members. A long-serving *Bundesrat* like Philipp Etter (1935–59) may well be able to serve often as president of Switzerland. New *Bundesräte* wait their turn until all their seniors have filled the office of president but, aside from that, the office moves in strict annual rotation. The powers of the presidency are not great and mainly consist of the chairmanship of the *Bundesrat* and ceremonial functions as head of state. It would be wrong to underestimate the office in spite of this. Its incumbent has general oversight over government as well as a few special emergency powers; in troubled times he or she can make a difference. Initially the presidency was tied to the Political Department, so that Switzerland effectively suffered a new foreign secretary every year. Under the forceful Numa Droz, the Political Department was separated from the presidency in the years 1887 to 1894 and after several decades of disagreement the 'système Droz' was made permanent.[64] In the modern *Bundesrat* it is not unusual to have a person serve as head of one department of state during his or her entire tenure.

The *Bundesrat* is not a cabinet in the British sense. The 'government' cannot 'fall' if its measures are rejected by the parliament. According to Article 97, 'members of the *Bundesrat* while in office may hold no other official position either in the service of the Confederation or of a Canton, nor may they follow any other career or exercise any other profession'. Unlike the British cabinet minister, they may not be members of either house of the legislature, and in this sense resemble the position of members of the American 'administration' who may not sit in Congress. Unlike the US president, they may and in fact usually do take part in debates in parliament and have the right to speak and to introduce resolutions. Chairs are set aside in the *Nationalrat* chamber for members of the *Bundesrat* to use as they choose. Normally the head of the department in whose bailiwick some legislation falls attends as a matter of course, but he or she speaks for the entire *Bundesrat*

Table 3.3. *Party political composition of the Federal Council, 1848–1995*

Party	to 1891	1891–1919	1919–29	1929–43	1943–53	1953–4	1954–9	since 1959
FDP/PRD	7	6	5	4	3	4	3	2
CVP/PDC	–	1	2	2	2	2	3	2
SVP/UDC	–	–	–	1	1	1	1	1
SPS/PSS	–	–	–	–	1	–	–	2

Abbreviations: CVP/PDC = Christian Democratic People's Party; FDP/PRD = Radical Party; SPS/PSS = Socialist Party of Switzerland; SVP/UDC = Swiss People's Party
Source: *Statistisches Jahrbuch der Schweiz 1995*, p. 365.

rather than for himself or herself. Custom asserts that the *Bundesrat* has one voice and one opinion.

If the *Bundesrat* is not precisely a cabinet, it is also not exactly an 'administration' either. Certainly the *Bundesrat* has some of the aura of the president of the USA. The Bern press corps rises respectfully when a *Bundesrat* enters the room and hard, direct questions are rarely put. Frequently, as one very senior political correspondent told me, the press knows exactly where each of the members stands on an issue but well established custom forbids them to use such knowledge. The notion of a collective identity has never been entirely plausible. There have always been members of the Federal Council who stood out by sheer force of personality, men like Motta, Hoffmann, Pilet-Golaz or Minger. Yet even such 'strong' Federal Councillors cannot direct Swiss politics the way a 'strong' German chancellor or British prime minister can. There are several reasons for this. The first is that nobody controls a Swiss cabinet. Federal Councillor Otto Stich explained to me that, as finance minister in a 'magic formula' cabinet, he has no prime minister to lean on, no parliamentary majority behind him, indeed, no political leverage of any kind. He cannot impose a tight budget on recalcitrant colleagues. Everything must be negotiated within a collective body, which in turn accepts collective, executive responsibility towards parliament. Of course, the other councillors are in the same position with regard to him. Each must read the other's position papers and all must arrive at a consensus before each can act. The executive is a collective of persons of different parties, but united in responsibility.[65]

Federal Councillors have an ambivalent relationship to their parties. A member of the Federal Council is not the leader of his or her party in either house nor, as Federal Councillor Flavio Cotti pointed out in an interview he granted me, can he or she be said to represent a canton or linguistic community. He or she retains full party membership, linguistic and cantonal identity, the right, indeed duty, to attend parliamentary party meetings and conventions, but cannot act as party spokesperson. A Federal Councillor may often end up having to represent policies which his or her party opposes. As Signor Cotti said to me, when he was president of the CVP he used to think: 'how unfortunate that the party president is not the Federal Councillor. Now I think how fortunate that he is not.'[66]

The relationship between Federal Councillor and party becomes even more strained when the elected councillor has not been the party's first choice. Since the Federal Assembly votes by secret ballot, it can and often does reject a party candidate for another, 'more moderate' representative, of course, from the same party. (To do anything more provocative would threaten the fragile 'magic formula'.) In 1973 the 'official' candidates of the Socialists, Christian Democrats and Radicals all fell to 'unofficial' candidates. Herr Stich himself was not the Socialist Party's first choice, which does not seem to disturb him all that much. A dramatic recent case followed the resignation of René Felber in January 1993. The seat 'belonged' to the Socialists and nobody contested that nor that the new Federal Councillor had to be French-speaking, preferably from a canton which had not been represented for some time. The SPS chose Christiane Brunner, a lively trade unionist from Geneva, a feminist, an opponent of the army in the 1989 referendum and the child of a dysfunctional family. Her sentiments had been formed in the 1960s but even the conservative *Neue Zürcher Zeitung* gave her good marks for belonging to the 'pragmatic, consensus-orientated' branch of Social Democracy.[67] When the Federal Assembly met on 3 March 1993, the grumbling about Christiane Brunner's 'lack of style and format' (code for class and feminism) had leaked to the public, and there were women's demonstrations when the Assembly elected François Matthey of Neuchâtel, the SPS's second choice. Matthey eventually stood down in favour of Ruth Dreifuss, a

German-Swiss but long enough resident in Geneva to square the magic formula's circles.[68]

There must be losers in any electoral system and with only seven seats on the Federal Council, not all national, linguistic, religious, gender, or political features can be satisfactorily represented. Some cantons have never 'had' a Federal Councillor and others only infrequently. There is still only one woman out of seven Federal Councillors. A more fundamental objection is that the elections distort the will of the parties and eliminate candidates with sharp profiles and hence leadership qualities. After a similar, though less dramatic, upheaval in 1966, Nationalrat Breitenmoser (CVP, Basel-Stadt) observed: 'Federal Council elections are rather like games of chance based on the formula: at the right moment find the right man with the right language from the right canton. The one elected is a very lucky fellow.' Perhaps there ought to be more Federal Councillors, more than one permitted from a given canton or no consideration given to commune of origin (*Bürgerort*). Certainly one or all of those alterations would loosen the automatic couplings by which candidates seem to drop into or through the right slots. Another, even more fundamental alteration would be direct popular election of Federal Councillors by the citizens. Good precedents exist for electing the executive directly; most cantons have direct elections of members of the Executive Council (*Regierungsrat*). All of these devices would make the election of Federal Councillors less like a pinball machine through which candidates drop on to the right or wrong cushions, but it would not resolve the much deeper *malaise* about the institution itself. Seven diligent honourable people do not constitute a political as opposed to an administrative focus. A president by rotation reduces the chance of genuine national leadership. In his novel about Swiss politics, Giovanni Orelli likens presidential orations on festive occasions to frozen food. The citizenry eats lunch while the president alone is talking. In fact his patriotic sentiments 'have been stored for a week in a cupboard, in a sort of strongroom, cut on to tape before being served: just like a dish which looks as if it had been cooked to order but has really been waiting there for weeks or months in the storerooms and refrigerators of the big stores'.[69] Perhaps the Swiss can confront the turbulence of the 1990s and the new millennium with the traditional pieties, now wrapped in cellophane and stored on tape, but there are those who doubt it.

In the first place doubts have grown about the very institution itself. In 1896 A. Lawrence Lowell noted that members of the Federal Council were 'decidedly overworked and at this very moment plans are being discussed for relieving them of a part of their labours'.[70] Not much came of those plans and a century later the problem has worsened. The various Swiss departments now contain ranges of incompatible agencies, doing things which in other executive systems would have a minister or junior minister to represent them. Take the case of the federal Departement des Innern; the Federal Councillor who heads this ministry of the interior is responsible for culture, environment, the meteorological services, health, statistics, social security, sport, science and technology, the federal office buildings, military insurance and the national archives. If the Western European Union has a meeting of ministers of health in Strasbourg, while what is left of EFTA has convened an informal meeting of ministers of environment in Oslo, and the ministers of social security of the European Union have convened in Paris and invited Switzerland to attend as an observer, what does the minister do? There is nobody of ministerial rank to replace him or her. Only the Department of Foreign Affairs and the Department of Economics have a kind of deputy minister, holding the rank of 'state secretary'. The rest have literally nobody.

In the early 1990s, the Federal Council proposed a new government and administrative reorganisation law which has been making its torpid way through the committees of both houses. Discussion has focussed on the terms of a proposal to appoint state secretaries as deputy ministers and place between ten and twenty-one such persons in the major ministries as department chiefs. Yet if they are appointed by the Federal Council and not elected by the Federal Assembly, they will lack political legitimation in a country which considers it right to elect everybody from the highest state officer to the *Brunnenmeister* of Malters. 'State Secretaries' have an alien, Germanic ring to them and belong, together with honorific titles and deferential behaviour, outside the 'Swiss way of doing things'. The 'sovereign' in its present mood may well reject the final legislation, even if both houses eventually agree on the number of state secretaries, their duties and the mode of election or appointment.

The difficulty with the Federal Council goes well beyond matters of organisation. A 'magic formula' guarantees that there will be compromise and consent but it also ensures that action will be slow and frequently hesitant. The behaviour of the Federal Council in the last decade has not been as coherent, decisive or focussed as many might wish. A recent survey showed that the public had almost no confidence in their government. Whereas in 1979 16% of those interviewed had 'absolute' confidence in their government and 45% had 'reasonable' confidence, a similar survey in 1995 showed that only 2% had 'absolute' and 26% 'reasonable' confidence in their institutions.[71] The gap between 'above' and 'below' has been exploited by the fringe parties of the right. The Federal Council has become 'elitist' in the demonology of such groups. Yet nothing could be more homely and unpretentious than the entourage or office arrangements of a Swiss ministry. The halls of Bundeshaus Ost and Bundeshaus West or the Finance Ministry date from the bombastic period of nineteenth-century public monuments but the Federal Councillors and their staffs, from senior civil servants to the porters downstairs, have the relaxed and easy reaction to the intruding public of genuine democrats. If small is beautiful, the Swiss have beautiful government.

The dissatisfaction has not arisen because Swiss Federal Councillors or parliamentarians have assumed imperial grandeur, but because they have assumed too little. I asked Bundesrat Otto Stich, until August 1995 Federal Minister of Finance, what he proposed to do to get the people to accept the introduction of Value Added Tax, an essential element in his financial reform package. He smiled and said 'Nichts!' It would be counterproductive, he believed, if members of the Federal Council campaigned for measures.[72] Yet if the Federal Council will not take to the soap-box and defend its programme, the box will be used by the anti-Bern, anti-Brussels demagogues.

Nor is it just the Federal Council that seems to be creaking under the strain of domestic and foreign demands on it. Modern Swiss government has rested for the past century and a half on the principle of 'militia service'. Just as the citizen served in the army, so he or she served in the legislature or executive of the commune, canton or federal government. But now the tasks of government have grown so alarmingly that the citizen–parliamentarian either turns professional or becomes increasingly ineffective. Over the past twenty years more and more cantonal executives have become full time and the *per diem* payments to parliamentarians have gone up. Here too professionalisation increases competence and specialisation but also widens the gap between citizens and their representatives, between 'them' and 'us'.

In one crucial respect Swiss government has become more representative in the last few decades: representation of women. The move to enfranchise women began after the first world war and by 1959 twenty-four cantonal referenda giving women the vote had been lost. Then in a very Swiss way things gradually changed. Just as in the 1860s the cantons slowly accepted referenda and initiatives before the federal government did, so in the 1960s many of the cantons moved to enfranchise women. On 7 February 1971 women gained the vote on federal level, and on 14 June 1981 a constitutional amendment was approved by the people, which has become paragraph 2 of Article 4:

Men and women have equal rights. The law provides for equal treatment in family, training and work. Men and women have equal rights to equal pay for equal work.

Formally, women in Switzerland now enjoy better legal status than they do in the United States where the ERA (Equal Rights Amendment) has not been passed by the states. The cantons still lead the Swiss federal government in female participation. Whereas the *Nationalrat* has thirty-five women out of two hundred members (17.5%), cantons like Geneva and Solothurn have more than double that percentage of female members in their parliaments.[73] The city parliament of Bern recently passed an ordinance requiring that there be no fewer than thirty-two female deputies out of a total of eighty, the first city in Europe to introduce a gender quota. It would work like this: because the city of Bern elects its city representatives by proportional representation, when there is a vacancy, the next person on a party's list simply steps forward to fill it. The city parliament has decreed that, if a vacancy occurs when there are not enough women among the members, the selection procedure will skip male candidates, no matter how high on the list of those not quite elected they were. The liberal *Neue Zürcher Zeitung* was appalled:

In elections the sovereign should really choose and not simply fill up some pre-fabricated rump of a structure. In any case it is in the hands of the voters to redress any imbalance among the sexes.

The voters agreed and turned down the proposal by more than two to one.[74] So far Swiss voters have not done badly in redressing the imbalance – about as well as most northern European states – but not brilliantly either. Swiss women occupy places in political life, especially on communal and cantonal level, but are still under-represented in industry, the big banks and chemical companies. Left-wing parties and organisations have made greater efforts to represent women than centre and right-wing groups. It is characteristic that the Bernese city parliament which tried to introduce the quota system had a 'red–green' coalition government.

Women may be under-represented but foreigners are not represented at all. Switzerland has the second highest ratio of foreign to native residents of any country in Europe (Luxemburg has the highest). According to the official census figures in 1993, there were 1,318,265 foreigners out of a resident population of 6,988,858 or 18.8%, a percentage which has been creeping up steadily over the last ten years.[75] The majority of these foreigners were either born in Switzerland (22.1%) or have lived there for more than five years (50.4%). In the work place foreigners make up 27% of all gainfully employed persons, although, as one would expect, unemployment among foreign workers is more than twice as high as for Swiss nationals. On the other hand the second generation of 'foreigners' has done much better than the first in achieving professional, trade or other qualifications.[76] Compared to the large number of foreigners in Switzerland, the numbers who acquire Swiss citizenship is tiny. The official figures show the following numbers of new Swiss citizens: 1988 – 6,689; 1989 – 6,863; 1990 – 5,497; 1991 – 5,346; 1992 – 9,830; 1993 – 11,920.[77] Even with the slightly easier provisions of the 1992 legislation, the number of foreigners gaining full citizenship rights remains well under 1%. It is not unfair to say that Switzerland has a large, increasingly well educated, underclass.

Swiss prosperity rests on foreign labour. The post-war boom sucked in hundreds of thousands of aliens and the Swiss government controlled them by limiting their status. Four types of foreigners were admitted – those with residence permits, those with seasonal permits (who were subject to a variety of restrictions on movement, choice of job, family status and time allowed in Switzerland), those with annual permits and the *Grenzgänger*, *Frontaliers* and *Frontalieri*, people who work in Switzerland but go home to Germany, France or Italy at night. In 1993 there were

921,982 foreigners with permanent residence, 315,229 with annual permits, 50,016 with seasonal permits and 160,087 frontier-crossers.[78]

In the 1950s and 1960s when the hordes of poor Italian, Yugoslav and Spanish workers first arrived, the governments in Bern and the cantons complacently assumed that, if a depression put an end to rapid growth, the foreigners would go home. After the crash of 1973 it became clear that they would not.

The reaction was predictable. Some native Swiss felt threatened, swamped by the flood of aliens. They used the term *Überfremdung*, inelegantly rendered as 'over-foreignisation', to describe a complex of defensive and anxious attitudes. Between 1965 and 1988 some Swiss right-wing parties decided to use the traditional Swiss weapon, the ballot-box, to solve the problem of foreigners. In June 1965 the Democratic Party of Canton Zürich proposed an initiative to limit the number of foreigners to 10% of the resident population. In the following twenty years the Nationale Aktion, the Republican Party and other right-wing organisations tried either to set quotas on foreigners or to tax employers who engaged foreign labour. The voters rejected such proposals on every occasion, the last of which took place on 4 December 1988.[79] On the other hand, the voters also rejected in 1994 a referendum which would have made it easier for young foreigners between the ages of 15 and 25 who had spent five years in Swiss schools to become citizens by an accelerated (and cheaper) procedure. The popular vote went 52.9% to 47.1% in favour of liberalisation but the vote by canton revealed that thirteen had voted 'No'. As in much recent Swiss politics, the 'sovereign' voters split into French v. German, rural v. urban. The *Neue Zürcher Zeitung* noted sadly that

once again the vote showed how little in these matters the views of parliament, the large parties and organisations can predict the behaviour of the voters. One ought to add that the political leaders and party members did all too little for an enterprise that they must have known would not be automatically accepted.[80]

The result of these contradictory voting attitudes – 'No' to attempts to limit the numbers of foreign workers and 'No' to initiatives to improve their status – reflects deep contradictions in contemporary Swiss life. The Swiss know they need the foreign workers but a great many refuse to consider integrating them.

These reactions have grown as the number of non-European immigrants grows. Between the mid-1980s and the mid-1990s the number of Asian and African foreigners in Switzerland doubled. As brown and black faces appear on the streets of Luzern and Bern, there is nostalgia for the simpler days when the poor were, after all, 'European'.

The division in attitudes to foreign workers corresponds exactly to the divisions on European integration, on Swiss participation in UN 'blue beret' operations and on liberalisation of land sales. In the face of such divisions, the Federal Council and cantonal executives hesitate and, in hesitating, are lost. The authorities have seen the 'absolute' confidence they once enjoyed erode over the past few years. Their hesitancy or inaction in crucial votes merely reduces what remains. None of this makes Switzerland more 'Euro-compatible' nor eases the lot of those poor Swiss diplomats who try to negotiate bilateral agreements with Brussels. The repeated pattern of 'Yes' to a more European-orientated Switzerland in the French-speaking regions and 'No' in German-speaking regions deepens the *Graben* and makes many Swiss wonder about the survival of the Confederation.

The European Union has become a 'threat' across the range of Swiss political life. Its councils, commissions, directories and boards, its regular meetings, the mountains of paper it produces and its centralised *dirigiste* bureaucracy place the homely, semi-professional, Swiss structures under great strain. The Federal Council has to act and be seen to be acting but it lacks, by its very collegial nature, leadership and direction. Parliament operates by 'magic formulae', conciliation and 'concordance'. The system shuns conflict and hence very unwillingly takes hard decisions, and never quickly. Then the voters or, more accurately, the cantons say 'No'. Switzerland seems to go nowhere, its system turns on heavy slow wheels which somehow never quite engage.

In this chapter, we have seen the 'Swiss way of doing things' in its political aspect and observed the set of 'do's' and 'don'ts' at work on communal level and in Bern. You don't force people out of office and you accept the vagaries of proportional representation. Every-thing is 'political' but the citizens understand that political activity must be tempered by fairness. The Swiss live in a world conditioned by historic continuities, some very ancient indeed. 'It has always been so' serves as a good justification for trying to keep it so in the future. Most of this is wholly unreflective, simply assumed as part of the texture of daily life. That self-evident assumption of continuity has been undermined by the transformation of Europe. Nobody in Switzerland can fail to see the signs of inadequacy in the political structures on all three levels of government, in the behaviour and apathy of much of the citizenry, in the disorder and confusion in parties and parliament and in the demagogic noises coming from the right-wing extremes.

If Switzerland were a multi-national state like Yugoslavia, one could imagine a terminal crisis in which the linguistic groups split. If it were, as many Swiss imagine, a fragile structure which must be 'willed' – the cliché is *eine Willensnation* – the uncertainty of political will which we have observed might be another sign of terminal crisis. Switzerland is, I believe, neither of these things but an ancient, historic entity which happened to escape the centralisation of the modern era. It is a bit of the old Holy Roman Empire which survived the rise and fall of the centralised modern state. Switzerland is still intact long after the totalitarian dictators with their centralised and unified states have strutted off the stage. Beneath the political crises and inadequacies there are levels of Swiss consciousness which bind and control behaviour in subtle ways. Swiss identity has much deeper and stronger roots than many Swiss imagine. One of these powerful roots is attitude to language, and that is the subject of the next chapter.

CHAPTER 4

Language

English-speakers rarely think about their language. Unlike the French who poured millions into propagating the French language overseas, the British in their empire (and the Americans in theirs) never worried much about the language as such. There is no recognised academy in any part of the English-speaking world to defend the purity of the language. As a world language, English is casual, slovenly and varied. In Switzerland, and in most European countries, language is a very different thing. By excluding those who cannot understand, it sets the outer limits of membership in a certain type of community. The precise meaning of that membership will depend on the status of the language: written or unwritten, used in a wide geographical area or restricted, spoken by all social classes or only by some. It will also depend on the economic, social, legal, political, religious and ideological structures in which it is used, for example, the language acceptable in a court of law. Language can change social and political institutions. It can help to alter the productive forces of an economy and can enlarge or contract markets. A startling example of life imitating speech is Italian unification. In his fascinating study of language in the history of Italy, Tullio de Mauro estimates that in 1861, the heroic epoch of Italian unification, only 2.5% of the total Italian population could speak Italian. The other twenty-five million inhabited what he calls a 'forest of dialect' so dense that when the Visconti-Venesta brothers walked down the streets of Naples speaking Italian they were thought to be Englishmen.[1] Modern Italy first took form in language, and this may be said of modern Slovakia, Slovenia, Romania, Serbia and, for different reasons, modern Israel. Perry Anderson is right when he observes that 'spoken language, far from always following material changes, may sometimes anticipate them'.[2]

Language is not a colourless fluid through which reality is refracted but a thick, viscous substance like tar. It has its own ebbs and flows which never leave the surrounding environment utterly unchanged. Political frontiers, accidentally imposed, may dam its currents. The accumulating liquid at first stagnates; then separated off from its original main stream, it literally becomes another language. Slovak differs from Czech, because the border of the medieval Kingdom of Hungary divided hitherto undivided west Slavic-speakers. The differences among German, Alsatian, Dutch, Swiss German and Luxemburgisch all began as historical lines on the map and deepened into separate dialect or language currents. The process works in the other direction too. Italian, Ukrainian, Croatian, Serbian and at an earlier date English, French and Spanish spread out to submerge and ultimately absorb other languages and dialects. The Scottish language was largely destroyed by political repression, the Irish reduced by economic and social change. This is the context in which the precise position of language in Switzerland must be seen. There are other multilingual states in Europe, for example Russia; there are bilingual states like Belgium; there are linguistic minorities on the 'wrong' sides of borders, as in south Tyrol. Switzerland is not special simply because it has four 'national languages' but because language itself has a special place in Switzerland. Language defines and at the same time denies Swiss identity; it reinforces the peculiarities of political practice and reflects them. Above all, it contributes to the bewildering variety in a small area which makes it hard to say anything general about Switzerland. In Chapter 1 I first offered one or two examples of that variety; now I should like to look at it in greater detail. First the dimensions of the question. The figures are shown in Table 4.1.

The impact of foreign migration between 1950 and 1990 accounts for the sharp changes in percentages, the doubling of the percentage of Italian speakers between 1950 and 1970 and the doubling of the share of 'other' languages (Turkish, Serbo-Croat, Tamil) more recently.

The largest of the groups is still the Swiss 'German' but the inverted commas around the word suggest that there is more to the reality than the noun conveys. Technically what Swiss Germans speak is *Schwyzerdütsch*, a rather artificial term to describe an

Table 4.1. *Residents of Switzerland by mother-tongue (in %)*

Year	German	French	Italian	Romansch	Other
1950	72.1	20.3	5.9	1.0	0.7
1960	69.3	18.9	9.5	0.9	1.4
1970	64.9	18.1	11.9	0.8	4.3
1980	65.0	18.4	9.8	0.8	6.0
1990	63.6	19.2	7.6	0.6	8.9

Source: Statistisches Jahrbuch der Schweiz 1995 (Bern, 1995), Table 16.2, p. 352.

astonishing number of dialects in a small geographical area. It falls into three broad linguistic groups, Low Alemannic, High Alemannic and Highest Alemannic, dialect groups of the wider Alemannic family whose relatives can be found beyond the borders of the present Confederation in Swabia, Austria and in the southern parts of Baden and Alsace. Technically the distinguishing feature of High Alemannic which marks it off from the other Alemannic dialects is a collection of distinct sounds or phonological features,[3] but equally important is the social and political position of the dialect. *Schwyzerdütsch* in its three forms is the normal language of the Swiss Germans in daily life and at all levels of society. All users of High Alemannic can understand all other users, although there are occasional difficulties. The one main Low Alemannic dialect, the *Baseldütsch* of the city of Basel, can also be understood by all Swiss Germans, although the traveller from Basel who finds himself in a remote valley may have to refute the charge that he is German and not Swiss. About 100,000 people still use Highest Alemannic, the dialects of the very high Alps, Oberwallis and the Bernese Oberland in particular, and there the normal *Schwyzerdütsch*-speaker may not understand conversations among native users. Swiss Germans seem to relish that fact, and I have often noticed the extreme gusto with which tales are told of how thick the dialect is up there.

Dialect for Swiss German-speakers is identity, and the pleasure in Oberwalliser archaism is a kind of self-satisfaction, a delight in one's own *Eigenart* or special nature. Dialect is a constant subject of discussion among Swiss German-speakers and a distinct form of instant recognition. The Swiss, like the English, feel that 'you are how you speak'. The moment a Swiss German opens his mouth, every hearer knows where he comes from. As the English hear class characteristics, so the Swiss notice regional ones. Different dialects produce different reactions. Zürich dialect has a reputation for harshness, some say, 'aggressiveness', while the broad, lava-like flow of *Bärndütsch* gets high marks for a kind of genial, folksy, homely quality. The Baseler enjoys a reputation for witty use of words, and the Luzerner for liveliness and emotionalism. Linguistic and social perceptions tend to merge. I have heard resentment expressed by some Swiss in central and eastern Switzerland that the radio is dominated by the Bern, Basel and Zürich variants. The resentment of the sound reflects the history of the place. Zürich's aggressiveness is an historical fact, smoothly and unconsciously folded into the sound the listener hears.

Dialect is identity but it is also a form of social communication. The easiest way to start a conversation with a stranger at a party is to say 'Ah, I hear that you come from Zug. Do you know . . . ?' Once names have been exchanged, the next step is to examine family. 'Are you a relative of the Burris in Hergiswil?' The location becomes more precise and the contact is established. Swiss German-speakers make contact easily with each other, when abroad. More tell-tale than the passport is the characteristic sound of *Schwyzerdütsch* in the London Underground or on Madison Avenue. Since virtually no one but a Swiss ever speaks the language, and hence no Swiss remotely expects anyone else to understand it, Swiss travellers are more prone to chatter away in public than English, French, German or even American travellers would be. It is the private language of some four million people, not a very large group in the wider world, and they value it as the most personal mark of identity. A recent congratulatory article on the eightieth birthday of a well-known Basel civic leader remarked as a matter of course on the fact that after more than fifty years in the city, he still spoke an absolutely pure *Bärndütsch* not out of pride but simply because 'one should preserve one's mother-tongue in foreign parts'.

It is important to be clear precisely what is meant by dialect here. It is not accent as in the case of Yorkshire or Texas. Nor are dialects simply 'debased, corrupt forms of standard. Rather, it is standard which has risen from the dialects to its level of social and cultural prestige.'[4] The opposite idea is also false. Dialects do not necessarily preserve ancient forms of the language. They are no older nor younger than standard German. They have developed differently, feel the iron grip of norms less acutely and in remote areas have preserved a different mix of old and new. Dialects are not necessarily more vulgar than the 'high' speech although they are usually more 'popular' and less literary. Standard or High German can be vulgar in a vulgar mouth, and *Schwyzerdütsch* as refined as its speaker. What is true, as both a strength and a weakness, is that for Swiss Germans, *Schwyzerdütsch* is the mother-tongue, above all, the language of childhood, family, the heart. It is more direct and more intimate. If an ad-man wants to get his message across, he will slip a little *Mundart* (a folksier word for the foreign *Dialekt*) into the copy, as in this advertisement for an apple juice, 'Ova Urtrüeb bsunders guet' or this one for a Swiss cigar, 'Neu Rössli fund . . . e rundi Sach'. Typically, the homey, intimate articles of daily use are fitted out with copy in dialect, while advertisements for life insurance or computers use the language of high seriousness: *Schriftdeutsch* or written German. The Swiss pop group, the five-man Rumpelstilz, made a much bigger impact in the 1970s when they switched to dialect song texts. Dialect was their natural monopoly unavailable to the Rolling Stones or Pink Floyd.

Schwyzerdütsch has a grammar very different from that of High German. There is only one relative pronoun (*wo*), no present participle, no preterite and no construction 'in order to . . . ' There is no verb 'to love' and there are a whole series of common German words which do not exist in it: *wobei, irgendwie, sondern,* although some urban dialects now use the German words very frequently. The sentence structure is entirely different and, of course, the pronunciation utterly so. For historical reasons *Schwyzerdütsch* has a limited vocabulary. Written German has remained the language of higher culture and also the *spoken* language of elevated discourse. A university professor will lecture in German and conduct his oral examinations and seminars in that language too. He will probably speak dialect in the privacy of his study to an individual student. The Swiss German Radio distinguishes with great subtlety between the occasions for German and those for *Schwyzerdütsch*, not always comprehensibly to the foreigner. The early morning music and traffic news in the now defunct programme 'Autoradio Schweiz' was in chatty dialect, an odd usage, when one considers the number of drivers in any Swiss city who are foreigners. International news and weather always come in German but sport normally in *Schwyzerdütsch*. Advanced discourse of any kind tends to be in

German, as, indeed, are most prayers and, until recently, most sermons. The 'Our Father' is always said in High German and the language of prayer and religious discourse cannot really escape the immense impact of the German Bible.

The existence of a 'national' language which cannot be written has other consequences. Swiss Germans find themselves at a peculiar disadvantage in the world of business and commerce. They cannot speak 'their' language with foreign customers or customers from French or Italian Switzerland. They frequently compete in markets where rivals use international languages like English or French with the agility of native speakers. Successful Swiss business people take this reality for granted. I recall a meeting with a senior Swiss executive who offered me (in High German) my choice of languages as if he were offering me coffee, tea or milk. At ordinary levels of society, High German tends to falter a little and emerges in that thick Swiss accent so beloved of the German and Austrian music-halls. The average Swiss speaks German woodenly. His prose is stilted, heavy and lifeless. He never makes a joke and by comparison with a witty German or Austrian seems about as lively as the grumpy dwarf in 'Snow White'. The same man using dialect in his 'local', chatting away and laughing, is simply another human being, easy, often very funny and spontaneous.

Spoken Swiss German is full of 'foreign words', especially French ones. Many Swiss Germans say *merci viel mal* not *danke schön*. A conductor in a tram is a *conducteur* not a *Schaffner*, and so on. There are obvious historical reasons for the prominence of French. For more than two centuries French dominated European culture and for many patrician Swiss families French was the language of civilised discourse. The French were very present politically during the Helvetic Republic and Napoleonic era. French cultural influence varied geographically and also socially. Some communities, especially Bern and Basel, absorbed more French into daily speech than Zürich or St Gallen. During the nineteenth century, the growth in political and cultural prestige of German began to right this imbalance, but uniformity of usage never became as characteristic of written or spoken German as it had been of French. Two great literary contemporaries illustrate this variety neatly. Theodor Fontane and Gottfried Keller were both born in 1819, but the 'German' writer, Fontane, wrote a prose so frenchified that modern editions require elaborate notes to explain words like *Affront* or *Eklat* for contemporary readers. The Swiss author Keller wrote a more germanic German using traditional words like *Base* for *cousine* (cousin) and *Muhme* for *tante* (aunt). Keller's prose probably reflected the smaller influence of the French on the underlying Zürich version of *Schwyzerdütsch*. The gap between written and spoken usage also permits the survival of words like *Ilp*, the Basel German word for elephant now obsolete elsewhere. There are specifically Swiss usages, such as *Besammlung* for an assembly of persons and the verb *äufnen* to accrue, neither of which occurs in standard German dictionaries. It is arguable that because *Schwyzerdütsch* is not normally written, it may be less resistant to foreign imports than written languages are, but other explanations, not least Hitler's campaign against 'foreign words' during the 1930s, also account for the higher proportion of them in Swiss German daily use than in High German.

The most remarkable characteristic of *Schwyzerdütsch* is its variety. Dr Ludwig Fischer in a study of Luzern dialect distinguished five groups among the 289,000 inhabitants: the dialects of Mittelland, the Hinterland, the Luzern and Hochdorf, the Rigi area and, finally, the Entlebuch. In isolating the character of each he emphasised the crucial geographical elements. In the Entlebuch valley, for example, there was practically no linguistic influence from neighbouring Obwalden, because until the 1940s the roads were not always passable. 'Earlier isolation, history, cultural life, economic development and the character of the population all helped to erect dialect borders.'[5] Even in the less mountainous regions, this linguistic diversity is marked. Each village or region has its own characteristic vowel sounds, speech rhythms and frequently its own vocabulary. As a result, the Swiss look puzzled if one asks whether dialect can be learned. The idea that dialect can be acquired is clearly alien to them. If they accept, for the sake of discussion, that dialect might be learned, they are quick to point out that there is no generally accepted dialect so there would be no use in trying. It is not surprising that there are only three or four courses in dialect in all of Switzerland. To teach dialect would mean to make it formal and to give it a grammar. The relationship of written German to *Schwyzerdütsch* is very like that of Latin to the vernacular Romance languages in the early Middle Ages, as Dr J. A. Cremona describes it:

It was not simply a question of there being no grammatical codification of the vernaculars: in the forms in which they were known, the vernaculars were believed not to be amenable to grammatical analysis. They were too irregular, too protean and variable, for analysis to be possible. These notions were encouraged by the diverging structures of Latin and vernacular.[6]

It would appear that the first attempts to provide grammars for Romance languages arose from the need to teach the vernaculars to foreigners and to serve as models of 'best' usage for vernacular poetry. Several grammars of this sort appeared in the thirteenth century. The presence of foreigners has not had the same effect in Switzerland. Even the intrusion of mass communications, especially television from Germany, has not done more than 'corrupt' dialect by introducing words from the written speech into the spoken one. The tension between *Schriftdeutsch* and *Mundart* continues without either displacing the other. Swiss German linguistic usage rests on an uneasy equilibrium between the decentralising pull of dialect and the pervasive centralising impact of High German. The explanation for this uniquely Swiss balancing act can be found, in the first place, in politics.

Schwyzerdütsch binds Swiss Germans together, especially in the face of the Germans, and is particularly precious to them. Swiss tell you that they 'love' their dialects in the way that people elsewhere love their homes. Spiritually the dialect is a home in the narrow sense and a national home in the wider. Dialect variety reflects and reinforces political and communal variety. The *Gemeinde*, the district, the canton and the federal government may all be said to have a linguistic reality to flesh out the civil forms. A striking example is Canton Bern where, for profoundly political motives, the members of the Grand Council, the cantonal parliament, insist on using Bern dialect. It reinforces the peculiar identity of Bern but at the same time irritates those citizens of the canton who speak French as a mother-tongue. It is well understood in Switzerland that you can expect the *Welschen*, as Swiss Germans often call Swiss French, to try to understand written German but not dialect. Hence by using *Bärndütsch* the Grand Councillors spread themselves more broadly across the political scene. The dialect includes but it also excludes.

Dialect excludes foreigners very effectively, whether the 'foreigners' are other Swiss in Oberwallis or in Romansch-speaking

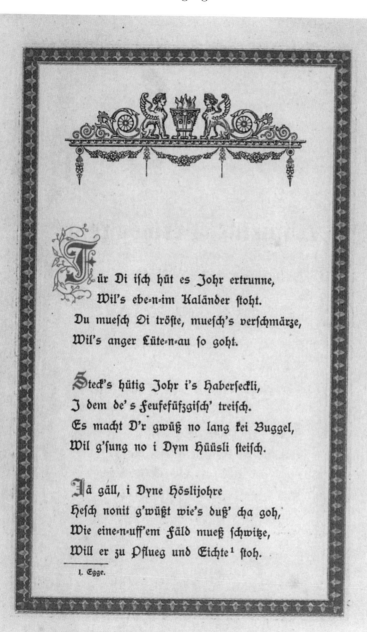

ür Di isch hüt es Johr ertrunne,
Wil's ebe-n-im Kaländer stoht.
Du muesch Di tröste, muesch's verschmärze,
Wil's anger Lüte-n-au so goht.

Steck's hütig Johr i's Haberseckli,
J dem de' s Feufefüfzgisch' treisch.
Es macht D'r gwüß no lang kei Buggel,
Wil g'sung no i Dym Hüüsli steisch.

Jä gäll, i Dyne Höslijohre
Hesch nonit g'wüßt wie's duß' cha goh,
Wie eine-n-uff'em Fäld mueß schwitze,
Will er zu Pflueg und Eichte[1] stoh.

1. Egge.

Plate 12 A poem in Swiss German dialect

Graubünden. More than any other single factor, dialect makes it hard to get 'inside Switzerland' or to get to know Swiss Germans. The foreigner who tries to approach the Swiss through the German language gets a misleading impression. Swiss Germans instinctively respond to a High German-speaker in their version of it. They find it psychologically very difficult to hear the one language spoken to them and to respond in the other. In a group, the presence of one non-dialect speaker can kill the spontaneity of a conversation. The moment the Swiss German-speakers remember the alien presence, they tend to throw the language switch back to High, leaving it there until they forget again.

If *Schwyzerdütsch* establishes identity, it does not do so simply nor without a considerable price. The price is seen in the ambivalence of virtually all Swiss about the written language, *Schriftdeutsch*. Its use is a tricky operation. Swiss Germans suspect any fellow Swiss who uses High German too well and are embarrassed by anyone who uses it too badly. A native German-speaker will recognise at once that radio announcers on Swiss radio have accents, but to the Swiss they sound too German to be real Swiss. Not the least of the accusations levelled at the poet Carl Spitteler in 1914, when he urged his fellow Swiss Germans to be less pro-German, was his constant use of High German. The ironies multiply. It was, after all, the prestige of literary German and the achievements of German and Austrian culture in the nineteenth century which made Jacob Burckhardt rejoice that *Schwyzerdütsch* had never become a literary language. The educated Swiss shared the international culture of the most advanced of the European peoples. When in the twentieth century that people reverted to a modern form of barbarism, Swiss Germans found themselves culturally caught up in the German catastrophe. Their literary language could not be spoken without shame in any non-German continental country, and many Swiss travellers in the 1940s suffered great embarrassment because Dutchmen or Danes jumped to wrong conclusions.

The extraordinary situation of German Switzerland is most poignantly revealed in the schools. Swiss German children have to learn to read and write in what is effectively a foreign language. The Czech philologist, Olga Neversilova, has compared it to asking someone to learn to play the piano and drive a car at the same time. In her studies of the behaviour of children, she noticed that the children coped with the alien written language by creating home-made High German: *ich bin gesein, Zeuge* for *Züge* and so on. What seems to happen is that the children draw natural analogues from one system and place it in the other. For adult Swiss Germans the written and spoken languages tend to be wholly dislocated. What is written is simply different and pronounced differently from what is spoken. Public lecturers and preachers will tell you that if they wish to speak to an audience in dialect, they cannot use a written manuscript but must rely on key words or phrases. The moment a proper text appears, the mind apparently switches into the channels which control the written language. These problems multiply what is already a complex and much discussed process: learning to read. In Miss Neversilova's view the present practice in Swiss schools is distinctly unsatisfactory and should be reconsidered:

In the first classes at primary school written German is taught with the aid of Swiss German. As far as the Swiss German is concerned, there is no attempt to convey a 'theory' of Swiss language, which might lead to the formation of a meta-language or to thinking about the language or even to an awareness of Swiss German as a system with rules of its own . . . [7]

The children have problems moving from dialect to High German, but so do writers. They write in a language which is not exactly foreign but is not their mother-tongue either. Some Swiss writers evade the issue by weaving in the odd dialect word or phrase and by giving the timbre of dialect to what is basically pure High German. Others, like Peter Bichsel, achieve their effects by radical innovations in German prose. In 1964 Bichsel published some brilliant short stories entitled *Eigentlich möchte Frau Blum den Milchmann kennenlernen*, in which the literary language was reduced to its simplest building blocks. The title, drawn from one of the stories, is actually a typical sentence in both length and content. Even in translation something of Bichsel's style comes through. Here is a specimen from his controversial *Des Schweizers Schweiz*:

I come out of the boring *Nationalrat* onto the crowded street. The many cars drive past each other. I stand there for ten minutes and don't see a single collision. The autos do not collide because they drive on the right. Some time or other this parliament decided that automobiles must drive on the right. That is why there are no collisions. Parliament has ordered my world for me; it fulfils its task; my world is ordered.[8]

Literary German more remote from that of, say, Thomas Mann

can hardly be imagined. Subordinate clauses, heavily modified adjectival phrases, the long, dangling sentence, have been cut away with a scalpel. Bichsel has a considerable reputation and was awarded a prize by the famous German literary group, the 'Gruppe 47'. How does he see his own very idiosyncratic language in relation to German literature?

I never heard the charge in Berlin that Swiss authors could not write High German but often the accusation that they wrote too high a German; they were prissy and fussed about grammatical exactness, they had contributed very little to the German language. I sometimes suspect that some Swiss authors come from Hanover rather than Zürich . . . I too lack the guts. I too am very concerned to be understood by north German readers.[9]

A Swiss writer cannot escape this dilemma by writing in dialect, although some pretend to do so. Ernst Eggimann says in commenting on his poetry, 'All I had to do was to sit under the broad roof of our farm house on our porch and listen. I could surrender myself to the language. The language made the poetry . . . '[10] No poetry is written like that, not even dialect poetry. A dialect poet's head is full of German literary history and tradition; his normal reading will be largely in High German. Hence his dialect poetry comes out of the same two-tiered consciousness which enfolds the High German writer. Hermann Burger sums up the recent success of the dialect poets by drawing a parallel with pop art: 'In museums things are suddenly to be seen that would not have been seen there a few years ago. If one took away the frame, the museum atmosphere, one would see the same things with very different eyes.'

The problem of writing dialect as a literary language can be seen in theatre as well as in lyric poetry. A perfect example is the case of Paul Haller, who wrote a great deal of second-class lyric poetry in High German but also two tragedies in dialect. Many critics think Haller's *Marie und Robert*, written in 1915, is the best play by a twentieth-century Swiss author. Haller himself was so embittered by the play's lack of success that he gave up dialect as a literary medium. A few years later he took his own life at the age of thirty-eight. The play was either forgotten or performed only by *Volkstheater* and amateur groups until 1958, when for the first time an important professional company attempted the work. In the spring of 1975, the critic Peter Ruedi discussed a new production at the Baseler Komödie in a review which superbly illustrates the problem of dialect theatre. 'The Basel production shows in an exemplary fashion the strains in handling such dialect material, above all, the language struggle. Haller wrote Aargauer dialect. Where could one find, within the confines of the professional stage, a complete Aargau cast? Where could one even find nine pros who speak the same dialect?'[11] The producer forced his actors to speak a common approximation to Aargau dialect. The result, wrote Ruedi, was 'devastating'. The enforced Aargau *Mundart* turned out to be a more artificial speech than stage German could ever have been. The spontaneity of dialect was lost.

The dilemmas of dialect literature arise because dialect is both general to all Swiss Germans but by its very nature rooted in a specific locality. The history of the country and the particularism of its politics find reinforcement in the habits of its speech. There is no Swiss dialect, but lots of Swiss dialects, no Swiss German language but German. The Swiss writer, whether in High German or dialect, cannot escape the confines of the two sets of conflicts: the conflict between dialect and the written language and between local and national identity. Swiss writers seem to be condemned by the paradox that there is no such thing as Swiss writing. A perfect example is the study of Swiss literary outsiders by the poet Dieter Fringeli. He managed to insist that 'there is no autonomous, no typical Swiss literature'[12] in the introduction and then to plead for its existence in the individual essays. I counted the word *unschweizerisch* (un-Swiss) five times in the first thirty pages. The very fact that Fringeli selected neglected Swiss authors and not just neglected German authors underlines the dilemma.

Two questions easily become confused here. Is there a Swiss literature as such, that is, what have Swiss Italian, French and German writers in common? And is there a Swiss German literature distinct from the larger world of German writing? The broader question is harder to answer. Undoubtedly, writers like Giovanni Orelli, Plinio Martini and Piero Bianconi share themes with Swiss German writers, village life, peasants, depopulation and so on, but it is hard to go beyond that. The answer to the second question seems to me clear. Yes, there is Swiss German literature and it includes all those caught up in the special Swiss form of bilingualism. I emphasise the special character of Swiss bilingualism, because many English-speaking people are unaware of how widespread bilingualism is. De Mauro provides figures for Italy which indicate that in the early 1950s a third of the Italian population had abandoned the use of dialect as the sole instrument of communication but only half of those (that is, 18.5% of the total population) used Italian exclusively. The rest used dialect normally in all social situations.[13] The difference, and it is absolutely crucial, between Swiss German and Italian dialect usage is class. In Italy, the use of dialect is a matter of class. The higher the educational and social level the more likely it is that Italian only will be spoken. This phenomenon was well known in Switzerland in the nineteenth century. Gottfried Keller's protagonist in *Der grüne Heinrich* observes that his father's aspirations and new style of life included wearing shirts with ruffles and speaking 'purest High German'.[14] In the twentieth century, the situation reversed itself. It became a matter of national pride to speak dialect and an assertion of Swiss political independence. A government study group has confirmed the existence of this *Mundartwelle* or 'dialect wave' but resorts to 'guesses' in its attempt to explain it.[15] At any rate dialect shows every sign of spreading into areas where High German has been dominant before. The tensions and ambiguities are unresolved, but the Swiss Germans seem to survive it. Indeed, they flourish in its peculiarities. In literature since 1945, they have been unusually creative: Max Frisch, Friedrich Dürrenmatt, Otto F. Walter, Adolf Muschg, Peter Bichsel, Urs Widmer and E. Y. Meyer are just a few of the names that come to mind. Frisch and Dürrenmatt have probably been the most successful writers in the German language during the past thirty years. Only Günter Grass and Heinrich Böll have had an equivalent international impact.[16] Certainly Frisch and Dürrenmatt are much better known to English readers than are most of the big names of contemporary German literature: Martin Walser, Uwe Johnson, Peter Handke, Hans Magnus Enzensberger and Siegfried Lenz.

The linguistic situation of Swiss Italians really belongs to the general history of Italian linguistic development, although it has many similarities with that of Swiss Germans. The written language called Italian, like the written language called German, is not, on the whole, what Swiss Italians speak. Their position, on the other hand, is closer to that described by de Mauro in that, like the Italians across the frontier, their literary language was for all practical purposes a dead language until the early nineteenth century. The establishment of the Tuscan dialect of the thirteenth and fourteenth centuries as a vehicle for national awakening owed its success to the prestige of Dante, Petrarch and Boccaccio and also to geography. 'As a central Italian dialect Tuscan had enough points of common development with both northern and southern dialects to serve as a bridge between them.'[17] The interesting difference between German and Italian Switzerland is that, while the Germans have two levels of speech, the Swiss Italians have three: the local dialect, the general Lombard dialect or *koine*, and the literary or High Italian. The Lombard dialects belong to the family known as the *gallo-italici* and are very close to French in both pronunciation and vocabulary. On the basic level, the local variants are enormous, as in Alemannic. A man from the valley of Bedretto in the extreme north of Canton Ticino will not understand the local dialect of the Valle di Muggio in the extreme southern tip of the canton, the Mendrisio. The general *koine*, or Lombard patois, saves them from embarrassment and acts as the medium of communication. All Swiss Italians are effectively trilingual, and move from local to Lombard to Italian with almost unconscious ease.

Italian and German remain 'high' languages in both parts of the country but with subtly different significance. Dialect is less universal in Italian Switzerland and runs along the edges of social divisions, age, sex and class in fascinating and complex ways. Two acquaintances meeting on the street in Zürich would speak dialect at once, but in Lugano they would speak Italian. Going from Italian to dialect is a little like moving from the polite to the familiar form, from the *lei* to the *tu* in Italian, and presupposes a degree of familiarity. Dr Federico Spiess, of the Vocabolario dei dialetti della Svizzera italiana in Lugano, describes it this way:

If I have to go to the window of a post office and I speak Italian, I make the postal clerk understand that I want to ask for some information or to buy a stamp and that I want our relationship to remain at this strictly official level. If I have to go back to the same window two or three times, and, if in addition to the few indispensable words exchanged, even a single allusion to the excessive heat or cold, to head-ache or sniffles, to the health of wife or children, the war in Viet Nam or an earthquake in Peru, the price of meat or the latest referendum should insinuate itself into our exchange, dialect is immediately used to underline the new sort of relationship between us.[18]

Dialect is the language of neighbourliness and the commune, but here too its use reflects very subtle canons of social behaviour. The country man or woman in a city shop may use dialect with impunity, but the middle-class city dweller will use Italian, certainly at first, lest the shop girl feel insulted by such excessive familiarity. Similarly the middle-class city dweller who returns to the village of his origin would give even greater offence if he did *not* speak dialect from the beginning.

It is in family or school that the use of Italian shows its most remarkable features. In traditional middle-class families, parents speak dialect with each other, as do the children, but children speak to parents and parents to children in Italian. Respect and distance imply the use of the literary language as in the quotation from the famous Ticinese poet and novelist, Francesco Chiesa, which heads this book. To show respect is to speak Italian. Similarly, as Dott. Rosanna Zeli has found in her study of dialect usage in schools, the dialect means intimacy or equality of status. Teachers chat in dialect in the common room but speak Italian to pupils in the classroom and in all other encounters. Children speak dialect among themselves and, of course, Italian to teachers. Dott. Zeli found that in secondary schools the boys spoke dialect among themselves but Italian to the girls, and the girls dialect among themselves but Italian to the boys. The uncertainties of teenage sexual relations push them into Italian as the language of distance. Adult men use dialect more often than women, especially in towns and cities. A similar pattern is clear among French-speaking peasants in the Pyrenees. Women adopted the urban back 'r' in place of the local front rolled 'r' more rapidly than men.[19] This may reflect women's greater responsiveness to fashions, or possibly a more positive reaction to modern life in general.

Italian is the language of public life and dialect the language of private social relations. Hence it is not surprising that, as soon as a political organisation or government body becomes larger than, say, twenty people, which it will generally not do on village level, Italian replaces dialect as the means of communication. Radio and television are almost wholly in Italian, although dialect is occasionally spoken, when a country man is being interviewed. The presence of foreigners in large numbers has also played a part in the development of language in Italian Switzerland. From the 1880s to the present day, there has always been a large Italian colony in Canton Ticino: 28% (41,869 persons) of the canton's population in 1910 was made up of Italian foreign residents, a percentage of foreign residents that has not been exceeded to this day.[20] The influx of Swiss Germans as tourists, hotel owners, retired persons, industrialists and commercial people has added to the mix of population. In 1980, over 15% of the overall population came from other cantons, mostly German-speaking.[21] Italian naturally gets a boost from these two factors since energetic German Swiss will want to learn Italian but not dialect, while the Italian-speaking foreign workers, unless they are Lombards, will not be familiar with the local dialect variants. As the mountain and high valley communities die out, their local dialect goes with them. Many dialects have already simply become yellowed research cards in the capacious card index of the Vocabolario in Lugano which issues the definitive guide to dialect. The dialects die out more rapidly than the director, Dr Federico Spiess, and his colleagues can publish volumes. By the time the vast multi-volume study of the dialects of Italian Switzerland is complete, many of the local dialects will long since have ceased to be used. As a final irony, Dr Spiess and his colleagues, in spite of years of collaboration, speak Italian not dialect in their office.

The Italian-speaking areas of Switzerland belong physically to the Italian world. They lie to the south of the Alps, and their borders with Italy have historical rather than geographical origins. The rivers empty into the north Italian lakes and in general the actual valleys themselves face toward the south. Swiss Italians speak of the rest of Switzerland as *oltre Gottardo*, beyond the great Gotthard Pass. Italian television is received in Ticino and in the three Italian-speaking Graubünden valleys. Swiss Italian television enjoys a high reputation in the areas of Lombardy which can receive it. The cultural capital of Ticino is Milan, which is less than an hour by car from Lugano and Locarno. The natural Lombard affiliation, proximity and the size of the public have had a tendency to suck the writer and scholar from Italian Switzerland into the Milanese orbit. The most famous of modern Ticinese poets, Francesco Chiesa, who died at the incredible age of 102 in June 1973, wrote many of his most important short stories and poems for the *Corriere della Sera* of Milan and had his works published by Italian firms. The wonderful collection called *Racconti del mio orto* (1929) ('Stories from my Garden'), originally published in the *Corriere*, are so written that there is no trace of 'Swissness' about them. The main character is a philosophical bookkeeper and passionate gardener. The place where he lives could be anywhere in northern Italy. The one reference to something concrete, to the cost of an article, is given in lire not in Swiss francs, as if Chiesa wished to underline the non-Swiss character of the work. Shortly after his death, the Rome newspaper, *Il Tempo*, devoted a very long two-column obituary to Chiesa's place in Italian literature, which closed by citing his considerable achievement, 'which granted him not only a pre-eminent position among Swiss Italian writers but reserved one for him not much inferior to his distinguished contemporaries in Italy'. *The Times* in its brief obituary noted that Chiesa had celebrated his 100th birthday by publishing a collection of sonnets. *Die Weltwoche* in Zürich failed even to report the death of one of Switzerland's most important writers.

The sense of being ignored gives to the culture of Italian Switzerland a certain edginess. Some residue of the centuries of involuntary membership in the Confederation lingers on in the culture and attitudes of the 'Third Switzerland'. Swiss Italians expect to have to learn German and French to cope with their fellow citizens from the other regions but they never expect them to return the compliment. On the other hand, they know that their contribution to the Swiss identity is indispensable in spite of the small proportion of the population who speak Italian. If the Italian component had not survived the French Revolution and the ensuing wars Switzerland would not have become multilingual. A state composed only of one-fifth French-speakers and four-fifths German-speakers would have been less resistant to the centrifugal pull of cultural and linguistic nationalism. The 'Third Switzerland' represented a kind of cement, proof that a multinational state could survive and flourish even in the nineteenth and twentieth centuries. This indispensability is reflected in the disproportionate frequency with which Swiss Italians serve in the *Bundesrat* and other high positions. Overall, while only 4% of the entire population are Swiss Italian, as opposed to Italian-speakers, 7.6% of all federal administrative employees, 6.0% of postal employees, 11.9% of railway employees, are Swiss Italians. Only at the upper levels of the administrative grade of the civil service is the proportion of Ticinese and Swiss Italians from Graubünden precisely equivalent to their share of the population.[22] Nevertheless, the Italian Swiss have the feeling that they are not taken seriously. As Dott. Flavio

Zanetti puts it, the other Swiss tend to look at Ticino with eyes full of folklore, as 'a little paradise where carefree people live solely from the warmth of the sun, and whose only contribution, in the opinion of other Swiss, is to produce scandals and quaint customs'.[23]

The Raeto-Romansch-speakers who make up 1% of the population are edgy too but for different reasons. They are engaged in a struggle for ethnic survival whose outcome is pretty uncertain. The history of Raeto-Romansch reaches back to the Roman Empire when the Raetian people inhabited a huge mountainous area from the Rhine to the Adriatic. The Raetians became fully latinised and remained so until the barbarian invasions fragmented their unity. By the end of the period of barbarian incursions, Raetia had become three utterly separate, linguistic islands, an eastern or Friulian group in today's Italian province of Udine, a middle group in the Dolomites and a western group in the area of today's canton of Graubünden. The incursions of the Walser and other Germanic speakers in the thirteenth century further divided Romansch-speaking communities so that large differences began to develop within Raeto-Romansch. Romansch dialects came to resemble coloured bits in a larger mosaic rather than a broad patch of ethnic reality. The communal autonomy of old Graubünden enabled German and Romansch *Gemeinden* to live in peace. The commune had the right to adopt whichever language they wished. In this process the Ladino of the Engadin and the Val Müstair grew apart from the Surselva of the Vorder Rhine valley and both developed into written languages with different orthography and pronunciation. The other two idioms, Surmeirisch and Sutselvisch, became written languages only in modern times.

By the twentieth century, Alpine depopulation seriously threatened the Romansch communities. The language faced extinction and there was no allied culture beyond Switzerland to which the Romansch community could turn. In 1919 the Lia Rumantscha (Romansch League) was founded to unify under one roof the various small organisations which fought the good fight for linguistic survival. The rise of fascism and nazism gave Romansch an unexpected boost. As the Swiss became more conscious of the threat to their continued existence, they listened to each other's grievances more intently. In 1938 Romansch was elevated to the status of a national language, and the federal authorities granted a subsidy to the Lia Rumantscha, which by 1974 had risen to 450,000 francs a year. Yet by 1983, an expert analysis of Canton Graubünden described the language as on the way to 'complete extinction'.[24] The Romansch speakers contributed to their own disappearance by fierce battles among the three main written variants. For a long time Swiss banknotes had Italian on two of the four sides, because Romansch speakers refused to agree on a spelling of 'ten Swiss francs' and 'twenty Swiss francs'. The invention of a common Romansch, *Rumantsch grischun*, annoyed many traditionalists and as late as 1991 the Lia Rumantscha had to defend the common idiom against attempts by Surselva speakers to get it banned.[25] Iso Camartin, professor of Romansch literature in Zürich, defends the new standard as 'the most radical reconsideration of what a small language can still achieve in the modern world'.[26] The trouble begins precisely in that modern world of television, film, radio, Internet and fax, all of which take place in other languages. Fewer schools use Romansch and in any case German replaces it as students proceed to secondary level. The facts of life compel all Romansch-speakers to learn German, without which they cannot survive. They usually tend to pick up several other languages as well. I saw an example of what this means in practice in a shop in Disentis-Muster. A charming young lady serving in a small supermarket spoke six languages within a quarter of an hour: Romansch, *Schwyzerdütsch*, High German, Italian, French and English. She assured me that this was not unusual for anyone in a public job. Such virtuosity cannot by itself save Romansch, as the melancholy figures in Table 4.2 suggest.

   The struggle to save Romansch has many of the features of the great linguistic efforts of the nineteenth century to revive the Slavic languages. The Lia Rumantscha has concentrated on devising decent grammars, preparing dictionaries such as the *Dicziunari rumantsch grischun* and encouraging poetry and prose. In precisely this way Slovak, Slovenian, Ruthenian and Czech were lifted from peasant dialects or archaic literary idioms and made into the vehicles of nationalist movements. In Switzerland and in Canton Graubünden much of what Slovaks and Slovenes had to fight for has always existed: self-determination. No German chauvinists threaten the future of Romansch. There is no need to blow up power stations or daub walls with patriotic slogans. Perhaps

Table 4.2.

	Swiss population	Swiss Romansch	%
1941	4,265,703	46,456	1.1
1950	4,714,992	48,862	1.0
1960	5,429,061	49,823	0.9
1970	6,269,783	50,339	0.8
1980	6,365,960	50,927	0.8
1990	6,873,687	39,632	0.6
	Population of Graubünden	Romansch	%
1941	128,247	40,187	31.3
1950	137,100	40,109	29.3
1960	147,458	38,414	26.1
1970	162,086	37,878	23.4
1980	164,461	36,017	21.9
1990	173,890	29,679	17.1

Source: Statistisches Jahrbuch der Schweiz 1995 (Bern, 1995); *Zustand und Zunkunft der viersprachigen Schweiz* (Bern, 1989).

Romansch is more threatened because it is politically without external foes than it would be if Canton Graubünden had the power to refuse Romansch-speakers privileges. The real enemy of Romansch is the modern world. People go where the jobs are, and the jobs are no longer in Romansch-speaking areas. Dictionaries and grammars cannot prevent emigration from the Alpine fastness. For those who have never seen Romansch physically here are some proverbs taken from the two main variants:[27]

Engadin (Ladino):
Basdrinaglia – la pü bella parantaglia.
(The more distantly related the better.)
Chi serva ad sumün, nun agradesch'ad ingün.
(He who will serve everyone, serves no one well.)
Id ais meglder da magliar tuot quai chi's ha co da dir tuot quai chi's sa.
(Better to eat everything one has than to say everything one knows.)

Surselva:

Il pur en la lozza mantegn il signur ella carrotscha.

(The peasant in the mud feeds the lord in the coach.)

In crap che rocla fa buca mescal.

(A rolling stone gathers no moss.)

In the 1980s as the anxiety of Romansch representatives about the future of the language grew, the Department of the Interior set up a working party to revise the linguistic provisions of the Constitution. This turned out to be much harder than the Department had anticipated. The rights of language groups, as so often in Swiss politics, rested on the 'unwritten' constitution, that set of behaviour patterns that Swiss observe in public life almost without thinking about them. The working party found that there were in fact two antithetical principles in operation in Swiss daily life: the 'territorial principle' and the principle of 'freedom to use one's own language'. Under the former the cantonal authorities determine which language will be permissible and where; under the latter, every Swiss should have the right to speak his or her language before any public body. In ordinary life, the latter principle generally holds. Whenever a body of Swiss from different language areas meets, each member speaks in whatever language he or she chooses. In parliament the same freedom to use one's own language is self-evident, although Italian and Romansch speakers recognise the need to reach their audience and normally use either French or German.

The attempt to legislate for these usages failed. In 1993 and 1994 parliament rejected the suggested clarifications and reaffirmed the present, undefined situation.[28] Representatives of French, Italian and Romansch areas prefer the territorial principle because it protects their linguistic integrity against the German Swiss, who dominate industry, commerce, banking and tourism. In a subsequent case, the Federal Court ruled that a German-speaking motorist who ran into the car of the French-speaking public prosecutor in Fribourg had no right to demand that the investigation be carried out in German, although in principle Fribourg is bilingual and the public prosecutor ought to be competent in both languages. The court's decision in favour of the territorial principle meant that for the time being the language question had been settled.[29]

The most important linguistic minority is, of course, the French-speaking Swiss, the *Suisses romands*. They comprise just under 20% of the total population and are the dominant linguistic group in six cantons. Unlike the other Swiss groups we have looked at, the Swiss French do not, on the whole, speak dialect. In the three Protestant French-speaking cantons, Vaud, Geneva and Neuchâtel, the dialects are just about extinct. In their place there has grown up a regional French whose characteristic inflexions reveal to the philologist the underlying dialect which once existed. Swiss French is, then, French with a regional flavour, like the French spoken in Belgium. Like the Belgians, Swiss French say *septante, huitante* or *octante* and *nonante* instead of the more cumbersome 'proper' French *soixante-dix, quatre-vingts* and *quatre-vingt-dix* for 'seventy', 'eighty' and 'ninety'. The French *traîneau* (sledge) becomes the Swiss *luge* and so on. There is the sort of vocabulary and accent difference which exists between American and English use of the English language. In the more remote, Catholic areas, the French-speakers of Fribourg, Valais and the Jura still use dialect, but it is rapidly dying out. The Swiss French belong unequivocally to the cultural world of France, and, while they may have to swallow the accusation of provincialism, they share that with other French-speakers unfortunate enough to live elsewhere than Paris.

The relations between the French-speaking and the German-speaking Swiss have always been complicated, not least because while Swiss Germans are confined, but also defined, by the world of dialect, the Swiss French have the advantages and disadvantages of the absence of dialect. What is 'Swiss' about French Switzerland is less obviously defined by language than in the other cases we have considered. Certainly Protestantism played its part in creating a sober, industrious, thrifty, God-fearing type of citizen. A frugal and industrious Protestant population was very much part of French life until the revocation of the Edict of Nantes in 1685, when French Protestants were forced into exile or discreet withdrawal from public life. As Denis de Rougemont says in his brilliant little book on Switzerland, the common theme of his childhood was 'work': 'How often in the Neuchâtel of my childhood have I read engraved on a tombstone or printed on the funeral card of the deceased in place of the usual biblical citation: "le travail fut sa vie".'[30]

These bourgeois, Protestant virtues, well known in Scotland, in the north of England and in the American states, are the virtues of a puritanism which represented 'another France' as much as it reflected general Swiss values. Historically, then, French Switzerland is defined in opposition to France as much as in union with it. De Rougemont offers five ways in which the Swiss French differ fundamentally from their French neighbours:

1. Culture in our cantons has never been tied to the state and has never been an instrument of state power;

2. Culture among us had its existence in little compartments either natural or historic – the city of Geneva, the country of Vaud, Neuchâtel or La Chaux-de-Fonds . . . which have never been unified, united by a central power or made uniform as was the case of the French provinces under successive regimes;

3. We are old republics founded on the autonomy of the communes;

4. Protestantism is dominant in French Switzerland; it has determined the greater part of our customs, our profound moral concerns and our distrust of ceremonies . . .

5. We are not only neighbours of a Germanic world; we are in a state of osmosis with it, much more so than many of us realise or would like to admit.[31]

Unlike the Swiss Germans, the 'Swissness' of the *Suisses romands* is not primarily based on language. History, not an exclusive dialect, has made them Swiss, and religion, politics and economic forces have kept them that way. Hence the Swiss French are free of the coils of one identity problem (they are part of a great world linguistic community) but tied up in another (since they are culturally French, is there any Swiss culture?).

French Switzerland has difficulty in establishing an identity, not least because it is too simple to talk of the *Suisse romande*. The *welsche Schweiz*, which looms so large in the imaginations of German Swiss, is a myth. The most striking characteristic of French-speaking Switzerland is its diversity. To begin with, the six territories are geographically divided, look toward different compass points and follow rivers which, unlike those of the German areas, do not all empty into one great central valley. They are divided by religion, which, in turn, means that they are divided by culture, education and social custom. They are divided politically, including the most radical and most conservative communities in Switzerland. Each canton has its own school system, its own university and higher secondary systems and its own tax laws. In a sense the Romandie is the most intensely federalist of areas in Switzerland. An example of what this means can be taken from the changes in the newspaper world of the *Suisse romande*.

On the surface, Switzerland still boasts a flourishing and varied array of newspapers. A typical kiosk will have a huge selection of domestic papers in the three national languages as a matter of course. In 1970 there were more than 300 newspapers in Switzerland as a whole, of which more than 100 were dailies. In 1993, there were still 241 newspapers and 96 daily newspapers of which 16 appeared in French. The total circulation in 1993 of all Swiss dailies was about 2,700,000 copies a day, 400 copies per every 1,000 inhabitants. This exceptionally dense penetration by print media is reflected in the high share which advertising firms allot to newspapers and magazines, 42% of total advertising expenditure in Switzerland.[32]

Beneath the surface things have changed radically. In the 1960s one could draw a map of the circulation of each daily in the *Suisse romande*. Like the mosaic of Swiss political and social reality, newspapers had specific environments. The *Tribune de Lausanne* circulated in Catholic, rural areas in Fribourg and Valais but sold almost no copies in neighbouring Geneva, thirty minutes away by car. In those days, an enterprising daily like the *Journal de Genève* survived on 18,000 copies. As the editor, M. Claude Monnier, put it to me, it was less a newspaper than 'un miracle quotidien'. Four other papers appeared every day in Geneva, *La Suisse* with 61,000 copies in 1970, a tabloid, mass paper; the evening *Tribune de Genève* with 63,000; the Catholic *Le Courrier* with 16,000 and the Socialist *La Voix ouvrière* with 10,000. Gradually the competitive situation worsened, aggravated by a sharp fall in advertising revenues in the late 1980s. The *Tribune de Genève* effectively went under and had to be saved by the Lausanne concern, Edipresse, and the *Journal de Genève* merged with the Lausanne *Gazette de Lausanne*. Bit by bit Edipresse absorbed the small, staggering independents. The company now controls 43% of the circulation in the *Suisse romande*, and over 70% in Geneva and Lausanne. As Ernst Bollinger put it,

There is only one newspaper publisher in French Switzerland which is financially healthy enough to pursue an aggressive press marketing policy in the narrow French Swiss market and to seize the publishing initiative: its name is Edipresse.[33]

Something essentially Swiss has disappeared as a result of the changes which Herr Bollinger indicates. Not so long ago the world looked different in Geneva and Lausanne. The tiny newspapers literally reflected the tiny, particularist identities of citizens of La Chaux-de-Fonds and Le Locle, of Sion and Fribourg. The *Suisse romande* had no 'national' identity because it had no capital (other than Paris), no regional centre and, above all, no regional newspapers. Edipresse, whatever its motives, cannot help but undermine that mosaic of tiny communal identities.

It could safely be said even twenty years ago that there was no such thing as 'French Switzerland'. The different micro-identities constituted no overall pattern. The *Romandes* knew a great deal about the outside world but knew little and cared less about the village commune up the hill, let alone across the mountains. When newspapers fuse, the world view of the readers either fuses or no longer resists that blurring of identity that fusion implies. A subtle sea change affects the readers. They become without realising it less parochial and less narrow, less locked into their Catholic or Protestant 'milieu', less divided and sub-divided from neighbours, more homogeneous, more fluid, more anonymous. In that process, they become in a deep sense less Swiss, for 'Swissness' has been historically rooted in the particularism of self. To be Swiss was to be part of a specific community. Urbanisation, mass communications, computers and fax, mass transit and suburbs, have made Switzerland more and more like everywhere else. The erosion of the great organising ideologies of European history, the gradual dilution of liberalism and socialism, the loss of religious convictions and coherence, affect Switzerland as much as anywhere in Europe. Edipresse's position is both consequence and cause of such changes. Evil press lords are not destroying the Swiss 'way of life' but the destruction of that 'way of life' gives the press lords new opportunities to sell newspapers and make money. If the readers no longer cling to 'their' newspapers, it makes sense to merge, rationalise and consolidate them, and that has happened.

If French Switzerland is an abstraction, it becomes a reality of a kind only in contact with German Switzerland. French-speakers are a minority of the whole country but they are a large enough minority to have claims. These claims matter, not because there is such a thing as the *Suisse romande* but because over a million Swiss citizens use French as their native language. In the canton or

city the French-speaker is untroubled by the existence of other
language groups. It is at work, if he is employed by a large company
or in the federal civil service, that problems arise. In the federal
civil service there are directives governing the employment of
persons from the different linguistic groups. Italian-speakers are
over-represented as a whole, while French-speakers have roughly
their share of posts at all levels. They are lightly over-represented
in the Political Department, no doubt as a historical survival of the
idea of French as the diplomatic language and partly because
French candidates for the upper ranks of the civil service tend to
gravitate toward diplomacy and away from the customs and excise.
Swiss Germans dominate the boiler rooms of government.

In the economy as a whole the same pattern reveals itself. There
are large international businesses whose headquarters are in
French Switzerland, Nestlé, for one, but the great weight of
economic power, the chemical giants, the machine tool firms and
the big banks are all essentially Swiss German enterprises. Upper
levels of trade and commercial associations tend to be dominated by
Swiss Germans. Spokesmen for industrial concerns and lobbyists
tend to be Swiss Germans. The hotel trade is dominated by Swiss
Germans and even watchmaking is far more Swiss German than
the names of firms would lead the outsider to believe. Swiss French
banks tend to be smaller, to serve a more exclusively private
clientele, and to specialise in more traditional forms of asset
management than do Swiss German private banks.

It is hardly surprising that such economic and demographic
preponderance gives rise to resentments and that frequently
such resentments take the form of Swiss French v. German.
These resentments are further inflamed by the entirely different
approach to language itself in the two groups. The Swiss French do
not, as a general rule, speak German. In most of my interviews in
French Switzerland I found that my conversation partners usually
spoke French everywhere in Switzerland and expected to be understood. Some confessed to the fact with embarrassment; others
announced it with indifference or even a certain pride. 'They all
speak French in Zürich, or try to', one man airily informed me.
They do not all speak French there, but the man was right in
emphasising that they try. Swiss Germans take language learning
deeply seriously. The moment Swiss Germans find themselves
anywhere with anyone on whom they can practise and 'improve'

their English, French or Italian, they do so. A German-speaking executive of a large Swiss company told me a characteristic anecdote. He had to entertain a vice-president of the firm from Lausanne. Being a dutiful Swiss German he made great efforts all evening to speak French, which he does badly and hence dislikes. Much wine was consumed. As the two executives parted, he suddenly felt compelled to ask the sort of direct question which normally Swiss never put to one another. He turned to his vice-president and asked, 'Are you pleased that I spoke French all evening?' 'Why should I be?' shrugged the vice-president. 'You Swiss Germans just like to practise on us.'

Swiss French, even if they have the best will in the world, find the language problem difficult. They must, to begin with, learn two Germans, High German and *Schwyzerdütsch*. If they learn the latter, they can use it only within Switzerland, and in any case, since it is so rarely taught, learning Swiss German is not all that easy. They find themselves forced to learn High German and hence run into precisely the same linguistic barriers that any foreigner does in making contact with Swiss Germans. Both sides are conversing in a foreign language. Many Swiss French reckon that they are, after all, flattering the hearer if they talk French right from the start. At least that way one of them is using his mother-tongue. A leading Geneva politician told me of her tribulations in the language question. As a senior national figure she travels widely, speaks German and is perfectly prepared to use it at meetings. The moment she begins, she told me, her Swiss German hearers ask her to use French instead. On the other hand, in committee or executive meetings of her party, the opposite problem arises. Documents have been prepared all too frequently in German only, and she finds herself trying to intervene in a debate, while translating the text under discussion at the same time. Official published papers are always trilingual, but at the draft stage, much more often than mythology admits, the work has been done in German. Her experience is that Swiss Germans are, perhaps, overly conscious of the need to placate the linguistic minority in some respects and forgetful of it in others.

Another difficulty is the strong centralism of French culture or, more precisely, the power of its norms. Several centuries of French preoccupation with the normative elements in language teaching have had their effect on the Swiss French too. *Dialekt* is a good word in German Switzerland, while *patois* has negative overtones. The purity and perfection of written and spoken French is important in Swiss French schooling. Swiss French-speakers instinctively look for 'best' usage and, very characteristically, refer to High German as *le bon allemand*. Swiss French also share the instinctive prejudice against dialect as vulgar or low speech, which I tried to disperse earlier in this chapter. *Schwyzerdütsch* is by definition 'bad German'.

Finally there is Paris, which for the Swiss French is, in its way, as important as it is for French-speakers generally. Roberto Bernhard, one of the great intermediaries between the two Switzerlands, points out that for the Swiss French Paris is the 'living stream of cultural development'. The cultivated French-speaking Swiss is far more likely to read a French paper regularly than he or she is to see a Swiss German one, and there is a certain sort of snobbery which expresses itself in *only* reading French newspapers and journals. Membership of a great cultural, Paris-centred, world gives French-speaking Swiss an aura of superiority over their more provincial Swiss German cousins, who have nothing to offer in reply. On the other hand, for the Parisian French, the Swiss are hopelessly provincial, 'les petits Suisses'. Swiss French live in an ambivalent position toward both their fellow citizens of different language and their fellow French-speakers of different citizenship.

Multilingualism is a fact about the Swiss as a people; it is much harder to say if and to what extent it is an attribute of individual Swiss men and women. The government working party on language stated in 1989 that 'multilingualism in our country is a social fact, i.e. that four linguistic regions make the whole, but the inhabitants of these regions are predominantly monolingual'.[34] The census of 1990 does not quite confirm that. Whereas 65.4% of Swiss Germans declared themselves to be monolingual, only 43.4% of Swiss French, 27.0% of Swiss Italians and 20.3% of the Swiss Romansch did so. Evidently the smaller the linguistic community the more likely it is that its speakers will use other languages regularly. The monolingual percentage of Swiss Germans matches the almost identical percentage from the same census, 66.4%, who state that they never speak High German. Whereas fewer than 1% of French Swiss and 5.4% of Italian Swiss state that they only use dialect, two-thirds of Swiss Germans live in the world of dialect exclusively.[35] A study in 1991 found that among Swiss Germans 40% state that they have 'no contact' with the other linguistic areas of the country.[36] These figures testify to more than a linguistic phenomenon. The core Swiss German population, the two-thirds who are monolingual, are *monolingual in dialect*, that is, the unique, private world of *Schwyzerdütsch*. If there is a *Graben* between French and German Switzerland, it also winds its way among Swiss Germans as well, separating the rural, dialect-speaking, small-town, central and mountain Swiss Germans from their urban, lowland, cousins who use both types of German and speak other languages. Two German Switzerlands co-exist, a closed and an open one. Figures from the votes on Europe and other contentious issues support this hypothesis. Closed Switzerland is Christoph Blocher's constituency, and it is to its sense of authentic 'Swissness', in effect, its nationalism, that he appeals.

At the other end of the spectrum are citizens who live on linguistic borders. Take the city of Biel–Bienne on the southern edge of the Jura. An historic German town which never quite made the grade to cantonal independence, Biel filled up in the nineteenth century with French-speaking watchmakers and craftsmen from the Jura, so that today about 30% of its 52,000 inhabitants use French as their daily language. All street signs are in both languages and every city employee and elected representative must be bilingual. Of its 326 electoral districts there is not a single one which is exclusive to one or the other language group. The inhabitants are well known for replying without thinking in one language to a question in the other. Below the surface there is less genuine bilingualism than the town propaganda would have one believe. The school systems remain rigorously separate. The *Gymnasium*, which until 1955 was bilingual, has now split into French and German sections. The one bilingual newspaper folded after only two years of life.

The greatest difficulty in discussing conflict and cooperation between the language groups is to know whether what looks like language conflict may not be class or economic conflict. This is particularly true of the three cantons where French and German Swiss are supposed to live together in peace. The German minority in Canton Fribourg suffer a degree of discrimination. The French-speaking majority makes up about 60% of the canton's population of 213,000.[37] Both languages enjoy equality in law and the rights of both groups have been written into the constitution. In practice very few of the judges and court personnel use German, and often hear cases in French even if both parties speak German. There was no training college for educating German-speaking teachers until 1962, and there are other examples of petty thoughtlessness of which German-speaking residents complain. In the Valais, similar incidents are recounted and there is even a language protection league for the German-speaking minority called the *Rottenbund* (the League of the Rhone), which resolutely insists on using archaic German terms for all place names, 'Martinach' for 'Martigny' and so on. In both cases the groups concerned express in linguistic terms issues which are at least as much economic and social. Canton Fribourg and Canton Valais are, perhaps, the two most conservative cantons in the Confederation. Both are strongly Roman Catholic and, in the case of Fribourg, historically rather anti-democratic. Fribourg was the last and most reluctant canton to introduce direct democracy and one of the last of the large cantons to accept the 'magic formula' approach to sharing power on the cantonal executive among the parties. In both cantons the German areas are more backward, more conservative and more clerical than the French-speaking areas, and hence some of the linguistic resentment is also regional conflict. In Valais the resentment is deepened by the historical reversal of roles. Until 1798 the *Oberwalliser* were top dogs and forced German down the throats of their French-speaking subjects. Children were beaten in the schools of Sierre if they were caught whispering in French. Now that Oberwallis has become a distressed area living on subsidies for inadequate peasant plots, the French majority has the upper hand. General resentment at this state of affairs finds its release in linguistic chauvinism of an intemperate kind.

The Jura conflicts offered an interesting example of inflamed linguistic sentiments. As I suggested in the previous chapter, the deepest fissures were those which divided French-speaking Jurassiens, but Bern and the dominant German-speaking majority in the canton stood for the other enemy, an enemy as much cultural as political. The *Jura libre*, a weekly separatist paper which appeared in Delémont, defended pure French against 'outrages to our language'. Here is an excerpt from the column 'Parlons français':

Many subsidiaries of large firms established in French Switzerland receive publicity and advertising texts from head office which are completely

German in thought . . . The firm Voegele posted a series of price tags in its Delémont shop recently, which read 'X. francs chaque pièce.' In French one should say: 'X. francs *la* pièce.' The other day in the shop front of the same store one saw with amazement the following inscription: 'Toujours à la hauteur du trend de la mode juvenile.' What is that jargon? (*Jura libre*, 23 August 1972)

No affront was too trivial nor grammatical lapse too slight for attention. Behind every mistake lurked the 'imperialist' and 'heavily teutonic' spirit of the oppressor.

Jurassien separatists were not simply unreasonable when they fought the good fight against linguistic outrages. Hard economic facts shimmered through the bad French of the Swiss Germans who owned the chain store. Now that a stable Canton Jura has emerged from the struggle, the Jurassiens have the political power to make an impact on firms trading within the canton and to develop educational institutions and other public fora to train a French-speaking new elite. Through a combination of historical circumstance, geographical isolation, religious tradition, economic discrimination and linguistic obsessiveness, they have created a new, small state. In this process the defenders of French will see themselves as vindicated, and, once again, as so often in the last two hundred years, economic and political realities will have been profoundly influenced by the intangible forces of language and culture.

The process is clear in the Jura. It is less so in the case of Switzerland as a whole. Minds conditioned by two hundred years of nationalist propaganda find it hard to think of a nation without a national language. Can there be a Switzerland which is more than the sum of its particular parts? No one who has visited the place could doubt that there is something more, but what is it? In the previous chapters on history and politics I tried to underline common historical experiences and political institutions which all Swiss share. In the next chapter, I shall offer evidence from the economy which points to the same conclusion. It may be that the combination of history, politics and economic development provides a sufficient explanation and that Switzerland survives as a state in spite of linguistic variety. The only common linguistic experience of all Swiss would then be the absence of a common language. A case, paradoxical at first sight, can be made for such a view. It is certainly true that the cumbersome forms of multilingual courtesy have become unifying elements, which reinforce the cellular structure of politics. People learn to be good pluralists in the 'language laboratories' of government institutions and large companies.

It could also be true that the question is wrong or that some of the assumptions underlying it need to be looked at. History offers lots of examples of 'ideas of the age' so widely accepted that only cranks and outsiders dared to question them. Take the case of social darwinism in the nineteenth century or social class in the twentieth. The 'unconscious mind' is a good example in our own day. Most of us now accept without further thought that human personality has two levels: a 'conscious' and an 'unconscious' layer. None of us has ever seen the unconscious and there is no proof that it exists. Yet we rear our children, improve our prisons, interpret our actions and words as if it did. The idea of the unconscious pervades our thinking so totally that we have lost the distance necessary to see it all. I believe that the link between a language and a nation is just such an idea. The French are those who speak French, the Danes Danish. And the Swiss?

The connection between a language and the people who speak it is an obvious one and appeared early in European history. In the late thirteenth century, the Florentine scholar Brunetto Latini evidently thought that he had better explain why he had chosen to write a major work in French: 'And should any ask why, because we are Italian, this book is written in Romance according to the idiom of the French, I would answer that it is for two reasons: one, that we are in France, the other because its speech is more pleasing and more common to all peoples than Italian.'[38] Goethe reflected the same attitude to language five centuries later, when he observed 'the German went to school under the French to learn how to live well and under the Romans to learn how to speak well'.[39] Both passages are really saying that Italians should speak Italian and Germans German. Between Goethe's time and our own, the idea of 'a people' has undergone a subtle but crucial change. The man most responsible for the change was Goethe's great contemporary Johann Gottfried Herder, who published a study in 1772 called *Abhandlung über den Ursprung der Sprache* ('Treatise Concerning the Origin of Language'). The work became the bible of nineteenth-century nationalists. Herder worked out the organic growth of language from family to tribe to what he called 'the Third Natural

Law . . . the formation of national languages'; their differences he attributed to 'mutual familial and national hatred.'[40] Herder saw the bearer of culture as the *Volk*, united by their common language. Herder's *Volk* was not Hitler's but a category rooted in the organic growth of the human being from beast to sentient creature. The *Volk* was a kind of family of families and its language reflected its history, the older and more 'original' the purer. *Volk* and *Sprache* in Herder's mind reinforce each other.

Herder's ideas spread rapidly. Educated people in Slavic countries literally rushed into the countryside to find the *Volk* with its *Sprache*, and found what they were looking for. As a Polish land-lord grumpily observed in 1848, the Ruthenian people had only been 'discovered last year'. In due course Herder's cultural categories filled up with nastier fluid; biological and racial definitions seeped into the idea of *Volk*; but even in Hitler's Reich, where racial definitions were most powerful, the link which Herder first postu-lated between *Volk* and *Sprache* remained largely unquestioned. It still exists in the automatic assumption that the French are those who speak French.

Switzerland raises questions about both terms of Herder's equation. What is a language? The great complexity of Swiss dialect usage, the variety of its forms, the geographical spread of its influence, in short, the whole tangle of issues abbreviated by the word *Schwyzerdütsch*, make a nonsense of Herder's romantic verities. The same applies to *Volk*. This great shimmering abstraction dissolves when you approach it. It can be applied to no specific cases and supported by no concrete evidence. In so far as individuals feel themselves part of 'a people', they assert a political or a historical or regional reality as much as a linguistic one. Language is certainly a part of that reality but not all of it. In Herder's terms the Swiss may be an impossibility (an *Unding*), a *Volk* without a *Sprache*, but this is only because Herder's terms are too narrow. The Swiss are a *Volk*, because geography, history, political structures and linguistic diversity have made them one, but also because all Swiss, whether French, German or Italian in language, participate in one national economy, whose features reinforce the other characteristics. It is to that economy that I turn now.

CHAPTER 5

Wealth

The first, and possibly the most important, economic fact about Switzerland is that it is a very rich country. No visitor to any Swiss town can fail to notice the glitter of wealth from behind shop windows. Everything looks solid, well-made and expensive. In late 1973, the *National-Zeitung* published figures which gave statistical support to the impression of the eye. In terms of gross national product per head of population, Switzerland was then the richest country in the world (Switzerland $6,890, Sweden $6,510, Federal Republic of Germany $6,260, USA $6,090). Twenty years later in its 1993 report the World Bank arrived at the same result. Swiss income in dollars per head stood at $36,410, ahead of Luxemburg at $35,580 and Japan in third place at $31,450.[1] Exchange rate fluctuations distort these figures, but Switzerland is one of the three or four richest countries in the world, no matter how 'rich' is defined.

The Swiss have been rich for a long time. Pierre Bairoch shows that from 1880 to 1950 only the United Kingdom had a higher gross national product per head of population than Switzerland. On average in this period Switzerland was one-fifth richer than Belgium, France and the Low Countries and one-quarter richer than the average for Europe as a whole.[2] Habits associated with the acquisition and maintenance of wealth go back well before 1880 but reliable statistics do not. Certainly chronicles record the presence of rich men, but individual wealth surrounded by poverty marks much of the Third World today. How rich were the Swiss in the Middle Ages?

Hektor Ammann did a good deal of research on just that question in his study of the cloth-making canton of Schaffhausen in the later Middle Ages. His figures for the period from the middle of the fifteenth to the first quarter of the sixteenth century show that the largest fortunes recorded in what was certainly a prosperous textile centre at the time fell between 13,000 and 19,000 gulden. His league table of wealth and class in Upper Germany (to which Switzerland still belonged) shows that fortunes of great size were rare, possibly occurring only in the Basel trading community. In Augsburg and Nuremberg, on the other hand, the Fuggers, the Welsers, the Höchstetters, the Tuchers and the Imhofs, were much richer. Jacob Fugger, who died in 1525, probably left a fortune worth several millions, depending on how you assess the marketable value of the castles, settlements, the mines in the Tyrol and Hungary as well as the trading capital, loans to princes and so on. Fortunes of 200,000 gulden were not unusual in late medieval Augsburg and Nuremberg. By these standards, the Swiss belonged to the second division in wealth. No Swiss family or trading company approached the magnificence of their German neighbours. On the other hand, wealth seems to have been rather widely distributed. The structure of capital ownership, measured by taxes paid, was not all that far from modern standards of tolerable inequality. Of Schaffhausen's 4,000 inhabitants, some 800 had assets which the city taxed. The top fifteen taxpayers owned a third of the wealth, and the next sixty-four taxpayers owned another third, while the remaining 721 owned the rest.[3] Most late medieval Swiss cities studied by Ammann show the same general features, especially the smaller ones. Schaffhausen's 4,000 inhabitants must have been comfort-able, if almost every fifth individual (roughly every head of family) earned enough to pay tax.[4] The guild constitution adopted in 1411 fits this social and economic structure neatly. The small wealthy establishment corresponded to the self-perpetuating, mercantile, political leadership described in Chapter 2.

The most important thing about Swiss fortunes was not size but survival. By the time a century of religious war had swept over them, the great cities of Upper Germany were ruined. The Swiss fought each other but not to the point of mutual destruction. Even Zwingli accepted the rights of his papist opponents to share in the government of the Confederation, in effect, their right to exist. Later on Swiss neutrality in the Thirty Years War paid fat dividends and by the eighteenth century accumulations of capital were impressive. The abbot of St Gallen, Cölestin II, spent half a million gulden in adorning his Lilliputian absolutist state but in 1767 still managed to leave his successor, abbot Beda Angehrn, another quarter of a million, mostly in cash.[5] An equally important invisible asset was the continuous tradition of mercantile enterprise. When the European economy began its great expansion after 1730, the Swiss city-republics took advantage of the upswing. The tiny city-republic of St Gallen (total population under 8,000) had sixty substantial mercantile houses during the eighteenth century engaged in the manufacture and sale of cotton, muslin and embroidery. About 100,000 spinners, weavers, calico printers and embroiderers worked for the city companies, mostly in the famous *Webkeller* (the weaving cellar) in each of the peasant houses dotted up and down the mountains of Appenzell and among the valleys of the Rhine, the Thur and the Linth. East Switzerland became one of the richest and most thickly settled parts of Europe. The commercial activities of St Gallen had deep historical precedents. As early as the fifteenth century, the *Mal*, the first quality seal in European economic history, stamped St Gallen linen cloth as merchandise of prime quality. By the eighteenth century, the same political structure and the same economic organisation were directed to the same end: quality production for export markets.[6]

The structure of textile manufacturing in eastern Switzerland underlines a second very important feature of the Swiss economy: a high degree of specialisation. The little town of St Gallen with its 8,000 inhabitants resembled the central nucleus of a complex nervous system. Almost alone of the great European trading cities of the eighteenth century, St Gallen had no agricultural hinterland. The baroque 'Vatican City', the abbey, in its midst and the prince–abbot's territories beyond its walls forced the city to specialise ever more exclusively in commerce. The pastor of the French church in St Gallen wrote in 1813:

St Gallen is an entirely commercial city. That unity of occupations facilitates our examination. From commerce is born avarice, not the sordid and bizarre avarice which forms skin-flints but the fatal habit of weighing sentiments on the scales of gold . . . Business absorbs them and they devote themselves exclusively to those studies most indispensable for their state . . . The revolutions which occur in the republic of letters do not disturb their sleep.[7]

Culture, habits, political institutions and religious injunctions combined to produce an utterly devoted merchant capitalist, a man, as one observer put it, born to be a 'commercial traveller'. This high degree of specialisation had its chroniclers in the uncomfortable few who did care about the republic of letters, and their complaint was always the same from Zwingli's days to those of Max Frisch. Switzerland is 'narrow', 'philistine', 'materialist', in other words, unusually highly specialised for economic survival.

The sheer variety of micro-societies in Switzerland accelerated this specialisation. As Rudolf Braun shows in his study of the eighteenth century in Switzerland, poor, peasant districts nestled close to rich towns or tightly controlled prosperous valleys. As 'proto-industrialisation' spread, the merchants found the weakly organised, poorer communities the perfect environment for recruitment of labour. Meanwhile the transformation of agri-culture in central Switzerland attracted the investment of urban patricians, who began to buy up high pasturage and encourage commercial specialisation.[8] Swiss economic development fitted into existing political units.

In Chapter 12 of Book 1 of *Das Kapital* Marx discusses the origins of what he calls *Manufaktur*, the classical pre-industrial form of manufacturing. He distinguishes two main types, 'heterogeneous' and 'organic', and chooses the Swiss watchmaking industry as his example of the perfect specimen of *heterogene Manufaktur* (he could just as well have used St Gallen textiles). The main feature of heterogeneous manufacturing is that the capitalist assembles bits and pieces made simultaneously in no determined order and in different workshops, while organic manufacture involves a con-tinuous flow of products in which each worker's finished product is the raw material of the next. 'Out of a temporal side-by-side grows a spatial side-by-side',[9] and hence the assembling of the continuous process under one roof, i.e. the factory. Neither the Swiss watch-maker nor the textile worker escaped factory labour entirely but for the most part the work was done by the 'putting out' system, in German called the *Verlagssystem* and in watchmaking *établissage* (from the watchmaker's table, *un établi*). The capitalist or *établisseur* had little capital himself and needed little, because the decentral-isation of production was so great that he needed only a tiny staff to assemble the finished product. (Marx lists over a hundred specialised stages of production: engravers, engine-turners, case makers, gilders, escapement makers, watch-hand makers, case finishers, pendant makers, mainspring makers, case spring makers, polishers, etc.)[10] The capitalist paid the hundreds of different tiny

Plate 13 New engineered road, Tremola, 1827

Plate 14 The plain of Magadino, 1835

firms and individual craftsmen twice a year at the so-called *termes*.[11] The decentralisation of watchmaking continued into the twentieth century and R. A. G. Miller estimates that about half of all persons employed in watchmaking at the turn of the century were still 'travailleurs à domicile'.[12] Alongside the outworker stood the tiny firm, highly specialised but employing fewer than five people, and both categories survived into the twentieth century. In the industrial census of 1965 six out of every ten firms in the watchmaking industry had fewer than ten workers.

The peculiar features of Swiss economic development constitute a vital element in understanding why Switzerland survived with so many of its antique institutions and structures intact. Swiss railway development provides a perfect example of the interplay of economic, geographical and political factors. As Pierre Bairoch shows, although Switzerland industrialised early and rapidly, its railway network was 'retarded'. Bairoch offers four interlocking explanations: the difficulty of the mountainous terrain, the small size of Swiss cities, the absence of coal and the lack of strong, central government.[13] In the period 1880 to 1950 Switzerland had a lower rate of urbanisation than its neighbours, just under half that of Britain and even below France, but a much higher proportion of foreign labour. As early as 1880 Switzerland had nearly six times more foreign workers as a percentage of its resident population than any other European state.[14] Its economy depended on exports. Only Belgium had a consistently higher rate of exports per inhabitant than Switzerland, and the exports were concentrated.[15] According to David Landes, on the eve of the first world war, Switzerland produced more than half the world's production of watches and for a brief period after the second world war attained a near monopoly.[16] With 1% of Europe's population in 1913, Switzerland exported 3% of all European exports, but had 10–20% of fixed capital abroad, and in terms of industrial production per head of population belonged among the most industrialised of European states.[17]

The long list of 'peculiarities' in Swiss economic history explains a great deal about the survival of Switzerland in its present form. The weak growth of towns, the high degree of specialisation, the slow spread of railways, the unique dependence on foreign labour, the absence of coal, the rapid and disproportionate accumulation of capital and the high rate of fixed investment abroad, the geographical concentration of economic activities in micro-units, a feature which also marked the pre- and proto-industrial phases of Swiss economic growth, and the very high level of industrialisation created an economy which nestled neatly in the network of jurisdictions and authorities, communes, cities and cantons which criss-cross Swiss political reality. Yet at the same time Switzerland maintained a flourishing, highly specialised agriculture based on milk products, exporting cheese and chocolate, but importing cereal. In 1950 21.5% of the Swiss population worked in agriculture compared to 6.5% in the UK, 12.3% in Belgium, and 17.8% in the Netherlands. Then, there is the special role of tourism which in 1913 reached 21.9 million nights of tourist lodgings, a level not reached again until the 1950s, and equal to 5–6% of gross national product and about a quarter of all exports. Tourism combined with milk and cheese production to sustain substantial populations in the remoter rural cantons.[18] The Alps have been an important 'invisible export' in the last century and a half.

The consequences of these peculiarities reach into every aspect of Swiss history. Watchmaking and textiles, the two great industries of the nineteenth century, often took place in country environments. Decentralisation meant that proletarian conditions rarely occurred. Adhémar Schwitzguébel, himself a watchmaker and leader of the anarchist Fédération jurassienne, had to apologise at a party congress in 1874 for the failure of class consciousness to develop among his 'half-bourgeois workers, living a bourgeois existence'.[19] Prince Kropotkin in his *Memoirs* wrote that the watchmakers were 'federalist in principle . . . each separate region, and even each local section, had to be left free to develop on its own lines'.[20] The economic development of the two most important Swiss export industries did not, as in Britain and Germany, destroy the cellular structure of the old political framework but reinforced, indeed reinvigorated, it. The communal political unit, the kinship network and the economic unit fused to form a powerful whole. Kropotkin described the Jura in May 1871:

In a little valley in the Jura hills there is a succession of small towns and villages of which the French-speaking population was at that time entirely employed in the various branches of watchmaking; whole families used to work in small workshops. In one of them I found another leader, Adhémar Schwitzguébel with whom, also, I afterward became very closely connected. He sat among a dozen young men who were engraving lids of gold and silver watches. I was asked to take a seat on a bench, or a table, and soon we were all engaged in a lively conversation upon socialism, government or no government, and the coming congresses.[21]

Kropotkin was enchanted by the sturdy independence, literacy and devotion of his anarchist watchmakers, men who walked five or six kilometres in blinding snow to attend socialist and anarchist meetings. Like Francesco Chiesa's experience with the Alpine shepherd (cited at the beginning of the book), Kropotkin found the peasant workman remarkably literate, informed and articulate.

General conditions were very nearly ideal for the development of light industry in Switzerland during the nineteenth century. The Swiss emerged from the Napoleonic Wars with a modernised system of government, with capital surpluses so abundant that the private bankers in Basel and Geneva had begun to invest heavily abroad as early as the end of the eighteenth century and with a labour force already well adapted to light manufacturing. Thousands of rushing streams provided cheap power to turn spindles, and Zürich rapidly became the capital of a flourishing cotton textile industry. The number of spindles rose from about 400,000 in 1830 to about a million in 1851.[22] As Zürich specialised in cotton, St Gallen took up embroidery and by 1913 embroidered goods at Sfr 215 million stood at the top of the list of Swiss exports, followed by watchmaking at Sfr 183 million, with other textiles and machine tools well behind.[23] Cotton and embroidery, like watchmaking, partly because mills grew up where nature had put the running water, left the basic cellular structure of Swiss communal life intact. When mechanisation came, it came less brutally and with less concentration of people than in Britain or Germany. In fact, embroidery produced the paradox that mechanisation actively fostered decentralisation. Instead of taking the worker to the factory where the machines stood in great rows, the machines were installed in the peasant worker's cottage. Here the traditions of the *Webkeller* of the eighteenth century renewed themselves in the nineteenth and twentieth. At the time that embroidery topped the list of Swiss exports, only two firms used more than one hundred machines. Embroidery, like watchmaking, depended on decentralisation and the putting out of work.

The Swiss variant of nineteenth-century economic development, which I think of as 'micro-capitalism', had enormous advantages for

Map 3 The major centres of industry in 1880

Linen, cotton, wool

Silk

Watch-making

S Rock salt

Blast furnace, foundry

the capitalist. The smaller the units, the less the percentage of production which could be subject to factory legislation. By putting the machinery into the peasant's cellar, the employer evaded the terms of the 1877 factory law and reduced wages at the same time. Child labour was very widespread in cotton and embroidery, less so in watches, and in many ways children in the Victorian cotton mill were better off than in their parents' homes in St Gallen. Parents proved to be more thorough, more ruthless and more insistent exploiters than a millowner could ever have been. Here is a passage from the diary of a twelve-year-old: 'After supper, I have to ravel until ten o'clock; sometimes, if the work is pressing, I have to ravel in the cellar until eleven. Afterward I say good night to my parents and go to bed. So it goes every day.'[24] The children rose again at five or six to get in a few hours of work before school. The myth of the happy peasant with roots in the land, actively propagated by liberal publicists, lost its meaning as the nineteenth century went on. The *horloger paysan* turned into an anxious, harassed exploited out-worker.

Apart from the brief flurry of anarchism, working-class organisations were slow to develop and one can easily see why. In Schwitzguébel's terms, the worker remained necessarily a 'half-bourgeois'. When the Fédération des ouvriers sur métaux et horlogers was founded in 1915, it tended to concentrate on bread-and-butter issues and shun the more violent forms of class conflict. Anarchism had fizzled out and now piecemeal achievements were to do the job instead. The great excitement of the General Strike of 1918 masked the essential conservatism of the Swiss working class, as I suggested in Chapter 2. Two other elements in the Swiss situation worked against labour militancy. First was democracy itself. The radical constitution of 1848 put Switzerland in the enviable position of being the most democratic country in Europe. The improvements in the revised constitution of 1874 and the introduction of referenda and popular initiatives during the 1890s kept a step ahead of potential popular unrest. Only when the advance toward greater representation lagged during the first world war did resentments begin to accumulate. The concession of proportional representation in 1919 drained that pool by making the Socialist Party one of the four main groups in parliament. The militants were tamed by the government's timely surrender on social welfare issues and soon accepted the *status quo* as more or less unalterable. The anarchists who had seen that danger never found the answer. To abstain from the many elections on all three levels of Swiss politics was futile; to participate was to accept the *status quo*. Another element was the pervasiveness of libertarian ideas at all levels of Swiss life. Decentralisation and putting out fostered the myth that, as a Genevese watchmaker put it in 1798, 'watchmakers work as free men. They are all more or less artists . . . '[25] The sturdy Appenzeller peasant could believe the same thing, even if he had to work a sixteen-hour day. After all, he owned his house, his land, perhaps even a share of his machinery. He was in the literal sense a 'half-bourgeois', both peasant proprietor and capitalist worker at the same time. *Travail à domicile* and small-scale production remained unusually prominent in Switzerland until well into the twentieth century. 1910 was the first year that the number of workers employed in factories exceeded outworkers and those employed in units too small to fall under the factory laws.[26] This 'arrested development' caught Marx's eye too. The failure of Swiss industry to get beyond what he saw as the random (*zusammenhanglos*) or heterogeneous stage of *Manufaktur* to the mature processes of factory production reflected the nature of the products. The main Swiss products had two characteristics which were 'obstacles' to factory methods: 'the smallness and delicacy of the work and its luxury character, that is, its variety'.[27] Mass production, Marx believed, demanded uniformity of product, and, in fact, the development of the *Roskopf* or simple pinlever watch, selling at Sfr 20, led to factory production of movements, the *ébauches*, the most mechanised, capital-intensive stage in watch manufacturing.

Marx was certainly right to put his finger on the luxury trade as the main source of Swiss wealth, but there was an irony there, which he failed to notice. The Swiss made luxury articles because their natural environment was poor and their transport costs high. Of the 41,287 square kilometres of modern Switzerland, 25.5% is classified 'unproductive', mainly the area of the high Alps, another 30.3% is 'forested', while only 38.3% is available for agriculture in all its forms. A tiny 5.8% of the land area is classified as surface areas of habitation and infrastructure.[28] We have seen that Switzerland has been dependent on cereal imports for some time. In 1990 only 29% of all agricultural land was committed to arable farming, whereas more than double that amount was classified as natural

Plate 15 Logs floating past Locarno, 1840s

meadows and pasture.[29] The agricultural base has always been too small to support the population and hence Switzerland began to specialise early in high-value agricultural products for export. Rudolf Braun cites evidence from 1619, when the peasants of the Emmental were startled to encounter an Alpine shepherd from Fribourg: 'the same maketh no butter but only fat cheese'. The shepherd boasted that he could buy any butter he needed to pay the rents for pasturage and still get 'syn Nuz' (his profit) in a summer.[30] Braun argues that by this time Alpine specialisation was not only possible but profitable and led to greater and greater commercialisation of milk products.

Transport costs were high. In the middle of the nineteenth century, J. M. Hungerbühler, one of the first economic historians of modern Switzerland, calculated that textile products from the Toggenburg or Wattwil arrived at the nearest seaports bearing ten times the freight charges of their competitors, and that Swiss goods remained competitive only because Swiss wages were 15% lower than those in neighbouring Germany and hours 15% longer.[31] Hard work by itself could not overcome the natural disadvantages of geography. A steady supply of sturdy, relatively well educated but poor mountain boys helped to keep costs down, but the real key to success on world markets (and effectively world markets were the main markets for Swiss products) was quality. The more the value added by Swiss skill the greater the chances of profit. High costs of imported raw materials and high transport costs pushed Swiss merchants and manufacturers into luxury products, where the margin created by specialised skill between costs and prices was bound to be greatest. The watch and the small piece of embroidery used little raw material, were light and easy to transport and very expensive to buy.

By the middle of the nineteenth century, Swiss manufacturers had developed recognisably modern attitudes to their enterprises. They spent money and time, developing and improving the quality of the products, and even more time on exploration of the market. In Keller's largely autobiographical *Grüne Heinrich* of 1854–5, there is a scene in which young Heinrich's mother visits a cotton manufacturer about a possible job for her boy. The date must be the middle of the 1830s. The manufacturer is delighted to hear that the boy wants to be a painter, which he regards as a most agreeable activity:

But this urge must be directed into solid and sensible channels. Now you, my dearest lady and friend, will be aware of the character of my not insubstantial enterprise. I make cotton prints and, in so far as I achieve a tolerable income, I do so by seeking always to bring the latest *Dessins* as attentively and quickly as possible and to outbid the ruling taste by offering something entirely new and original. To this end I employ some designers, whose only task it is to find new *Dessins* and sitting in this comfortable chamber can sketch flowers, stars, tendrils, dots and lines to their hearts' content . . . He [young Heinrich] shall abstract from the riches of nature the most wonderful and delicate forms and drive my competitors wild.[32]

Part of the training would be apprenticeship in Paris to learn the language, the techniques and, above all, to study the market.

As cotton textiles conquered Zürich, another industry began very modestly in Basel: the dyestuffs manufacturing industry. Between 1857 when J. R. Geigy and W. Heusler set up their small plant to extract dyestuffs from wood products and 1900, only the Swiss firms of Bindschedler & Busch (later reincorporated as the Society for the Chemical Industry in Basel or CIBA), Kern & Sandoz,

F. Hoffmann–La Roche and J. R. Geigy SA were able to keep up with what David Landes has called the 'leap to hegemony, almost to monopoly' of the German dyestuff industry, a leap without parallel in the economic history of the nineteenth century and 'Imperial Germany's greatest industrial achievement'.[33] By 1900 the Swiss alone were left with a vigorous, competitive dyestuff and organic chemical industry in the face of the overwhelming power of the great German giants later to be consolidated in the I. G. Farben cartel. The achievement is the more remarkable because, as always in Swiss economic history, none of the raw materials were native to the country and very large amounts of raw and semi-finished products had to be imported to sustain Swiss chemical production. Even more remarkable, and from our point of view more interesting, is the compartmentalisation of the industry. Like watches in the Jura, embroidery in St Gallen, and cotton textiles in Zürich, the new chemical industry was, and still is, exclusive to Basel. How did a wealthy but quiet mercantile community of about 27,000 in 1847 become the centre of one of the greatest industries of the twentieth century?

No one answer will do but some elements in the history of Basel stand out as plausible parts of a tolerable one.[34] There was a great deal of capital in Basel. When it joined the Confederation in 1501, it was already the richest city-state in the region. In 1862, there were twenty substantial private banks investing at home and abroad. The local silk ribbon industry, the so-called *Posamenterie*, had a demand for colouring and dyestuffs, which assured the infant organic chemical companies a safe market. It is worth noting too that the ribbon-makers, like the watch and embroidery workers, worked at home, outside the city's jurisdiction and hence in earlier times outside the restrictions of the guilds. The *Bändelherren* or 'ribbon lords', the equivalent of the *établisseurs* in the Jura, lived in town where, as in St Gallen, they supplied the mercantile venture capital for the industry. The introduction of the bar loom in the seventeenth century had greatly increased productivity. By the middle of the nineteenth century there were around 4,000 bar looms in peasant cottages in the countryside around the city. Silk-dyeing for the ribbons had become a separate branch of the industry and here a factory system had begun to emerge. In these respects, Basel was not all that unusual among the Swiss cities we have looked at; where Basel differed was *Kultur*. Basel had always had aspirations toward higher things. During the fifteenth and sixteenth centuries, Basel had been home to Erasmus and to Paracelsus and to Johannes Froben, one of the greatest printers (or what we should today call publishers) of the age. Erasmus's New Testament in the original Greek text printed at Froben's works in 1516 is, perhaps, the most important single work ever published in Switzerland. The first revised edition of Galen, the first edition of Vesalius, and the first edition of the *Book of Herbs* by Fuchs all appeared in the fine editions of the Basel printers. Woodcuts prepared by Dürer, drawings by Hans Holbein the Younger and frontispieces of the greatest opulence adorned the books printed by Froben, Cratander, Bebel, Herwagen and Isengrin. There was also the only Swiss university, founded in 1460. Basel could claim, along with Geneva, to be a metropolis.

Printing is by its nature a radical trade. It flourishes where censorship is lax and public tolerance well developed. Renaissance Basel welcomed the alien, the eccentric and the heretical with more insouciance than most other European cities. Basel naturally became the home of a native Swiss tradition of free thought and in the eighteenth century the Enlightenment took deeper root in Basel than in any other Swiss canton save Geneva. It is no coincidence that the radical moving spirit of the Helvetic Republic, Peter Ochs, and many of his passionate supporters were Baselers. During the late seventeenth and eighteenth centuries Basel and its university claimed the Bernoulli family, who, like so many of the city's craftsmen, preferred the tolerant patrician atmosphere of the city to the absolutist repression around it. The Bernoullis, rather like the Bach family in music, produced four generations of brilliant mathematicians, scientists and scholars, almost all of whom taught at the university of Basel. Johann Bernoulli (1667–1748) pioneered a great deal of modern pure and applied mathematics, was the first to use the 'integral calculus' as a concept and wrote the first textbook on differential calculus.

This rich cultural and scientific background helps to explain the spectacular expansion of chemistry. As early as 1845, Christian Friedrich Schönbein had produced the first man-made material. A professor at the University of Basel, Schönbein investigated the effect of sulphuric and nitric acids on various substances. He saw that cotton underwent a chemical transformation while retaining its fibre structure. The cellulose of the fibre became cellulose nitrate. Schönbein's new cotton (he called it *Schiessbaumwolle* or 'guncotton' because it was so inflammable) later became the basis of the first plastics.

In spite of this lively tradition Basel seemed very narrow to the young patrician Jacob Burckhardt when he returned to his native city in 1843. After Berlin, Paris and, above all, the literary intoxication of the 'Cockchafers – A Society not for Philistines', which he had joined at Bonn University, he was struck by what I have called the cellular qualities of Swiss life: 'How much a city like this silts up without stimulating life-giving elements from outside. There are learned people here but they have turned to stone against everything foreign. It is now good nowadays if such a tiny corner is entirely left to its own individuality.'[35] Yet the very individuality which Burckhardt deplored turned out to be the precondition for the most general of developments, the growth of an international dyestuffs industry. That 'tiny corner' had specialised in economic survival for centuries and now, as Landes says, by 'concentrating on special tints, requiring the highest production skills, and offering customers the latest technical advice',[36] Basel on its own competed with that greater Germany to which young Burckhardt was so partial. In the process, it may be argued, the tiny corner ceased to be what it was and became the capital of a vast empire of plastics, drugs, hormones, dyestuffs and glues which have literally transformed the physical circumstances of all mankind. Today the three biggest Basel chemical companies, Ciba-Geigy, Hoffmann–La Roche and Sandoz, have an aggregate turnover which is larger than the Swiss federal budget. In 1994 total federal expenditures amounted to Sfr 42 billion whereas the Basel giants turned over more than Sfr 54 billion. Even more remarkable is their relationship to the domestic Swiss markets, where they do less than 2% of their business. Dr Albert Bodmer, former deputy chairman of Ciba, told me in 1991 that in his two decades on the main board of the company he could recall no occasion when the domestic market had come up for discussion. In what sense are they still Swiss companies? In the first place, the ownership remains very largely Swiss, a practice reinforced by the existence of several types of shares with differential rights (and prices). They are Swiss in tone. At Ciba headquarters the emphasis is on substance, not show. As I mentioned above, Dr Bodmer startled me by pointing out that directors went to work by tram and that the company only maintained three company cars to use, of which one alone was a Mercedes.[37]

Until recently the Swiss chemical companies believed that publishing financial information was roughly the equivalent of violating the official secrets act. It used to be said of Hoffmann–La Roche's annual report that the only number in it was the date. Now the Big Three publish quarterly reports from which domestic and international investment analysts can draw real conclusions. Even more characteristic has been the way the three companies have selected very different long-term strategies. Hoffmann has chosen to focus on its pharmaceutical side, shedding the bulk chemical businesses, and acquiring highly rated pharmaceutical companies in other countries. Hoffmann now does 57% of its turnover in pharmaceuticals, whereas Sandoz does 45% and Ciba only 28%. Ciba and Sandoz have moved to acquire companies which can either be integrated vertically or allow them to enter parallel activities.[38] In March 1996, Ciba and Sandoz annouced plans to merge under the new name of Novartis, an astonishing twist in Big Three strategy.

The smaller Swiss companies have also become more open, but traditions of continental secrecy continue to have an impact. Many Swiss executives believe, as do their German neighbours, that too much financial information generates that tendency to short-term business behaviour so marked in American and British investment decisions. In addition, as one managing director explained to me, if the Swiss companies had to present absolutely accurate balance sheets, their 'still reserves' of concealed, accumulated capital would be so shocking that the Swiss government would have to tax them. The accumulation of 'still reserves' reflects two features of Swiss capital markets that need to be noted: the weakness of Swiss company law with its equivalent tolerance of anti-competitive behaviour (cartels, etc.) and the very different traditions of capital formation in Switzerland and in the English-speaking world. Swiss companies have never used the formal and public mechanisms of the stock exchange to anything like the extent that English and American companies have. The 'still reserves' took the place of a public capital market. Hence there was no equivalent to the American Securities and Exchange Commission which could compel a company to reveal its true finances before it got listed on the New York Stock Exchange. Continental banks are also stockbrokers. They had other ways of finding out about company finance than the annual report and, since continental banks also dominate the market in publicly quoted securities, they had no reason to worry. The attempts by the Swiss security analysts to achieve better reporting of company finances have not been unsuccessful, merely slow. A few years ago they reported that the twenty-four biggest Swiss companies reported less than half of the internationally accepted facts: cash flow per share, reserves of liquidity, earnings per share, production levels, inventory changes and interest receivable. Since then, as the chemical Big Three have dropped the veil, no doubt others will follow as they see their best protection in frankness.

Some of the pressure for greater openness comes from the existence of European directives and the Swiss government's intention to make Swiss institutions 'Euro-compatible'. More comes from a kind of low-lying anxiety about the competitiveness of Switzerland in general. Industrialists have themselves gradually come to see that the present cosy arrangements for dividing markets must give way to harsher and more open competition. Branco Weiss, a successful entrepreneur, argues for 'a new Swiss cartel law with teeth, which is long overdue, to open the market'.[39] While Swiss legislators make their crab-like progress, their own companies are voting with their francs. According to Thomas P. Gasser, president of the Verein Schweizer Maschinen Industrieller (the trade association of the machine tool, electronics and metal industries), between 1985 and 1992 Swiss firms invested Sfr 11 billion in the European Union, creating 100,000 new jobs there, whereas the members of the VSM companies report a loss of 30,000 jobs at home.[40] Anxiety about *Standort Schweiz* (roughly the Swiss economic environment) has become a common theme of newspaper articles, government warnings and industrial special pleading. The general thrust of such diagnoses is that Switzerland must follow the best practice elsewhere, deregulate, privatise, reduce public and private monopolies, lower environmental protection standards and the like. This familiar litany will, of course, undergo that process by which all such impulses become part of Swiss public life. They will be debated, discussed, re-discussed, formed into legislation, rejected, accepted and altered over such a long time-span that what eventually emerges will be the orthodoxy of decades remote from the 1990s. Swiss slowness has its advantages.

Both the old secrecy and the new candour express different responses to the same reality: the dependence of Swiss industry on exports. The Basel companies protected their affairs so anxiously because they knew that, however strong they might seem on paper, they were vulnerable to foreign attack. Unlike any of their competitors, they had no domestic market to fall back on nor a Swiss state with a lot of international force to protect them. That vulnerability has led them to try the opposite tack: 'see what friendly, local multinational giants we are' seems to be the present defence. Neither attitude alters the fact that 90% of chemical and pharmaceutical production goes abroad. The chemical industry is not unique in this respect. Between 70% and 90% of all textiles, between 70% and 80% of all machinery and engineering products and about 97% of all watches and watch parts are exported. The extreme disproportion between the volume of turnover and the size of the domestic market makes big Swiss companies uneasy. They know the line between wealth and ruin can be thin. The very specialisation which brings the fat profits makes the specialised company vulnerable to changes in the market. The basic realities of Swiss economic life can be summed up in two linked paradoxes: because they were poor, they specialised in luxury goods, and because they specialised they were easily ruined.

Currency fluctuations provide a dramatic example of the fragility of Swiss economic prosperity. Some of these currency movements blow up with the velocity of a tropical hurricane. As a result of the Yom Kippur War and the oil crisis, the Swiss franc appreciated against the dollar by 41.3%.[41] The 'floating franc' hit the watch industry hard, an industry which at the beginning of 1974 could claim nearly 40% of world production, two-thirds of world exports in volume and more in terms of value. During the first quarter of 1975 exports of the pinlever models (*Roskopf*), which accounted for half total exports, fell by 42%. Of this particular type of watch 99% were sold abroad. Pierre Waltz, general director of the Société suisse pour l'industrie horlogère, told a press conference in the early spring of 1975, 'with the dollar at Sfr 3.40 we find ourselves in a more or less normal recession like everybody else. With the dollar at Sfr 2.70 the situation becomes critical. With the dollar at Sfr 2.40 the struggle is hopeless and we shall lose more and more of our markets over the next few years.'

The catastrophe that in fact occurred was much worse than

Plate 16 The Montres Grana Kurth watch factory in 1906

anybody in the industry foresaw. In 1974, the Swiss made 87 million pieces out of 227 million in the rest of the world, still number one in watch production. By 1980 Swiss production had fallen to 51 million and dropped to 45 million the following year. Of the 2,332 independent Swiss watch houses in 1956, there were under 900 left by 1981 and the workforce had fallen from 55,320 to 26,228. In the meantime Japanese production had tripled from 1970 to 1980, from 23.8 to 87.9 million units of which 68.3 million were for export.[42]

Complacency, not currency fluctuation, ruined the Swiss watch industry, for, as David Landes points out, the Japanese companies like Seiko and Citizen and the American Timex and Texas Instruments were selling something that 'still looked like a watch but was in reality a new product': the quartz-based digital time-keeper.[43] In his wonderful analysis of the history of time-keeping, Landes shows how the same five elements go into every time-piece:

Plate 17 Workshop in the ASSA watch factory, 1924

1) a source of energy (spring or battery);
2) an oscillating controller (balance or quartz crystal);
3) a counting device (escapement or solid-state circuit);
4) transmission (wheelwork or electric current);
5) display (hands or liquid crystal segments).
All clocks, save continuous timekeepers such as the sundial or clepsydra, have these five essential parts.[44]

Although the Swiss had the technology, they simply refused to believe that the quartz could compete with their supreme crafts-manship nor did they foresee (nobody did) the implosion of miniature circuits, which made possible the greatest fall in production costs in the history of technology. While prices fell, performance rose. Micro-chips carried more transistors embedded in ever smaller micro-circuits for less and less cost per unit. As Landes observes, 'it is hard to love a quartz watch',[45] but if it keeps incomparably better time than any mechanical watch and costs a fraction of the price, it is hard to resist it.

When Landes finished his *Revolution in Time: Clocks and the Making of the Modern World* in 1982, he drew the veil on the Swiss watch industry. 'Now we bid farewell to those master craftsmen, who have brought us the wonders of the mechanical arts', he wrote elegiacally.[46] Today the Swiss franc stands at about $1.20 and the watchmaking industry still exists. In 1975, watchmaking stood third in Swiss exports at Sfr 3,702,000,000; today it still stands third, exporting in 1993 Sfr 20,495,600,000.[47] The resurrection of watch-making in Switzerland is a kind of economic miracle, so unexpected and unlikely that even a great economic historian like David Landes could not imagine it. It is also a very Swiss story, and its unfolding tells us much about the Swiss way of doing things.

As A. M. Schütz, former president of Eterna, explained to me, the first attempts to save the industry followed traditional Swiss federal, consultative lines. Government intervened to assure each firm and community something from the shrinking turnover, but, as the crisis became terminal, the big Swiss banks moved in to stop the losses. They abandoned 'concordance' and ruthlessly cleared out the entire social order of traditional Swiss watch-making. With the exception of the independents who make luxury watches, Patek Philippe, Vacheron-Constantin and the like, the families and companies in charge of the watch industry in 1975, especially the multiplicity of small firms so characteristic of

Plate 18 The ASSA watch factory in 1927

the Jura, were wound up. The owners were given roughly 10% of the
value of their shares, their debts were cancelled and the remaining
value was simply absorbed into a new holding company. Herr
Schütz, a German-speaker, was sent into the Jura to liquidate
companies, while a French-speaker from Neuchâtel was sent to
Grenchen to liquidate the German-speaking firms.[48]
   In 1983, the banks fused the remaining holding companies and
formed a new entity, the Schweizerische Gesellschaft für Mikro-
elektronik und Uhrenindustrie, the SMH. The new board engaged
the services of an absolute outsider. Nicholas George Hayek, the
managing director of Hayek Engineering, enjoyed a reputation as
an outstanding management consultant but had no previous
experience of watches. He and the new top manager, Ernst
Thomke, set to work to save the industry. They developed the Swiss
answer to the Japanese and American quartz watch: the Swatch.
The Swatch combined fashion, low price, reliability and variety.
SMH swept the Japanese aside, especially in Asian markets, with
its lively, imaginative and cheap plastic watches.[49] The remaining
traditional watch companies, merged with SMH, were rationalised

Plate 19 Modern watch factory in 1946

and limited to specific areas, say, Longines in the USA or Movado in Italy, but all controlled from the centre by Hayek and his team of aides. In 1994 SMH turned over Sfr 2.7 billion, and suffered the first break in ten years of what the *Neue Zürcher Zeitung* called 'breathless' growth. In 1994 sales of finished watches and raw works went up by 9% to 94.8 million pieces. SMH had restored Switzerland to leadership in the watchmaking world.[50]

This, then, must be the greatest success story in the history of Swiss business and one of the greatest anywhere. The industry over which Landes had said last rites still employs over 30,000 and exports as vigorously as its predecessor. Yet it is not the same industry. SMH is really an electronics company, a centralised,

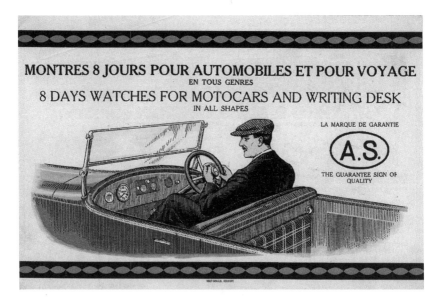

Plate 20a Advertising material for watches

powerful, holding concern. This giant business has replaced the over two thousand independent companies which sustained the old watch industry and the old structures of Swiss life. Indirectly the growth of SMH undermines one of the key elements in the survival of the micro-mosaic of Swiss reality: the micro-economy which buttressed it. The French-speaking valleys of the Bernese Jura have lost population and the will to live. The villages in the Vallon de St Imier, towns like Le Locle and La Chaux-de-Fonds, look run down, provincial, forgotten. Industrial concentration threatens the survival of the political and social structures at the heart of the Swiss way of doing things. To save the watch industry, the Swiss had to accept a drastic, centralised, top-down solution. In effect, Switzerland saved its watch industry in an un-Swiss way. Switzerland exports watches today but the world in which they are made has changed for good.

Not all such stories have happy endings. The case of embroidery in St Gallen provides us with an example of the peculiar 'fragility' which extreme specialisation imposes on Swiss economic enterprise. The embroidery industry in eastern Switzerland was actually larger than watchmaking on the eve of the first world war and

Plate 20b Advertising material for watches

exported more. Embroidery shaped the economies of St Gallen, Appenzell and Thurgau. The federal census of 1905 showed that 49.5% of all employed persons in St Gallen worked directly in embroidery (28,967 in factories, mostly small, and 33,547 in homes) and that the total number of persons employed in the industry in the north-eastern cantons approached 100,000.[51] As in watchmaking and chemicals, production was concentrated in certain areas which had become wholly dependent on one product. The specialisation which made the industry competitive also made it, and the economy of north-eastern Switzerland, vulnerable. The first world war hit the industry hard but the end of the war destroyed it. Not only were important export markets like the German and Austrian utterly ruined, but even in the prosperous ones like the USA there had been a huge change. The war acted as a giant social mixer. It mobilised the population, and that included women. During the war, the huge floppy hat, the stays and corsets, and the long skirts went into the cupboards and with them went the taste for embroidered articles. Swiss embroidery production fell from 9,157 tonnes in 1913 to 2,830 tonnes by 1921. The value of exports declined from Sfr 215 million in 1913 to 147 million in 1921, to 65 million in 1930 and to 26 million in 1937. An industry which had employed 117,375 people in 1910 had shrivelled to 32,626 by 1930.[52] In the middle of the 1930s St Gallen had become a ghost town. The pompous office blocks in *Jugendstil* which had housed firms with English names like 'Atlantic', 'Union', 'Ocean' and 'Worldwide' were empty. The misery in the countryside was unimaginable. The tens of thousands of small-holders who had adapted their lives to the outwork system of the embroidery industry were destitute. The fragility of the Swiss economy had never been more evident: an entire region ruined by a change in fashion.

Plate 20c Advertising material for watches

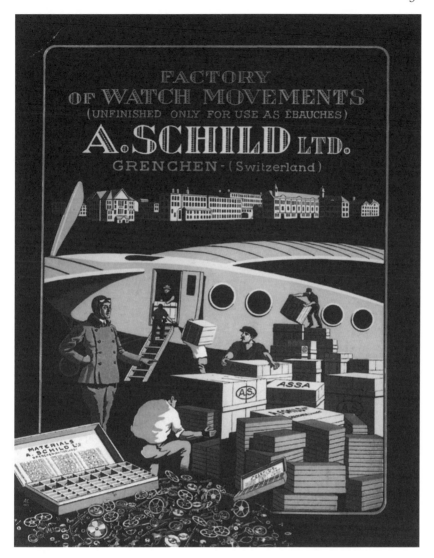

Plate 20d Advertising material for watches

Table 5.1. *Gross national product in nominal and real terms (1938–71)*

Year	GNP (nominal) (Sfr millions)	% change	GNP (real) (Sfr millions)	% change	Degree of inflation (%)	Real GNP per cap. (Sfr)	Change in real GNP (%)
1938	9,580	–	18,345	–	–	4,376	–
1948	18,975	–	22,480	–	–	4,906	–
1949	18,755	–1.2	21,685	–3.5	–2.3	4,673	–4.7
1950	19,920	6.2	23,245	7.2	–1.0	4,952	6.0
1951	21,935	10.1	25,130	8.1	2.0	5,292	6.9
1952	23,020	4.9	25,330	0.8	4.1	5,261	–0.6
1953	24,090	4.6	26,465	4.5	0.1	5,425	3.1
1954	25,555	6.1	27,955	5.6	1.1	5,672	4.6
1955	27,265	6.7	29,445	5.3	1.4	5,913	4.2
1956	29,285	7.4	31,215	6.0	1.4	6,178	4.5
1957	30,870	5.4	32,105	2.9	2.5	6,263	1.4
1958	31,520	2.1	31,520	–1.8	3.9	6,063	–3.2
1959	33,840	7.4	33,795	7.2	0.2	6,426	6.0
1960	37,055	9.5	35,770	5.8	1.0	6,671	3.8
1961	41,490	12.0	38,930	7.3	4.7	6,985	4.7
1962	46,050	11.0	40,335	5.1	5.9	7,126	2.0
1963	50,370	9.4	42,190	4.6	4.8	7,312	2.6
1964	55,540	10.2	44,330	5.1	5.1	7,547	3.2
1965	59,985	8.3	46,255	4.3	4.0	7,780	3.1
1966	64,625	7.7	47,585	2.9	4.8	7,932	1.8
1967	68,825	6.5	48,435	1.8	4.7	7,978	1.4
1968	74,220	7.6	50,365	4.2	3.3	8,193	2.7
1969	80,930	9.0	53,128	6.2	2.8	8,530	4.0
1970	88,850	9.8	55,925	4.6	5.2	8,800	3.2
1971	100,760	13.4	58,330	3.9	9.5	9,223	4.8
1972	116,095	15.2	61,713	5.8	9.4	9,665	4.7
1973	129,370	11.4	63,874	3.5	7.9	9,932	2.7
1974	139,490	7.8	64,384	0.8	7.0	9,966	0.3

Source: 'Die schweizerische Konjunktur im Jahre 1971', Mitteilung No. 231, Kommission für Konjunkturfragen, January 1975.

The year 1945 marked a break in Swiss history not unlike 1648 but with this difference. Where the end of the first Thirty Years War ruined the Swiss economy, the end of the second 'Thirty Years War' (1914 to 1945) opened a period of unparalleled boom. After a short pause, as Table 5.1 shows, the Swiss achieved rates of growth among the highest in modern history. These were the 'golden twenty years', as Peter Rogge has called them.[53] In spite of

Table 5.2. *Percentage of all employed persons*

	1888	1960	1970	1993
Primary sector (agriculture and forestry)	37	11	8	6
Secondary sector (industry, mining, building, electricity, etc.)	41	51	48	33
Tertiary sector (service, tourism, commerce, trade, etc.)	22	38	44	61

Source: Schweizer Brevier, 1972 (Bern, 1972), p. 42; *Statistisches Jahrbuch der Schweiz 1995* (Bern, 1995), Table 3.6, p. 102.

expectations, Europe recovered rapidly. Through Marshall aid and other sources, capital was pumped into reconstruction of heavy plant, rebuilding of ruined cities, resurfacing of gutted roads and twisted railway tracks. Incomes rose sharply and with them the demand for consumption goods, specialised products such as drugs, vitamins, prepared foods and the like. Switzerland with its intact industry and its unique blend of products was ideally placed to supply the Nescafé, the vitamin B, the new wristwatch or office calculator which the reviving Europe demanded. Price seemed to be no obstacle to the buyer and profits soared. Such rapid, Japanese-style economic growth began to cause huge social and structural changes in Swiss life. The last reserves of surplus domestic labour were simply sucked off the land, as Table 5.2 shows.

The backbone of Swiss life, the peasant small-holder, disappeared from the economic arena. Many areas of the mountains depopulated rapidly. By 1970, 22% of the Swiss population lived in communes of fewer than 2,000 people, as opposed to 48.5% in 1900. On the other hand 68.9% lived in 'agglomerations' of over 10,000 in 1990, compared to 6% in 1900. The Swiss had become a nation of city dwellers and office workers in a political and economic system designed for country men and tillers of the soil. At the same time, the booming economy began to outstrip the natural sources of energy, especially the hydroelectric power drawn from the thousands of fast-moving rivers. By 1975 electricity from all sources supplied only a fifth of the nation's energy needs, and of that a third came from nuclear power. Oil accounted for 80% of all energy consumed in the Confederation. Here too the Swiss economy rested on fragile foundations, as the country discovered when the price of oil was quadrupled during the winter of 1973–4.

Neither labour nor capital shortage interfered with the hurtling progress of the great post-war boom. After 1950 an endless supply of cheap labour flowed into the country from southern Europe. As we have seen, capital from domestic sources was already plentiful. To this was added the large sums transferred by anxious Europeans unable to believe in the reality or stability of the new post-war currencies. The Swiss government, whose contingency planning had been dominated by fears of another post-war depression, a kind of 'St Gallen complex', awoke to the new reality slowly, but managed to do so just in time to make the situation worse. Government departments at all three levels suddenly realised that the 'infrastructure', the roads, power plants, water and sewage systems, were inadequate for the booming private economy and hurriedly began to make up for lost time. Public works, which had stood at about Sfr 1,200 million in the middle of the 1950s, reached Sfr 2,000 million by 1961, 3,000 million by 1963 and 4,300 million by 1966. The federal budget tripled between 1960 and 1970, and the cantons and communes were not far behind. In 1961, all three levels spent Sfr 7,630 million, in 1971 they spent Sfr 24,230 million and by 1980 expenditure amounted to Sfr 47,240 million. Perhaps the most significant way to measure the change is to notice that in 1961 government expenditure on federal, cantonal and communal level equalled 18.6% of gross national product; by 1975 it amounted to 28%. Finally and inevitably, deficits began to appear in federal, cantonal and communal budgets, rising from Sfr 446 million for all three levels in 1971 to Sfr 2,063 million by 1973.[54]

These deficits grew sharply when in the mid-1970s the world went into a severe recession. Switzerland was in an especially vulnerable state. The franc had shot up because of the oil crisis, the huge expansion of world liquidity and nervousness caused by the Arab–Israeli war. When international investors start to worry, they switch capital into the safe Swiss franc. In real terms between 1977 and 1995, the value of the franc measured against the currencies of Switzerland's fifteen most important trading partners hit its highest level in September 1978.[55] The watch industry's decline accelerated and other branches of industry began to decline as well. The resulting depression reduced Swiss gross national product more sharply than that of any other member of the Organisation for Economic Cooperation and Development and even more sharply than in the crisis of the 1930s.[56]

Switzerland entered the 1980s shaken and sobered. The great post-war boom had ended, leaving a kind of detritus of unresolved economic and social issues. The emergence of marginal groups, of a drug problem, of welfare and other claims, pushed the Swiss toward greater centralisation. In 1978, a referendum gave the federal government new powers to manage the economy, but with these new powers came further expenditures and larger government deficits. In 1980 the federal and cantonal governments were running deficits but not the communes; by 1990 all three were in deficit. In the 1990s the sums have doubled yet again so that by 1994 the three levels of Swiss government had overspent by Sfr 15,966,000,000 and public debt had doubled from Sfr 77 billion in 1980 to Sfr 149 billion in 1993, equal to 43.1% of gross domestic production, or Sfr 21,339 per head.[57]

The Swiss finance minister has an unenviable task. No finance minister in the world exercises so little leverage over a cabinet as does the Swiss. 'Concordance' and 'magic formula' ensure that he or she will have only one other party colleague in the Federal Council. A federal minister has no party in parliament to give backing to a policy. There is a public which votes on taxation at federal, cantonal and local level and a federal system in which central government can cajole but not coerce the cantons. In April 1991 Herr Otto Stich, the Finance Minister, granted me a lengthy interview in which he set out his difficulties. It had taken eight years to put together a new 'financial package', elements of which had been forced on him by parliament. It included a provision for Value Added Tax, a tax already rejected by the voters on earlier occasions. When I asked him what he intended to do to get voters to accept the package, he smiled and said 'Nichts'; it would be counterproductive if the Federal Council campaigned for a measure. In the end, the package was defeated in a referendum in June 1991, but accepted in 1993.

Taxation is never popular but in Switzerland there is widespread resistance to the very idea of direct federal taxes; direct taxes belong to cantons and communes. Hence the share of taxation controlled by a federal finance minister is limited. Federalism further restricts the minister's choice by imposing complicated sets of payments and transfers which involve programmes that the federal government delegates to the cantons. Making a budget is a nightmare. The finance minister has no veto, no power of

compulsion, only the give-and-take of the Federal Council. Herr
Stich observed wryly that in Switzerland nobody, certainly not the
finance minister, has power to set priorities.[58]

The system lacks transparence and is unusually clumsy in its
response to sudden challenges. The complexity of the taxation
system and the variety of tax burden from one place to another
makes it difficult to compare Swiss taxation with that in other
countries. The idea that Switzerland is a tax haven is certainly
misguided. Herr Stich reckoned that taxes amounted to about 30%
of gross national product. In 1993, it came out at exactly 31.6% of
total national income, not by any means a light load.[59] More
striking are inequalities of income and capital ownership in
Switzerland. In 1991, official statistics show that 2.9% of the
population owned 42% of all capital wealth and a further 15.2% was
owned by the next 4.7%.[60] As for income, according to calculations
by Marliss Buchmann and Stefan Sacchi, inequality is also very
marked. The richest 20% of income recipients earn 44.6% of all
income, the poorest 20% earn 5.2%, or a ratio of rich to poor of 8.6
to 1. Switzerland has thus the most unequal distribution of income
in Europe and stands fourth in the world. Australia at 9.6 to 1 tops
the table and Japan at 4.3 to 1 comes at the bottom. Buchmann and
Sacchi suggest that inequality has worsened recently, aggravated
by high unemployment and indicated by mounting welfare payments.[61]

Buchmann and Sacchi cite research which shows that the Swiss
are very well aware that theirs is an unequal society. The lowest
income earners see it clearly, but strikingly they do not perceive
these inequalities as sources of conflict or tension. Buchmann and
Sacchi conclude:

We have explained this striking difference between perceived inequality
and low level of conflict by looking at the political system in Switzerland
and its tendency to relocate conflict. The system of direct democracy and
the political culture support policies orientated towards compromise
and prevent the articulation of conflict.[62]

There is an irony here worth noting. A more centralised system
might collect taxes more efficiently and possibly even more
equitably, but it could do so only by restricting those rights
which make the present inequalities tolerable. Membership in a
European Union must bring such restrictions. The risk that social

discontent, now tamed by a culture of consent and concordance, might erupt under a more remote, more centralised and more authoritarian government is not the least of the uncertainties which 'Europe' poses.

No consideration of wealth in Switzerland can omit perhaps the most characteristic of all Swiss industries, the banking business. The Alps, chocolate, cuckoo clocks and banks constitute the sum total of what most foreigners know of the Helvetic Confederation, nor are they wrong about banks. The stability of the Swiss franc in comparison to other currencies, its convertibility at a time when others were not and the famous 'bank secrecy' offered sophisticated investors a security, reliability and confidentiality which no other banking system could match. Swiss banks profited from the post-war boom, the uncertainties of the Cold War and the periodic floods of hot money. Banks sprang up like mushrooms. In the early 1970s there were 1,629 independent banking companies operating in 4,480 branches. That was roughly one bank for every 1,400 people. There were more banks (4,480) than dentists (3,658). In the 1980s the bubble burst. Small banks with ambitions beyond their modest provincial station got into trouble and, as the hectic growth of the 1980s slowed, big banks began to swallow competitors in order to show impressive figures of net asset appreciation. Between 1981 and 1993 104 banks, worth Sfr 8.22 billion, were taken over, mostly by the big banks and more successful regional banks. At the same time twenty or more banks went out of business each year (45 in 1993 alone). Hence by 1994 there were only 529 banks left in Switzerland, a third of the total of twenty years before.[63]

The concentration of the banking sector reflects those trends noted earlier in the chapter. As local and regional banks go the way of the small watch companies or machine tool businesses, the autonomy of the local community erodes. When relatively large cantonal banks like the Berner Kantonalbank or the Solothurner Kantonalbank stagger under the burden of bad debts and poor investments, the idea of Swiss micro-politics and the reality drift apart. A typical example is the case of the Neue Aargauer Bank, a creation of two local banks which merged in 1989. In September 1994, it went under and had to be rescued by Crédit Suisse. When the director of the Federal Banking Commission was asked about it, he remarked, the problems of the Neue Aargauer Bank show that fusion cannot definitely guarantee the survival of a bank ... In the case of the NAB the union of the two institutions had weakened rather than strengthened them.[64]

Yet, as in the case of watches, the Swiss banking industry still has many strengths. The currency still attracts foreigners. Basel is the headquarters of the Bank for International Settlements – in effect the central bankers' bank – and Swiss bankers still retain their agility. What has changed is the world around them. Whereas between 1945 and the 1970s Switzerland offered a uniquely free financial market, today all markets are deregulated. Whereas the franc was freely convertible, today other currencies are equally convertible. The story of the Euro-dollar is an instructive case.

During the late 1950s a new world currency began to appear. It began modestly. Managers of European banks noticed surplus dollars in their New York accounts and tried to think of ways to use them. Gradually an international telephone market sprang up in which surplus dollars were loaned out for short periods among banks. The borrowing bank would then sell the dollars against the domestic currency, and buy them back by a future contract timed to coincide with the day of repayment to the lending bank. It could lend the sums thus released to its domestic customers for the same time span. Dollars were on offer so cheaply that, even after subtracting the cost of selling and repurchasing them at the future date, the borrowing bank could still charge its customer a rate below that in the domestic money market. The lending bank was happy, since it earned more for three months' dollars in Europe than it could do on Wall Street. The Euro-dollar was born. Europe was still rebuilding after the war, and needed this new source of capital. At first money-market men distrusted a system which looked more like a chain letter than sober banking practice. They assumed that it would be a temporary bonanza. In time it became clear that the real source of Euro-dollars was the vast balance of payment deficits of the United States. During the 1960s and early 1970s the deficits became so permanent a feature of world trade that the pool of Euro-dollars turned into a chartless sea. The official estimate was about 200 billion dollars in 1975 and over 50 trillion today. Swiss banks were not the first to see the possibilities of the Euro-dollar (merchant banks in the City of London were), but the Swiss invented the 'Euro-bond', a fixed-interest security denominated in Euro-dollars. Characteristically, the Swiss banks found a specialised corner of the market, which they soon dominated. Their best customers were American companies who borrowed dollars for five to ten years in Europe more cheaply than they could borrow them at home and used the proceeds of the issues of Euro-bonds for their foreign operations. Zürich came to be the nearest thing to a proper stock market for Euro-bonds, and the Union Bank estimates that between the early 1960s and early 1970s 13,000 million dollars of Euro-bonds were underwritten and issued by Swiss banks.

Zürich is the Swiss financial capital, not Bern, and it is in Zürich, especially on the Bahnhofstrasse, that the legendary gnomes dwell. Gnomes are by the light of day just foreign exchange dealers, that is, people who trade one currency against another. The Swiss Germans are unusually good at it, because they are unusually well prepared for a profession which requires the simultaneous use of different languages. Early in life, as we saw in the preceding chapter, the Swiss Germans become bilingual in *Schriftdeutsch* and *Schwyzerdütsch*. Any Swiss who has ambitions for a life of commerce spends time in French-speaking Switzerland (even typists think in such terms) and they learn English as a matter of course. A dealer will sit in a room surrounded by telephones with a computer terminal, fax and telex by his side. 'Open lines' amplified through little speakers will stand on his desk and he may wear a headphone too. A dealer may have an open line to a London broker connected to his headphones. He speaks English to London, French to Paris and German to the dealer at the next desk. The foreign exchange dealer regards his Tower of Babel as normal.

What dealers do is very complicated, requires good nerves, a stout digestion and a love of games, but it is not mysterious. Essentially foreign exchange dealers make it possible for us to be paid in our own currency when we sell goods and services abroad or return from holiday. The bank collects the various sums required, passes them to the dealing room and there the dealers buy or sell currency as required to meet obligations. In fact, the dealer is really buying and selling large round lots of currency in accounts in New York or London or Paris, as the case may be. That is the so-called 'spot market'. A sum traded today in dollars will be delivered two business days later, that is, one New York bank will pay to or receive from another a sum in the name of and for account of the dealing bank in Zürich. The scale of these transactions can be very large but the margins are small. A prudent dealer, and here I have to simplify, keeps his 'position' balanced by attempting to match assets in each foreign currency against liabilities. If a dealer buys a million dollars at ten in the morning at Sfr 1.1820, he will try to have another million sold by closing time at Sfr 1.1860, a profit on the transaction of four-tenths of a centime per dollar, equal to Sfr 4,000. His position will be closed on the day with dollars balanced in his book. Reality is much more complicated than this. There is a futures market in which currencies are bought and sold now for delivery in a week, a month, three months, six months, a year or longer. It is the overall position which the chief dealer has to balance (rather like three-dimensional noughts and crosses). People forget that both parties to a sale cannot each be right. The dollars which our dealer bought could have gone down to Sfr 1.1780 and, if he had balanced his books that day, he would have lost the four-tenths of a centime per dollar or Sfr 4,000.

The Swiss are good at this game, but they no longer have a particular competitive advantage. The world of finance has become a seamless whole, linked by instant communications and operating twenty-four hours a day in places that scarcely had international telephones in the early 1970s. Deals may be made as conveniently in Seoul or Hong Kong as Zürich or London. As in manufacturing, the future of the Swiss banking industry worries observers. *Bankplatz Zürich*, like *Standort Schweiz*, has become the shorthand for anxieties about the future of this peculiarly Swiss specialisation. As a consequence Swiss banks have been going through a process of self-examination and reduction in personnel and expenses. Consolidation in domestic banking has its equivalent internationally. Big banks merge with yet bigger ones. Swiss banks have taken over American investment houses and London merchant banks.

The world of Swiss banking, like the world of the chemical industry, is dominated by the Big Three: the Union Bank of Switzerland, the Swiss Bank Corporation and the Crédit Suisse. 'Big' is no exaggeration. The balance sheet of the Union Bank of Switzerland at the end of June 1995 showed a total sum of Sfr 354 billion francs and was thus roughly equal to the Swiss gross national product, and its profits stood at an estimated Sfr 1.6 billions for the year. Its two rivals are slightly smaller but colossal by comparison with other institutions. No other banks in Switzerland are even remotely in their class. The Volksbank which used to run a distant fourth stumbled into difficulties and fell prey to Crédit Suisse.[65]

Clearly institutions so out of proportion to the size of the environment must have great influence, but it is not necessary to wield it crudely. In any case Swiss banks have to tread carefully because of the problem of 'bank secrecy'. The origins of the present banking secrecy law go back to 1934, when Nazi authorities put pressure on the Swiss to reveal the identity of Jewish customers. Economic relations with Hitler's Reich, as one Swiss diplomat put it, 'violated treaties in a way which had never been seen before in the history of trade relations'.[66] To protect the banks and their clients, the Swiss parliament passed a law making it a criminal offence to reveal the identity or other details of a client's holdings. As J. Murray Luck has written, the secrecy law 'is fully in accord with the innate desires of the Swiss people' and attempts to alter the law by popular initiative have been unsuccessful.[67] Pressure from suspicious socialists and international efforts to halt 'money laundering' have had an effect on Swiss practice. In 1977, the banks themselves introduced self-policing regulations, which member banks are supposed to observe in accepting new clients. The code of conduct has been renewed every five years and augmented since 1 August 1990 by government measures against money laundering. Any bank employee who acts contrary to such measures may be subject to legal penalties.[68] This has been further tightened by directives issued by the Swiss Banking Commission. In principle, Switzerland has the toughest code of banking behaviour in Europe. In practice, nothing has happened, partly because bankers are unlikely to betray clients and, secondly, because the law says what bankers may do, not what they must do. The present law allows what is called a *Melderecht*, that is, a right to violate bank secrecy for any person who as part of his or her professional activity has reason to believe that illegal transactions have occurred. What is clearly needed and has not yet been established is a *Meldepflicht*, a duty to report such violations. In any case, much 'dirty money' passes along para-banking channels, through lawyers, through trust funds and investment advisory firms, which are not banks and thus not subject to the legislation.[69]

One very characteristic Swiss difficulty with banking regulation lies in federalism itself. Although the constitutional amendment empowering the federal government to establish a bank was passed in 1891, the Swiss National Bank opened its doors on 20 June 1907 after a long, exhausting political battle. The bank differs from other national banks in that it is not a state bank but has shareholders, mainly the cantons and other public bodies. In the words of Rolf Zimmermann, the Swiss National Bank reflects the reality of 'organised capitalism'.[70]

The structure of the Swiss National Bank has a lot to do with the absence of conflict between the government and its 'over-mighty subjects' on the Bahnhofstrasse. The working executive of the National Bank is the directorate. There are three members: a president, the main spokesman who deals with political matters, a director who runs the Bern office which handles the bank notes, volume of gold and currency in circulation and bank investments, and a director in the Zürich office in charge of the money market and foreign exchange sides of the bank's work, a field generally left to a foreign exchange expert. There is a board or *Bankausschuss*, composed of ten members, mostly influential Zürich banking figures, who meet the directors monthly to talk policy. The directors, since they are appointed directly by the state, consult but need not follow the views of the *Bankausschuss*. The *Ausschuss* in turn reports to the *Bankrat* or bank council of forty, twenty-five of whose members are appointed by the government. It would be naive to imagine that the big banks cannot make their weight felt through such a system but it would be even more naive, as some critics suggest, to believe that the big banks dominate the central bank. The system works smoothly because it is structurally an extension of the Swiss practice in other walks of life. The National Bank, which incidentally also has private shareholders, is not unlike the *Dorfzwing* in Malters. One might see it as a financial *Gemeinde* where citizenship devolves on the managers of companies whose balance sheets are larger than Sfr 500 million.

The image of the National Bank as a gigantic village commune is certainly overdrawn, but it points to an interesting problem. Most people have semi-conscious ideas about how things ought to be done. Ask a typical Englishman to chair a meeting and he will call up a garbled version of House of Commons procedures. He gets confused if the participants start using amendments and points of order but in a roughish way he can follow widely understood rules. The Swiss are no different. It would be hard to run the discussions in the *Bankausschuss* on lines other than those of the local *Gemeinde*, especially if the members use *Schwyzerdütsch* at any time. The language naturally evokes the spirit of the *Gemeinde*, the home and hearth. Swiss banks are not just banks chartered in Switzerland; the atmosphere is different. There is a Swiss way of life, a Swiss way of business, a Swiss style of office hours (start early and work late).

The way of life is housed in a political structure. There is a modern state called Switzerland, so there must be an economy to go with it complete with currency, taxation, legal system and customs barriers, in short, what you would expect to find in any contemporary state. However fashionable it may be to forget it, the national state by its mesh of laws erects an invisible outer shell around the economic activities within its frontiers. There is a Swiss economy, just as there is a Danish or Dutch one. There are also characteristic products of that economy: watches, chocolate, cheeses, numbered bank accounts, Victorian hotels in the Alps and a railway that runs to time. On the other hand, the majority of products produced in Switzerland today are not so closely identified with their country of origin. A piece of anodised aluminium tubing or a kilo of urea-formaldehyde condensate could be produced anywhere. The structure of enterprise in Switzerland is much like the structure elsewhere. There are large, medium-sized and small firms operating in the manufacturing sector. Swiss large firms, as we have seen, are larger in relation to their economic base than any other. A Swiss multinational company dwarfs its surroundings. Nestlé's turnover is larger than the federal budget. The Netherlands and Sweden spring to mind as parallels, but the Dutch economy is half as large again as the Swiss. Unilever and Philips are giants but on a broader pedestal. The big Swedish companies are not as big as the Swiss. Few Swedish companies can claim to be the largest producer of anything in the way that several Swiss firms can, but in the end there is only a difference in degree and not kind. An international company is just that. In the process, the company loses its distinctive national character or, at least, some of it. There is a Swiss economy but it grows more like other European economies every day. Even watchmaking has been regrouped into huge holding companies like those of their Japanese competitors.

The Swiss no longer live in their own media world either. Figures show that they now watch more 'foreign' than domestic TV in pretty well identical proportions in all three linguistic areas (in 1993 the figures were: 68% of all TV watched in German and Italian Switzerland was 'foreign', 64% in French Switzerland).[71] In other words, they get their news and entertainment from abroad and it comes in all sorts of packages. Cable TV has always been important in a country like Switzerland where mountains limit television reception. The remotest Swiss village can tune into CNN, Sky, Euro-Sport and the literally dozens of commercial stations in Germany, France and Italy. Other surveys show that English has become a hidden national language, that young Swiss would prefer English as obligatory second language to any of the 'national' languages, and that adults wish they had learned English instead of French, German or Italian in schools – not to mention the use of English in radio and television, in ads and interestingly even in graffiti.[72]

   None of this is unusual in European terms. The Belgians, Dutch and Danes have similar experiences and, no doubt, similar anxieties. Small states seem to be swamped in the waves of international media coverage, and the day of the Internet and other forms of instant, international communication has just begun. It is the 'normality' of Switzerland that strikes me. When Conseiller Fédéral René Felber told the Socialist Party of Zürich in November 1990 that Switzerland had, at last, become a 'normal country', he spoke a deep truth.[73] More and more Switzerland looks and acts like its European neighbours, but with one difference: from 1 January 1995 all its neighbours belonged to the European Union but Switzerland did not.

   In recent years, under the mounting pressure of European integration, the Swiss sense of specialness has begun to swing from positive to negative. The Swiss passport has become a liability not an asset. As 'non-Europeans' the Swiss have to wait in long queues at airports with the 'others', while the fortunate travellers from the European Union sweep by without further formalities. In European Union countries, young Swiss cannot get work permits or scholarships; they pay foreign not 'home' fees, and Swiss businesses have had to move production beyond their borders to enjoy the full benefits of the common market.

   All of these factors, internal change and external pressure, must push Switzerland towards greater conformity with European norms in every aspect of life from regulations on meat storage to agreements on Alpine transit. As State Secretary Franz Blankart said to me, it would be an irony of history, worthy of Hegel at his best, if Switzerland celebrated the 350th anniversary of its independence from the imperial courts of the Holy Roman Empire at the Peace of Westphalia in 1648 by accepting the imperial courts of that empire's successor: the European Union in 1998.[74]

That peace put an end to religious wars among the German states, though interestingly not among the Swiss cantons, which saw Catholic and Protestant at war as late as 1848. In the end religious peace was achieved but in a characteristically Swiss way, and it is to religion in Switzerland, the last of the great peculiarities of Switzerland, that we now turn.

CHAPTER 6

Religion

The 1990 census showed that 47.3% of the Swiss population called themselves Protestants and 43.3% Catholic. An additional 6.7% stated that they belonged to no religious community, and the rest were Jews, 'old Catholics' and others.[1] The Swiss take religious division for granted; it is built into the very pattern of their daily life. On the edge of each Swiss town or city there are two signs, one with the place name and the other to identify its religion. Different symbols are used for Protestant and Catholic churches, and the motorist sees at a glance whether both confessions are present in the town or only one. Religious denomination is part of the geography of Swiss identity.

In a world where religious conflict daily destroys once peaceful communities, this peaceful co-existence deserves some attention. As in worldly matters so in religion there is (or has been) a peculiarly Swiss way of doing things. Its most notable achievement has been the construction of a lasting religious peace. That peace in its turn provided a crucial buttress for the modern Swiss state. Equally unusual, though less dramatic, are the institutions which provide the laity of both confessions with the power to participate in the government of their churches. Swiss democracy co-exists, sometimes uneasily, with the authority of pastor and priest.

The outlines of Swiss religious history coincide with general developments in European Christianity. Little distinguished Swiss communities from others in the Upper German region of the Holy Roman Empire in the late fifteenth century. The medieval Catholic church suffered from the same corruption and provoked the same resistance in Switzerland as elsewhere but, as so often in Swiss history, there were certain peculiarities. In the fifteenth century four Swiss cities created their own type of monastic establishment,

206

the *Kollegiatstift*, a kind of secularised monastery, in which the city governments exercised jurisdiction. In 1455–6 Luzern transformed the monastery of St Leodegar into a secular canonry and dispersed the resident monks. In 1484–5 Bern expelled the Teutonic Order which had enjoyed a priestly monopoly for over two centuries and, like Luzern, turned the parish church into a canonry. The city council elected the canons, who were either from Bern itself or the surrounding towns. City officials had the right to attend meetings of the chapter and to preside on certain occasions. Fribourg and Solothurn took control of their monasteries in the same way. The four cities had common characteristics. As members of the Helvetic Confederation, they were already powerful enough to defy the bishops under whose diocesan authority they nominally still stood, and their geographical positions on the outer margins of the bishoprics of Lausanne and Constance made it easy to sustain the defiance. They were not initially intent on establishing *Landeskirchen*, that is, state churches, but, in effect, it amounted to that.[2]

The Swiss framework provided the four cities with the leverage to insert a civic layer of authority between Rome and the clergy. Basel, which joined the Confederation in 1501, added its thriving publishing industry and new university to the ferment. Erasmus of Rotterdam, the greatest humanist of the age, lived in Basel and worked on his schemes for reform of the church by using renaissance scholarly techniques. The philological insights which the *quattrocento* Italian humanists had used to purify texts of classical antiquity, Erasmus applied to biblical texts. Erasmus, the prince of humanists, worked with the greatest printer of the age, Johannes Froben, and soon Erasmus's works and purified biblical texts circulated wherever people could afford to buy them.

Among Erasmus's enthusiastic readers was a young priest from the Toggenburg, Ulrich Zwingli. Born in 1484 into a large peasant family, Zwingli's career took him first along conventional lines until he met Erasmus in 1516 and began an intensive study of the bible. In 1519 he became *Leutpriester* (secular priest) in the Zürich Grossmünster, the highest priestly office in the city. Gradually he found his own way to the truth. On 6 September 1522 he preached a sermon 'concerning the clarity and certainty or sureness of the Word of God' in which he stated

Plate 21 Protestants destroy church images in Zürich

Plate 22 The Bernese *Grosser Rat* meets, c. 1600

I know for certain that God teaches me; for I have my experience of it . . .
I began to pray to God for enlightenment, and the scriptures suddenly
became brighter – although I was just reading – as if I had read many commentaries and interpretations. See, is that not a sign that God directs me?
For with the smallness of my understanding, I should never have arrived
there on my own.[3]

The following year the city government arranged a set of
disputations; during the course of these the orthodox could not
refute Zwingli and he was allowed to continue to preach his revolutionary doctrines. Urban and rural unrest accompanied these
changes in theology and practice, part cause, part effect. The
dramatic events in Germany associated with Martin Luther added
to the ferment and soon other Swiss *Orte* (places) turned to the new
faith. In French Switzerland Guillaume Farel, five years younger
than Zwingli, brought the same attitudes and same evangelical
enthusiasm to Lausanne, Yverdon and Neuchâtel. In Geneva, which
had a long history of independence, Jean Calvin imposed the strict
new doctrines of what has come to be known as Calvinism. Calvin
made the tiny city on the Rhône into a new Jerusalem and envoys
of the new order spread through the French-speaking world and
beyond.

The Reformation turned Switzerland into a patchwork of
religious division. Certain cantons remained Catholic and others
turned Protestant. Since the large Swiss cantons held subject
territories, it was not always possible or prudent to impose
uniformity on all the subjects. This drama repeated itself across
the whole of Europe and the hundreds of kingdoms, duchies,
principalities and free cities of the Holy Roman Empire also turned
into a complex mosaic of religious identity. What distinguished
Switzerland was not what happened but how.

Swiss cities had already managed to establish a civic right to
control religious activity, which predated the troubles. There was
also a tenuous but real sense of common membership in the Swiss
Confederation and there were regular meetings of the members.
This in turn helped the Protestant cantons to preserve a fragile
unity in spite of doctrinal disputes. In 1549 Calvin organised an
agreement between the Zwinglian and Calvinist churches on
the doctrine of the Eucharist and in 1566, just after his death, the
various Protestant churches accepted that 'since there is always one
God only, so it follows therefrom that there must be only one

unique church'.[4] This so-called Second Helvetic Confession saved Swiss Protestantism from splintering and certainly helped to preserve the Confederation by maintaining a balance of power between Protestant and Catholic territories.

The Swiss cities which remained Catholic acted to strengthen the traditional faith by increasingly drastic interventions. The weakness of the bishops of Lausanne and Constance encouraged conservative, urban patriciates in Fribourg and Luzern to take control of priestly appointments and to decree the maintenance of orthodox liturgy and doctrine. In the countryside the communes continued, as they had in the past, to elect their own priests. When Pope Paul III called the Council of Trent to order in 1547, the Swiss cities had not bothered to send representatives. They had the situation well in hand and welcomed the Reformation of the church from a comfortable distance. When theory in the Counter-reformation became practice, the Swiss began to resist. In 1567, the Swiss representatives refused to accept any strengthened authority for the bishop of Constance and, when Cardinal Carlo Borromeo made an episcopal visit to Switzerland in 1570, he found the Catholic territories absolutely determined to maintain their independence of Rome and of bishops. The central Swiss authorities prevented the establishment of a Swiss bishopric but accepted an episcopal commissariat, thus maintaining the fiction of obedience and the fact of local jurisdiction. The Catholic cities made clerical appointments, supervised the income of church lands and administered ecclesiastical institutions.[5]

Here too the difference between Swiss and general European experiences was not great but significant for the long term. Both Catholic and Protestant cantons were able to impose a kind of 'state church' on their subjects. The Counter-reformation succeeded in transforming the style and substance of Catholic worship but never entirely eradicated the Swiss tendency to interfere in 'their' church. The Catholic cantons embraced the decorative art and architecture as well as the theology of the Counter-reformation. Switzerland has as rich a selection of princely monasteries and gilded baroque churches as any Catholic state in Europe. The patricians of Luzern permitted the Jesuits to teach their children but refused to allow any outside authority to control the local church establishment. The Protestant cities maintained rigid control over the orthodoxy of the reformed faith with equal zeal.

Religion, like politics, language and the micro-economy, reinforced the cellular character of Swiss life. Each place had its own set of religious customs and practices within a wider world, practices which set it apart from its neighbours, even if they shared the same faith. The fact that all the urban patricians and wealthy merchants, the powerful local peasants and the rural gentry, had more to lose than to gain by centralisation reinforced those tendencies. On the other hand, they all stood to lose if the Confederation tilted too strongly in favour of Protestant or Catholic powers outside Switzerland. Hence the Swiss stayed out of Europe's great wars of religion, especially the Thirty Years War between 1618 and 1648, but fought their own wars between Catholic and Protestant in the mid-seventeenth and early eighteenth centuries, 1656 and 1712, when the danger from outside was not great.

During the eighteenth century, the spread of enlightened ideas and the practice of political absolutism attracted the Catholic patricians in Luzern, Fribourg and Solothurn to strengthen their control over their religious establishments. What the Emperor of Austria or the King of France could do in the great world, the von Balthasars and von Wattenwyls could do in miniature. In Protestant Bern and Zürich the Enlightenment affected the establishments differently. For them the Enlightenment produced a kind of *mentalité*, which led to the foundation of cultural and academic societies, reading circles, coffee houses and clubs. Enthusiasts collected botanical specimens and studied peasant agriculture. Jürgen Habermas has called the development of the new sociability in the eighteenth century the 'rise of the bourgeois public sphere'.[6] Protestant pastors played an important part in this intellectual sea-change and gradually relaxed the severity of their doctrines under the rays of the new reason. The independence of Swiss cantons made Swiss cities, as in the Reformation, free ports of intellectual life, places where radical printers and writers could publish new ideas. Montesquieu published the first edition if *De l'esprit des lois* anonymously in Geneva in 1748, because he dared not publish it in France, and Rousseau's *Du contrat social* appeared there in 1762.

The myth of the Swiss peasant, the cult of the Alps and the sturdy Alpine shepherd, and the legend of William Tell, which took its modern form in the eighteenth century, reinforced the idea that freedom was natural to mankind and that liberty had been

Plate 23 Mother of God chapel in Morel, Counter-reformation baroque

Plate 24 The church of St Ursus, Solothurn

encumbered by the artifices of civil society. The enlightened reformers rushed to the countryside with incompatible aims. On the one hand, they admired and encouraged the myth of the simple cultivator and praised his natural ways; on the other, they wanted that cultivator to be a more productive farmer and to introduce the latest discoveries of scientific agriculture. The cult of natural liberty and rationalisation of agriculture introduced knowledge and disrespect for authority into areas where the 'gracious lords' in Bern and Luzern preferred ignorance and obedience.

The Enlightenment also reinforced a strong sense of 'Swissness', a common identity, which challenged the traditional patrician right to rule. It subverted the ancient particularism in the name of Swiss liberty and thus caught the imagination of the world. 'Swissness', on the other hand, glossed over the fact that the sturdy Alpine peasants and William Tell himself were inconveniently Catholic and hence not ideal representatives of progress. The patricians, who oversaw these developments, Protestant or Catholic, in Geneva or Luzern, in Basel or Fribourg, found that they had more in common with each other, irrespective of religion, than they had with their own increasingly turbulent subjects.[7]

The religious balance of power rested on the common interests of the ruling oligarchies in the Swiss cantons and produced, as in the Holy Roman Empire, institutional compromises to enable both camps to live side by side. When the French Revolution swept over Europe, it flattened those antique structures of religious compromise. In its most radical phase, it abolished churches which blocked its headlong rush toward a society governed by (French) rationality. The French imposed a secular, uniform, centralised state on the Swiss, but it failed. In 1803, Napoleon restored the federal structure and raised the formerly subject territories to full cantonal status, which the Allies accepted and confirmed in 1815. Geneva joined the Swiss Confederation for the first time in that same year.

The restoration after 1815 was a curious period. On the one hand reactionaries turned the clocks back to 1800 or 1789 according to taste. That was no metaphor in the German principality of Hesse–Cassel or the north Italian Kingdom of Savoy, where restored rulers revoked every decree, appointment and alteration which had been made by the hated 'Jacobins' during their decade and a half of 'usurpation'. The restored papacy resumed its rule over its former territories and everywhere spies and agents looked for 'reds under beds'. On the other hand, the administrative improvements made by the French, their decimal and metric systems, their rationalisation of borders and fusion of territories, were useful to the restored rulers and not revoked. Kingdoms like Bavaria and Württemberg and even the Austrian Empire had no intention of disgorging the dozens of bishoprics, principalities, duchies, princely abbeys and monasteries that they had greedily accepted from the hand of the 'Corsican usurper'. As was said of Maria Theresa, 'they wept and took'.

Episcopal borders also had to be neatened in 1815. The abolition of dozens of old ecclesiastical states by the French forced the Holy See to revise all the bishoprics in central Europe. Whereas before 1789, most of the Swiss Confederation lay within the dioceses of foreign bishops, now for the first time all Swiss territories became part of Swiss dioceses. Geneva joined the diocese of Lausanne and Fribourg and in 1819 the former territories of the bishopric of Constance passed to a new bishopric of Chur in Graubünden. In 1828 a new bishopric of Basel was created, covering the cantons of Aargau, Basel, Bern, Luzern, Solothurn, Schaffhausen, Thurgau and Zug, with its episcopal residence in Solothurn. In 1847 St Gallen and Appenzell became a separate diocese, leaving Chur to cover the central Swiss cantons, Zürich and Graubünden.[8]

The Vatican and several Swiss cantons concluded a concordat on 26 March 1828 which established the new bishopric of Basel and which continues to regulate church–state relations to the present day. By signing the concordat the participating cantons acquired the (very Swiss) right, as Walter Gut puts it, in effect 'to elect their own bishop'.[9] The election takes place in two stages. Cantons Luzern, Solothurn and Zug have the right to appoint their own *Domherren*, members of the cathedral chapter, and the other seven cantons select names from a list submitted to them. The eighteen members of the cathedral chapter submit six names to a diocesan conference, composed of representatives of the ten cantons, who establish if any of those proposed are 'less acceptable' (*persona minus grata*). Although Herr Gut considers it 'untenable' in law, the Diocesan Conference has claimed that right since 1906, and on 14 January 1994 actually used it to declare a candidate 'not electable'.[10] The Diocesan Conference then submits its selected names in order of preference to the pope who confirms their selection.

There is no episcopal electoral procedure anywhere in the Catholic world which affords the secular, democratic state such an influence on the choice of a bishop. Walter Gut, who served as Luzern's representative in the Diocesan Conference for sixteen years, compared it to the old *Tagsatzung*, the Diet of the old Swiss Confederation, and there is much in the comparison. The federal government in Bern has nothing to do with the business; it is based on a treaty between the Holy See and the sovereign *Stände* (untranslatable; somewhere between 'states' and 'estates' in English) of Luzern, Solothurn and the rest. Each representative of the canton serves as an ambassador to the Diocesan Conference and may be either a member of the executive (Walter Gut was Luzern Minister of Education and Religion) or in some cantons a representative chosen by the *Landeskirche* or synod of that canton, a mixture of roles which the system in theory avoids.[11]

The period, the 1820s, in which the Holy See concluded its concordat with the Catholic cantons in the bishopric of Basel, coincided with the 'awakening' in the Protestant churches. All over the world 'beautiful souls' confessed that they had been saved by the direct intervention of the Holy Spirit. In the United States this was the second great era of 'revival', the campfire meeting and the emergence of new 'enthusiastic' churches of God in which the experience of salvation counted more than the authority of the pastor or synod. A similar movement of inwardness, the 'new Pietism', swept Germany from the east Elbian noble estates in Prussia to the shores of Lake Zürich. The 'awakened' met in halls, in homes, in the fields, to worship God without the restraints of tradition and liturgy. They railed against the 'walled churches' empty of the Spirit. The official churches, the United Churches of the German states and the 'national churches' of the Swiss cantons, fought back against the wave of popular, charismatic Christianity, asserting that it was subversive, backward, intolerant but, above all, divisive. They used their positions as 'state churches' to forbid the Pietists to hold services.

None of this was new. Luther's message that conscience and the bible were the only sure foundations of faith had undermined the ultimate claims of institutional authority. If every man is a priest, only God can truly ordain him. If, as Zwingli claimed, God interpreted texts directly for the faithful, no theological faculty could refute them. The Swiss theologian Alexandre Vinet in his

Essai sur les manifestations des convictions religieuses of 1842 put it
unmistakably:

Christ sanctified the principle of religious individuality. This principle is
inherent in the very idea of religion. A religion which in point of departure
and goal is not personal is no religion. Religion is the choice which the soul
has to make over and over again between the world and God, between the
visible and the invisible. Man must be able to choose; where the invisible
is visible, there is no choice. Freedom and individuality stand in so
intimate a relation that they can be seen as synonymous . . . Individuality
and religion – the two ideas cannot be split. A collective religion is no
religion.[12]

This deeply Protestant doctrine of the freedom of the Christian soul
refuted the authority of the Roman church, where the 'invisible is
visible', and ultimately weakened all ecclesiastical authority. The
contrast between Protestantism and Roman Catholicism could be
summarised in two propositions: if Protestantism degenerates,
there is anarchy; if Roman Catholicism degenerates, there is
tyranny. The evolution of politics in the nineteenth century drew
this contrast ever more sharply. The emergence of liberal movements in the 1830s and 1840s, the great waves of nationalist
agitation in the 1850s, the wars of unification which led to a united
Germany and Italy in the 1860s and the struggle by the state to
control education in the 1870s, threatened the Roman church as
a bastion of authority and a temporal power. After all, the pope
still ruled most of central Italy until 1860. Protestantism could
apparently come to terms with these manifestations of 'progress'
much more painlessly. If Protestantism preached the liberty of the
Christian soul, it could hardly deny the liberty of the secular citizen.
   These issues became acute in the nineteenth century in
Switzerland. As the cantons moved to adopt democratic forms of
rule, and as at the same time the Roman Catholic church under
Gregory XVI and Pius IX rejected all concessions to liberalism,
secularism or nationalism, a conflict was inevitable. Protestantism
and the evangelical churches felt themselves to be on the side of
progress and civilisation in the struggle against reaction and
barbarism. Anti-catholicism, liberalism and secularism mingled to
intoxicate the Swiss Protestants with a feeling of superiority. The
gradual erosion of faith, the compromises which so-called 'liberal'
theology had to make with natural science and the capitalist
market, weakened the state churches more than they realised. Sin

came to seem an old-fashioned idea, and evil merely the absence of good. Liberal Protestants led the fight against the consequences of industrialisation and introduced legislation to protect the poor. The churches substituted the 'social question' for arguments about the nature of God.

Swiss Protestant theology remained as an island of optimism when the certainties of bourgeois society and enlightened progress died in the trenches of the first world war. The horrors of the war called for a new approach to the reality of radical evil. In this gloom a new, neo-orthodox piety emerged. Shortly after the end of the first world war, a conference of Protestant theologians took place in Schloss Tambach not far from Gotha in Germany. One of those who attended described the occasion as one in which the people present knew they 'wanted something different' but did not know what. They had heard of radical developments in Swiss Protestantism and invited various prominent Swiss theologians who turned them down. In the end a 33-year-old Swiss pastor, Karl Barth (1886–1968), gave a talk on 25 September 1919 which the German church historian Klaus Scholder considered 'one of the most important acts of witness in twentieth-century theology'.[13] Barth's talk, called 'Der Christ in der Gesellschaft' (either 'Christ' or 'The Christian in society'), rested on the double meaning of the German word *Christ*. It could mean, and the listeners, good left-wing Christians as they were, assumed it did mean, 'The Christian in society'. Barth had other ideas:

Der Christ: we all agree that the Christians cannot be meant by the phrase, neither the mass of the baptised nor the tiny band of the elect with religious–social consciences, nor the finest selection of the devoutly pious of whom we might think. *Der Christ* is Christ himself.[14]

Barth put God back into the centre of Protestant faith and called the churches to return to the original Protestant message. In his famous lectures of 1920, Barth called God 'the entirely Other', the experience of religious confrontation with the crucified Christ 'on the very borders of humanity'.[15] The impact of this 'neo-orthodox theology' in the German-speaking world grew as the Weimar Republic disintegrated and Hitler came to power. Barth and the other Swiss neo-orthodox thinkers like Emil Brunner (1889–1961) became spokesmen of a radical, biblical, uncompromising Protestantism which resisted Hitler in a way that the liberal, worldly, patriotic Protestantism of Germans in Hitler's Reich had not. As in Zwingli's and Calvin's day, the existence of Swiss German, Swiss French and Swiss Italian cultures provided alternative voices for those countries whose churches and cultures had suffocated under fascism. As in military matters so in Protestant theology, the years between 1919 and the 1960s may be seen as Swiss Protestantism's finest hour.

If Protestantism had been compromised by its pact with secular progress, Swiss Catholicism was equally compromised by the Vatican's rejection of that progress. The authority of the pope collided with the claims of the modern world. At the heart of the collision between authority and the Swiss version of democracy is an insoluble dilemma. As the church historian Victor Conzemius remarked in an essay on the problem,

The church is no democracy. There is no voting on truths of the faith; at most on their temporal formulations. The church is, on the other hand, no monarchy, as an extreme papalism would have us believe.[16]

As Conzemius indicates, Swiss Catholicism has sought a *via media* between authority and democracy. The long history of local rights, the survival through the entire twentieth century of synods, concordats and agreements gives the Swiss Catholic church a special character. Swiss Catholicism has historically had to fight a two-front war, against Protestantism, liberalism and secularism on one front and against papal integralism on the other. That in itself does not make Switzerland unusual; the special element was, as often in Swiss history, not the problem but the solution.

The democratic and liberal movements of the nineteenth century encouraged the Protestants and threatened the Catholics. In Switzerland it led to the war between Catholic and Protestant in the so-called *Sonderbundskrieg* of 1847. The tacit agreement between the Protestant and Catholic patricians against democracy was shattered and many aristocratic conservatives lost their 'natural' places in public service. One of these was the remarkable Luzern patrician, Philipp Anton von Segesser (1818–1887), who has already made an appearance in Chapter 2. Segesser took an active part in the *Sonderbundskrieg*, and the humiliating failure of the Catholic forces to fight properly stung him. He began rebuilding his life within the protection of the sovereignty of his canton. In an outburst from February 1848 he wrote

For me Switzerland is only of interest as long as the canton of Luzern – this is my fatherland – is in it. If Canton Luzern no longer exists as a free, sovereign member of the Helvetic Confederation, then Switzerland is as irrelevant to me as the lesser or greater Tartary. Second, I shall be either a free man or a subject. If as a Luzerner I cannot be a free man, I should rather be a subject of the King of France or the Emperor of Austria or even the Sultan himself than of some Swiss republican diet.[17]

The shame of defeat, the pride of class but also the fear for the church combined in Segesser's rejection of the modern, radical, progressive Federal Constitution of 1848. Radicalism in Switzerland meant separation of church and state, civil marriage and divorce, a licentious free press and attacks on the church of Rome. Segesser found himself pushed, alone and without a stable party, a viable Catholic newspaper or enough money, onto the national scene as spokesman of his faith, his fatherland and his fellow citizens.

Not that defending the church was easy. As Pius IX moved towards a confrontation with bourgeois liberalism, and as Italian unification threatened the temporal power, the pope issued the encyclical *Quanta cura* on 8 December 1864, which condemned every proposition dear to modern liberalism. As a Swiss caught in the middle, Segesser felt more and more uneasy. In a letter of March 1860 he complained:

In Rome they cling to the unsustainable and compromise the sustainable and essential. It is certainly unjust if the pope loses his states, but I believe it would be providential. Italian princely politics have always been fatal for the church.[18]

Quanta cura did not 'suit me and my people and is making our situation ever more untenable', he wrote in early 1865,[19] but he never wavered in his loyalty. Gradually he and other central Swiss conservatives found their way to direct democracy, to the initiative and referendum, as devices to control the rampant, liberal and capitalist circles in Zürich and Bern. As he wrote in 1866,

My firm conviction is that we of the conservative camp must put ourselves entirely onto a democratic basis. After the collapse of the old conditions nothing else can provide us with a future and a justification except pure democracy. Even if democracy has its dark side it is preferable to the quasi-bureaucratic aristocracy of the representative system.[20]

As we saw in Chapter 2, this combination of conservatism and democracy allowed Swiss Catholics to survive the crises of church–state relations in the nineteenth century and ultimately by 1891 to put a Luzern Catholic onto the Federal Council. Yet the techniques by which that success was achieved made conservative Swiss Catholics unlike their brethren in the church outside Switzerland. Segesser disliked the whole idea of a 'state church' but he disliked extreme clericalism even more. In 1862, he wrote to a friend

More and more I become convinced that our forefathers were right to take the care of the Catholic Church in Switzerland into their own hands and to keep the very reverend gentlemen within their four walls.[21]

During the 1870s after the First Vatican Council, the declaration of papal infallibility, the unification of Italy and Bismarck's attack on the church known as the *Kulturkampf*, Switzerland got sucked into the maelstrom of church v. state. The liberals saw 'ultramontanism', the extreme claims to papal authority, as a direct challenge to everything they held dear. The machinery which gave Swiss cantons the constitutional rights to elect a bishop was used or misused to depose one. When the bishop of Basel, Bishop Eugène Lachat, excommunicated priests who refused to accept the doctrine of papal infallibility and the encyclical *Quanta cura*, the cantonal governments represented in the Diocesan Conference of the bishopric of Basel deposed him on 29 January 1873, and confiscated his property. The dissenting priests established a separatist movement outside the Catholic church, which still exists, is officially recognised in Switzerland as the *Christkatholische* church and numbers about 12,000 members. When in the same year, 1873, the pope named Gaspar Mermillod, a well known advocate of extreme papal authority, to be Apostolic Vicar of Geneva, the Swiss federal government expelled him. Segesser watched with mounting anxiety as the conflicts worsened. In a letter of May 1873 to the Liberal Zürich *Bundesrat*, Jakob Dubs, he compared the crisis to that of 1847 but now made worse by the threat to expel the Jesuits and the campaign for a new, more secular constitution.

Today the Catholics face the alternative of giving up their faith in exchange for a new state religion and state church or fighting. That is clearly where things are heading, for freedom is no longer allowed to everybody. Ultramontanism is declared to be subversive of the state and so defined that it becomes identical with the entire structure of the church.

That was, of course, intolerable. On the other hand, Segesser could see certain advantages in the expulsion of Bishop Lachat from his diocese.

The Conservative Party in Solothurn will have to learn to stand on its own feet. That way it will grow stronger and more confident of victory. Up to now the bishop was the middle point, around whom the mass of ultramontanes collected. Now he is gone and the consequence is that politics will be secularised, as it has been here [in Luzern – JS] for years.[22]

In the end, the conflict slowly eased. Pius IX died in February 1878, and his successor, Leo XIII, proved much more conciliatory. Bismarck gradually lost his enthusiasm for the battle against ultramontane catholicism because it made him too dependent on the German liberals. The onset of a serious economic depression in the 1870s shook the self-confidence of ruling liberals everywhere, including Switzerland, and brought down the liberal certainties. Free trade, free speech, free markets and 'a free church in a free state' had not ensured permanent prosperity and enlightened rationality after all.

Switzerland survived the crisis in church–state relations with its inherited institutions intact. The rights and duties of the Diocesan Conference of the bishopric of Basel survived into the late twentieth century unaltered, and the provisions of the Federal Constitution of 1874 which forbade the Jesuit order from operating on Swiss soil were only lifted by referendum on 20 May 1973. Yet the issues of authority and popular democracy in Swiss catholicism were not settled in the nineteenth century and have re-emerged at the end of the twentieth in a new and startling way. Several cases illustrate the new crisis.

The first of these became front-page news even outside Switzerland, when the bishop of Basel, Hansjörg Vogel, announced in June 1995 to a dumbfounded public that he intended to resign. In a letter to all the faithful in the diocese, he declared

Since my election I have experienced very severe spiritual burdens. I sought support in a relationship with a woman whom I had known before. This relationship led to a pregnancy.[23]

The continuing debate about celibacy and the role of the clergy became more public and intense. The reaction of Catholic Switzerland to Bishop Vogel's resignation was unusually mild and understanding. Surveys showed large majorities, especially among women, which wanted to see the abolition of celibacy. In such circumstances, the spiritual and practical complexities of the choice of successor can be imagined, especially since the election of Bishop Vogel had been preceded by a very substantial (and very Swiss) consultative process involving 1,500 individual submissions.

In such consultative procedures Switzerland challenges the traditional authority of the Roman Catholic church in a way quite unlike that presented by the radical challenge of 'liberation theology' in Latin America. The Swiss challenge, rather like the difficulties in the Roman Catholic church in the USA, arises not from doctrine but daily life. The Swiss are accustomed to doing things in a certain way and rarely think about it unless confronted. The Holy See, on the other hand, has, since the Second Vatican Council in the 1960s, struggled to arrive at a new, more open concept of authority. In that struggle Switzerland has been peculiarly important.

Teaching has been a particular area of conflict. There are three institutions in Switzerland for the training of priests, the Theological College in Chur, the Theological Faculty in Luzern and the Theological Faculty in the University of Fribourg. The University of Fribourg is a hybrid institution. a state university but also, as a result of a treaty between Canton Fribourg and the Swiss bishops, formally a 'Catholic university'. As the only university in Switzerland with a Catholic theological faculty, it is at the heart of conflicts between church and state. In 1971 a Dominican, Stephanus Pfürtner, gave a series of lectures on sexual ethics which rejected the official teaching in certain respects. Amidst loud, public protests, he was forbidden to teach and ultimately left the order. Although it is a state university, Fribourg cannot confer honorary degrees without the *nihil obstat* of the General Master of the Dominican Order, which in 1990 was refused in the case of the South African Dominican Albert Nolan and the controversial American bishop of Milwaukee, Rembert Weckland.[24]

The most prolonged and bitter of the clashes between the Swiss way of doing things and the Holy See was the appointment of Bishop Wolfgang Haas to the bishopric of Chur. In April 1988, Pope John Paul II announced his intention to appoint the chancellor of the diocesan *Ordinariat*, Monsignor Wolfgang Haas, a forty-year-old of outspoken conservative views, to be suffragan bishop of the diocese with the right to succession (Coadjutor). The then bishop of Chur, Johannes Vonderach, had apparently agreed the procedure with influential figures in the Vatican in an attempt to evade the rights of the cathedral chapter. According to Walter Gut, the papal decree *Etsi salva* of 28 June 1948 gave to the cathedral chapter a limited electoral right. The cathedral chapter cannot elect a bishop entirely freely but must choose from a list of three presented by the Holy See. In addition, an agreement of 3 August 1824 granted Canton Schwyz special rights, incorporated in the Bull *Impositata humilitati nostrae* of the following December. In Herr Gut's view, while technically the agreement has not the same force as a formal concordat, it constitutes 'a binding treaty . . . which has been mutually observed in essence for 150 years'. In a brief, 'Concerning the Nomination of a Coadjutor in the Bishopric of Chur', dated 4 April 1989, he concluded that the nomination of Monsignor Haas had 'violated the concordat'.[25]

Bishop Haas immediately took steps to assert his episcopal authority and to suppress those modernist trends which he detested. In February 1991 he expelled lay theological students, both male and female, from the Seminary of St Luzi, dismissed the rector and returned the institution to its 'real' function, the training of priests. The fact that St Luzi served as the only seminary for candidates for the priesthood from Zürich, the most populous, urban and open of Swiss cantons, made matters worse. The ex-Dominican Gonsalv Mainberger saw in these and other appointments and dismissals 'a sharp course of re-catholicisation ordered from above'. He reckoned that over 80% of all Catholics in the bishopric opposed the new course and even more decisive was the opposition of priests. 'There has never been an ecclesiastical decision which has produced such a demonstration of solidarity', he wrote, and cited a chain of demonstrations, protests, and official declarations. The Catholic Synod of Zürich even cut its contributions to diocesan funds.[26]

The battle between Bishop Haas and his faithful ended in deadlock. In March 1995, the president of the Catholic Synod of the Canton of Zürich, Eugen Baumgartner, declared

Since we have now been waiting a very long time for the dismissal of Wolfgang Haas, I simply cannot understand it any more, and ask myself how long must we wait for a decision from Rome. If there were ever a bishop who could not unite his diocese, it is Wolfgang Haas.[27]

The conflict between the Swiss state and Bishop Haas sharpened a few months later, when three inspectors appointed by Canton Graubünden declared that the Theological College in Chur (St Luzi Seminary) no longer met cantonal standards for academic accreditation, that students had been admitted without the customary examinations results and, above all, that the institution had lost its academic autonomy because of repeated interventions by the bishop in his capacity as grand chancellor. The cantonal education department warned that, unless measures were taken to raise the academic quality of the college, it would no longer be recognised by the state. Two professors appointed by Bishop Haas condemned the report as 'a tool in the private war against Bishop Haas', and charged that the inspectors were 'partisan and prejudiced' and the report 'sheer waste of money'.[28]

Switzerland has been the arena of another clash within the hierarchy not less dramatic than the Haas case. In 1988, the same year that Pope John Paul II made Monsignor Haas suffragan in Chur, he excommunicated Archbishop Marcel Lefebvre for disobedience. Archbishop Lefebvre had refused to recognise the changes in the liturgy inaugurated by the Second Vatican Council and had continued to celebrate Latin mass in the tridentine form. He had rejected the ecumenical direction indicated by the Council and any introduction of collegiality in episcopal rights. He founded a traditionalist 'Order of St Pius X' and became the focus of all those in the church who rejected the drift from traditional practice. His seminary in Ecône in Valais trained a traditionalist clergy and when, on 30 June 1988, Bishop Lefebvre consecrated four bishops, the pope excommunicated him. Archbishop Lefebvre, not Swiss himself, used the traditional religious liberties of the Swiss cantons to establish his movement.[29]

A third case in 1988 was the elevation of the Swiss theologian Hans Urs von Balthasar to the rank of cardinal. Balthasar, a descendant of one of the Luzern patrician families, had written *Herrlichkeit*, a work of original theology dedicated to beauty as an attribute of the Godhead. Balthasar, who may be compared to Karl Barth in theological significance and international resonance, had fallen out with the Jesuits and founded a mystical order. He had for years seen himself as a marginal figure in the official life of the church and at conferences used to register as 'Urs Balthasar – *niente*'. When the pope made him a cardinal, he remarked, 'we are in the Catholic church and obey the pope even if it isn't very democratic and Swiss'.[30] Two days before the ceremony, on 26 June 1988, he died at the age of eighty-three.

It is not chance that Switzerland has been the stage on which so many dramatic clashes between church and state have occurred. Swiss democracy plays a unique role in the actual operations of both Protestant and Catholic churches. Take the case of the *Landeskirche* of Bern, an evangelical–reformed church. Its base, as in secular society, rests on the *Kirchgemeinde* or church community, the religious equivalent of the secular *Einwohnergemeinde* or residential community. The 691,812 registered Protestants of Canton Bern and a portion of the 80,000 Protestants in the Catholic Canton of Solothurn are divided among 240 *Kirchgemeinden*. Each *Kirchgemeinde* jealously guards its theological and practical independence. Reformed churches have neither bishop nor hierarchy. For many years the cantonal parliament of Bern, the *Grosser Rat*, fulfilled the functions of the synod of the church, that is, state and church were one. In some Protestant cantons, such as Graubünden and Schaffhausen, the Protestant members of the cantonal parliament still act as a synod. From 1803 to the adoption of the Constitution of 1874 in Bern state and church were literally the same institution.

When the Constitution of 1874 was adopted, a separate church organisation had to be created. Its rights and duties have been made more precise in the Constitutions of 1945 and 1995. The *Landeskirche* is governed by an elected synod or church parliament of 200 members. Just as in a secular Swiss parliament so in the church's parliament: decisions of the Synod are subject to facultative (i.e. optional) referenda if they make permanent changes, involve expenditure above a certain level or alter the prayerbook or liturgy. The Synod elects an executive council, the *Synodalrat*, for a term of four years. There are nine members, five of whom are theologians or pastors. This council operates within the state church exactly as the *Regierungsrat* of a canton or the Federal Council in Bern. It meets fortnightly. It has nine departments, each headed by a member of the executive called, as in the federal or cantonal councils, the *Departementsvorsteher*, who acts as a kind of cabinet minister in charge of his or her department. Each department has its own administration with a church civil servant as administrative head. There is a *Kirchenschreiber* whose function resembles that of a *Gemeindeschreiber* in a commune or the Federal

Chancellor in Bern, who serves as head of the civil service and secretary to the synodal council.[31]

The very existence of such an institution annoys certain traditional pastors and their flocks. The president of the synodal council is never, never, to be compared to a German Protestant bishop. The evangelical–reformed church builds from the bottom up. The sum of the faithful organised in congregations is the church and not the hierarchy, not even the elected synod. These suspicions about hierarchical ambitions apply even more to the Swiss national Protestant organisation, the Schweizerischer Evangelischer Kirchenbund, which represents all the cantonal churches in Bern.

The *Kirchgemeinde* has considerable powers. It sets a *Kirchensteuer* or church tax at some percentage of the cantonal tax. Poor communities set high rates, sometimes as high as 14 or 15% of the cantonal tax, while rich communes can afford rates as low as 6%. All those who register as members of one of the publicly recognised religions have an obligation to pay the tax. That includes legal entities, i.e. companies and business organisations not engaged in charitable activities, which happen to have factories or offices in a particular *Kirchgemeinde*. The legal entities contribute a healthy 10% of church revenue in Canton Bern. The constitutionality of forcing the local machine tool company to support the evangelical church in Canton Bern is not established and it is hard to see how a company can leave the church on a matter of conscience. Cases on the issue before the Federal Tribunal in Lausanne have not yet produced a clear ruling.

The state, that is, the residential community, collects the taxes on behalf of the government. The *Kirchgemeinde* in Bern (as in Vaud, Zürich and Basel-Land) does not, however, pay the pastors. The state does. Not only that; the civil state sets rates of pay for pastors by salary class within the Bernese civil service (a pastor belongs with middle school teachers) but the *Kirchgemeinde* can (and does) supplement the state salary with an additional payment. The state treats pastors and priests as civil servants. Pastors and priests swear the civil service oath and are bound by laws about receipt of gifts, retirement and the like.

The pastor in Bern has three distinct sets of demands to confront. There is, first and most important, his or her church council. Although the *Kirchgemeinde* may not pay the pastor directly, it maintains the fabric of the church, pays for prayer books, and looks after repairs and a variety of educational and cultural activities. The pastor must also obey directives from the *Kirchendirektion*, the part of the state bureaucracy which deals with church matters, and finally he or she is subject to the liturgical and theological decisions of the synod and the synodal council.

Not everybody in Switzerland likes these arrangements. Individuals who no longer go to church on Sunday resent paying for an establishment that they no longer support. They can apply formally to leave the church and statistics of *Kirchenaustritte* or 'church resignations' make gloomy reading for the remaining faithful. In the Protestant canton of Zürich, the number of church members has fallen steadily. In 1970, there were 659,814 registered church members; in 1990 there were 583,624.[32] Since that time the trickle of resignations has become a flood, rising to 3,100 in 1991, 3,500 in 1992, and by 1993 to between 50 and 60 a day or about 18,000.[33] These resignations take money out of the collection box and taxes out of the system. Every resignation costs the church literally thousands of francs. In spite of the resignations the churches still receive substantial sums from the church tax. In 1994 the budget of the Zürich *Landeskirche* amounted to Sfr 39 million and the *Kirchgemeinden* as a whole raised Sfr 167 million, a very substantial sum indeed.[34]

Another way to vent one's frustrations with the *Landeskirche* is to change the system. In all substantial Protestant cantons, action committees emerge from time to time to propose the separation of church and state. Since Swiss democracy offers such committees the weapon of the initiative, these moves can be very effective. There have been several such attempts in Bern and Zürich. The latest in Zürich in September 1995 narrowly failed to put an end to the tie between state and church.

The exact place of the Swiss churches in an increasingly secular society has begun to raise questions about the desirability of state churches. The non-official churches, the other Christian and non-Christian confessions, do not need the prop of the state. In 1991 the Radical Party of Canton Zürich organised a conference to consider the future of the state church. The Protestant theologian Robert Leuenberger pointed out that churches have always mirrored the prevailing political structures. The papacy became a monarchy when monarchies were the natural model, the Swiss churches became democracies as 'a particularly remarkable mirror-image of the state system', when democracy spread as the form of Swiss politics. Professor Leuenberger concluded that democracy had gained at the expense of the role of the clergy; in other words, the pastor could hardly make him- or herself heard in the noise coming from the church democracies.[35]

That noise from the base also applies in the Roman Catholic church where neither tradition nor structures of authority easily accommodate it. The Roman Catholic church in Canton Bern is an officially recognised state church and the state regulates pay and conditions of priests as it does pastors. In the city of Solothurn the *Kirchgemeinde* owns and operates the splendid baroque cathedral which it places at the bishop's disposal. The Solothurn *Kirchgemeinde* maintains a hermit, the *Einsiedler*, who lives in a romantic gorge just outside the city itself. The *Einsiedler* must be the only municipal hermit in the entire Catholic world.

The vertical lines of authority in traditional Catholic hierarchies waver when they descend into the Swiss context. The faithful have democratic rights guaranteed by cantonal law and by centuries of established practice. The laity in Switzerland are not mute, obedient flocks waiting on the priestly word. As Rolf Weibel points out, the system requires compromise. The priest cannot simply issue orders but must argue a case with his flock; the church community will not simply concern itself with building costs and administration but takes a position on theological and liturgical issues. Where the cooperation works, it fulfils that aspect of the Second Vatican Council, which introduced a new conciliar structure and partnership throughout the church.[36]

The changes introduced by the Second Vatican Council have brought Protestant and Catholic practices closer to each other. The mass in the vernacular and the increasing use of congregational or general confession makes the typical Catholic mass feel like an Anglican or Lutheran service. Hymns sung in the vernacular and a more ecumenical attitude to the Eucharist have been striking developments of the thirty-five years since the end of the Second Vatican Council.

The Haas controversy illustrates how difficult Pope John Paul II has found it to impose a more traditional authoritarian style and doctrine on the dioceses in Switzerland. As Cardinal Carlo Borromeo found in 1570, the Swiss Catholics resist the authority of foreigners, even those in clerical vestments. Switzerland, although numerically a very small part of the great Roman Catholic universe, has contributed more than its share of difficult cases for the Holy See, and, as I suggested, none of that is chance. The 1994 annual general meeting of the Roman Catholic Central Committee of Canton Zürich argued strongly for the preservation of its status as a *Landeskirche* and against the separation of church and state in the canton. The annual report maintained that the institutions built up in Canton Zürich since 1963, when the Catholic central state organisation was established, were valuable in themselves and would be destroyed if church and state were split. Without their state church the Catholics of Zürich would be utterly dependent on the diocese of Chur and Bishop Haas.[37] This kind of language is not welcome in the episcopal palace in Chur. Father Joseph Bonnemain of the diocesan *Ordinariat* in Chur called the behaviour of the Zürich state church 'democratic, popular Josephinism',[38] which in short-hand sums up much of the argument of this chapter. What Emperor Joseph II wanted was to control the church, his 'Josephine' policy. He failed but the Luzern and Fribourg patricians succeeded, as Segesser shrewdly observed, until they passed that control precisely to the *Volk* whose democratic pretensions collide with the demands of episcopal authority.

The battle between the Zürich state church and Bishop Haas plays itself out against a background of decline, crisis and uncertainty. Church membership among Catholics has also fallen and, more seriously, the number of priestly ordinations and the decline in the numbers in the monastic orders has reduced the available number of priests quite sharply. Rolf Weibel constructed a table based on the 1985 figures which showed that pastoral care in all six Swiss dioceses now depended on a very large number of lay people. In the German-speaking dioceses of Basel, St Gallen and Chur 24%, 27% and 19% of all pastoral activity was carried out by lay people, who acted as deacons and liturgical assistants. With the exception of the administration of the Sacraments, these lay people were performing priestly functions.[39] Ten years later the situation had become much more acute. The Roman Catholic Central Committee of Canton Zürich reported in early 1995 that 26 parishes had no elected priest and that the situation had now reached a stage at which temporary measures would no longer suffice. It might be necessary to alter church law to

Plate 25 Woman pastor celebrates the Eucharist in Geneva

allow church communities to elect lay people as well as ordained priests.[40]

On the eve of a new century and millennium both great Swiss confessions face critical problems. In Protestant cantons, the fall in the number of members of *Landeskirchen* is such that the non-official sects and so-called 'free churches' outnumber them. Swiss church attendance continues to decline as the behaviour patterns of the Swiss become more and more like those of their neighbours. The Roman Catholic church faces conflicts between authority and Swiss democracy but against a background of growing indifference, disintegration and uncertainty. If the 'Swiss way of doing things' has achieved notable successes, it has done so by solving the problems caused by too much religious passion. The great religious peace between Catholic and Protestant achieved in the nineteenth century drew its urgency from the bitterness of the *Kulturkampf*. The crises of the present occur against a background of lack of interest.

The Swiss have become like everybody else. The Swiss way of doing things in religion no longer supports the cellular structure of Swiss life. The physical reality of Switzerland has eroded the religious as well as the political and economic identities that made Switzerland distinctively Swiss. The religious divisions, which once etched their sharp borders onto the cellular structures criss-crossed by politics, language, history and the micro-economy, are gradually disappearing. Switzerland is in the process of becoming a 'normal state', as René Felber argued.

Today some five million Swiss live in a great suburban sprawl which extends from Lac Léman to Lac Constance. Peter Baccini, an architect, and Franz Oswald, an energy expert, have called the new settlement pattern 'the Swiss city', one great urban/suburban agglomeration.[41] It is a way of life not all that different from that of the Washington–Boston corridor, the Home Counties in Britain or the Wiesbaden–Frankfurt–Bonn triangle. In the great suburbia of the twenty-first century, where houses will be linked by cable to hundreds of TV stations, and computers will surf the Internet, where the universal language will be English and the universal technology will be energy saving, Switzerland's style of life will be indistinguishable from that of its neighbours. If the arguments advanced in the previous chapters add up to anything, they suggest that the *Sonderfall Schweiz* must be near its end. The next chapter will attempt to look at the nature of Swiss identity in the past and present to see if it too must go when the conditions which produced it gradually disappear.

CHAPTER 7

Identity

On 26 November 1989, 68.6% of Swiss voters turned out to decide if the Swiss army ought to be abolished immediately. To the astonishment of the entire country, 35.6% said 'Yes'. Nobody, not even the organisers of the initiative, the Socialist Youth of Switzerland, could believe the figures. The members of the government, the officer corps and the establishment in its broadest sense were stunned. Divisionär (ret.) Gustav Däniker, Switzerland's most distinguished 'defence intellectual', took part in the campaign from the start and defended the army at the first mass meeting in January 1989. From the beginning, he noticed 'a completely different atmosphere'. The participants were different and so was the tone. There was none of the hatred which poisoned public debate during Vietnam protests or the peace campaigns of the 1970s. Thoughtful people showed up to listen and discuss.[1]

The army leadership had publicly declared that a 75% 'No' vote was the minimum that it would regard as an acceptable outcome. In the event, only Uri, William Tell's home canton, rose to the army's call. Of the Urner, 76.1% voted 'No', followed by Obwalden with 74.4% and Appenzell Inner-Rhoden with 74.1%. The two Basels and Neuchâtel had 'No' votes of under 60% and Jura and Geneva under 50%.[2] There is a wonderful irony in the fact the Swiss army, the very image of the modern, federal state, had its greatest defenders in the remote, mountainous, Roman Catholic cantons, the greatest opponents of that state in the nineteenth century. As Karl Iten has observed, the central Swiss cantons have by 'a kind of division of labour' taken over the function of defenders of traditional Swissness, leaving the lowland, industrialised areas to get on with the modern world.[3]

The fall of the Berlin Wall on 9 November 1989 startled the world and no doubt contributed to the size of the Swiss 'Yes' vote. As the fall of the Bastille in July 1789 seemed to contemporaries, and rightly, a sign of a new age, so the end of the Berlin Wall had the same effect on this generation. The world could never be the same again. Suddenly grand possibilities of peace and reconciliation opened up. There was talk of 'peace dividends' and a 'new world order'. Under these new, happy circumstances, even responsible Swiss citizens might vote to abolish the army. Nobody seriously expected that the army would be abolished but a 'Yes' vote sent a message to the authorities that the voters wanted change. The army chiefs realised that the 35.6% who voted 'Yes' must include many who were not extremists or pacifists and certainly some who had served in the ranks or as officers.

There were domestic causes as well. A variety of scandals had rocked the Swiss government. On 12 January 1989 Frau Elisabeth Kopp, the first woman to serve in the Swiss Federal Council, resigned because, it was alleged, she had tipped off her husband about investigations into his business affairs. A parliamentary investigating committee was looking into rumours about a vast archive of secret files on Swiss citizens suspected of anti-patriotic activities. These files had apparently been collected by the Swiss secret police for years. In the event when the so-called *Fichenaffäre* burst into the open in late 1989, the outrage was so great that an ombudsman and later a special delegate had to be appointed by the Federal Council to deal with granting access to the fiches and with violations of rights. About 144,000 files had been kept but nobody knew who had been kept on file and who had not. In some circles, it became a matter of honour to be a *fichiert*. 350,000 individuals sent in written requests asking the 'Fiche delegate' if files on them had been kept and requesting access.[4] A new word entered the language: *Filz* (literally 'felt' as in 'felt hat') came to symbolise all these scandals. To many Switzerland seemed to be land of secrecy and insider deals. A protest against the system earned the protester a fiche but had no effect on the cosy club of insiders who knew the score. Many of those who voted 'Yes' on 26 November 1989 were voting against *Filz*.

The reaction to the fall of the Berlin Wall and disenchantment with domestic scandals are not phenomena unique to Switzerland, but the Swiss army is. It is a militia based on universal service and as such unlike any other army except that of Israel, which adopted the Swiss model. To attack the Swiss army is to attack the Swiss state and the image of the armed free citizen on which it rests. To attack the army is to attack the *status quo*, for a militia stretches like a tight garment around the shape of the existing social order. To attack the army is to assail the very identity and self-image of the Swiss people. The old folk song puts it well:

> Was bruucht e rächte Schwyzerma
> nes subers Gwehril a der Wand,
> nes heiters Lied fürs Vaterland.
>
> (What does a true Swiss man need?
> A clean little gun on the wall
> And a cheerful song for the Fatherland.)

The Swiss have always been a nation in arms. Switzerland was created in battle, reached its present dimensions by conquest and defended its existence by armed neutrality thereafter. During the great age of Swiss expansion contemporaries saw clearly that the armed free peasant made a formidable fighting machine. The free man fought as no slave could, for only the free could be safely armed. Machiavelli wrote: 'gli Svizzeri sono armatissimi e liberissimi' (the Swiss are most armed and most free). For him and for generations of foreign observers afterwards the connection remained the key to Swiss survival. The Swiss agreed, and even today the free man goes armed to the *Landsgemeinde* in token of his status. The connection between freedom and the gun is enshrined even in the American Bill of Rights. Article 2 states: 'A well regulated militia being necessary to the security of a free state, the right of the people to keep and bear arms shall not be infringed.'

The true Swiss is armed. Popular culture has been saturated with military activities, with rifle competitions, with gun lore, with a certain Alpine bellicosity, with the wrestling, the drinking and the ponderous camaraderie. As Max Frisch says in *Dienstbüchlein*, if you do not know what a true Swiss is (and, interestingly enough, he uses the same term of art as the folk song, the *rechter Schweizer*) you learn about it in the army: 'To feel yourself a true Swiss, you don't have to be a peasant or the son of a peasant but a certain rustic (not rude, of course) manner goes with being a true Swiss, whether you are a lawyer or a dentist or a clerk, at least when you are talking man to man among other true Swiss.'[5] The modern Swiss army still has a vestigial atmosphere which goes back to the unruly crowd of armed,

Plate 26 *Jodlerklub*, Flühli

free peasants who slaughtered the flower of Burgundian chivalry by flailing at them with five-foot pikes.

It is easy to see how the army and the state became synonymous. In a federal union, in a state divided by linguistic, religious, geographical, economic and social distinctions, the army alone united all citizens. It was (and is) the only institution which really transcends the cellular structures of Swiss life. For many young men, the only time they ever meet their co-nationals of a different language, region or creed is in the army. Unity and the universal militia stand and fall together; at least, many Swiss think that. There is therefore some justification for beginning a chapter called 'Identity' with a discussion of the crisis in the army. The dilemmas of the Swiss military establishment have much in common with those in most NATO countries, but they have, as always, features unique to Switzerland. Because Switzerland is like no other European country, its army is like no other European army.

According to Article 18 of the Federal Constitution, 'every Swiss male is subject to military service'. That obligation was absolute and put Switzerland in the bizarre position of being the only civilised country in the world not to recognise conscientious objections. To refuse military service was a criminal offence, punishable under military law by imprisonment. The severity and inflexibility of these provisions had certainly contributed to the 'Yes' vote of November 1989, but the conservative temper of Swiss voters and the deep sense of identity with the army had frustrated all previous attempts to relax these harsh provisions. Now, after the shock of the initiative to abolish the army and the end of the Cold War, the military leadership itself began to rethink its attitudes; indeed it had no choice but to do so or watch its still intact support dwindle. The problem was that the Constitution would need to be amended before real concessions to conscientious objection could be made. Raphael Barras, chief of the military justice section, suggested that a way forward might be to allow military courts to offer alternatives in civil work to jail sentences. On 2 June 1991 the 'sovereign people' accepted the so-called 'Barras bill', to the great relief of government and army, by 55.7% 'Yes' to 44.3% 'No' with only four cantons – oddly enough all French-speaking – saying 'No'.[6] The way was now clear for a constitutional amendment which was approved overwhelmingly by an 82.5% 'Yes' vote on 17 May 1992.[7] A new clause was added to Article 18 which states 'the law provides for alternative civilian service'.

The structure of universal service itself needed rethinking. Until the army reforms of the 1990s, the Swiss conscript entered a militia which would engage him most of his adult life. Between the ages of twenty and thirty-two he was in 'active service'. From thirty-three to forty-two he went into the *Landwehr* (rather like the Territorial Army in the United Kingdom or the National Guard in the USA) and those between the ages of forty-three and fifty served in the *Landsturm*, a second-line reserve. The obligation to serve lasted for thirty years for enlisted men and thirty-five for officers, which gave Switzerland the curious distinction of imposing longer conscription on its citizens than the hated Tsars of Russia had done on their subjects before 1914. The three waves of service and their names went back to ideas first formulated by Scharnhorst and Gneisenau in their attempts between 1806 and 1815 to turn the ramrod automata of the Prussian army into citizen-soldiers. The time had really come to reform and reduce this vast operation. Did Switzerland still need to be able to deploy the second largest land army in Europe? What was the army for? How should it be trained and equipped? What operational objectives should it have?

After 1945, the Swiss general staff had adopted a 'total defensive strategy', known as Swiss general defence. As Marko Milivojević observes, this was

a multi-faceted or holistic strategy . . . one of deterrence or the avoidance of war by convincing an enemy that the cost of invading Switzerland would be far higher than any possible gain.[8]

This strategy, very much the product of the successful experiences of the *réduit national* during the second world war, involved both conventional and nuclear weapons. It led to a vast and expensive programme of civil defence, the compulsory maintenance by home owners of nuclear shelters equipped with stipulated supplies and an increasingly expensive investment in the latest technologies on land and in the air. Even if the Cold War had not ended in 1989, the Swiss armed forces would have had to make ever more painful compromises.

In the aftermath of November 1989, 'reform' became the slogan. The *Ausbildungschef* (the instructor-general, one of the two senior posts in the Swiss army), Korpskommandant Rolf Binder, created a working party under Ständerat Otto Schoch 'to sift through the criticisms expressed against the army and to develop reform suggestions': The working party wanted the army to change its ways: the style of command was to be replaced by cooperation and communication; there was to be less drill, no parades for visiting senior officers, and no 'senseless saluting on arrival and departure'.[9] The working party saw their task as making the army more amenable to civilian expectations, but it had neither the remit nor the personnel to ask the hard question: did Switzerland need an army and, if so, what kind?

Just before the Schoch group reported, the Federal Council issued *Swiss Security Policy in Transition*, known as *Report 90*, the government's formal answer to that very question. It appeared as a

Plate 27 Swiss soldier with equipment

pamphlet addressed to the members of the two chambers of the national parliament but in form and language it sought the attention and ultimately agreement of the citizenry as a whole. This was one of those moments which the Swiss take for granted, but which to the outside observer are extraordinary. How many other European governments ask the public to discuss a defence white paper?

Report 90 asked the hard questions about security. The answers it

Plate 28 Woman army officer giving orders

gave included the new, non-military threats to security – over-population, environmental catastrophe, economic crises – as well as conventional and non-conventional military crises. Neutrality, it declared, 'is not the object of Swiss foreign policy but one among many means to realise foreign political objectives'.[10] It urged a flexible interpretation of the idea of neutrality which would include Swiss participation in UN operations or disaster relief overseas. What it rejected was a fundamental change of structure. 'The form of defence best suited to the present development is the militia . . . military training policy and civilian career development must be better attuned to each other to avoid conflict.'[11]

At the very moment when these new parameters were being considered, the Gulf War broke out. The Swiss army watched with dismay how relatively defenceless even the powerful Israel Defence Force looked against the Iraqi Scud missiles. They studied the rapid deployment tactics used in the desert war and in May 1991 Federal Councillor Kaspar Villiger announced the first results of the rethinking. The Swiss army looked now to rapid deployment and flexibility to fight the small wars erupting under the new world order. Rapidity, skill, professionalism and high technology formed part of the new *Army 95* programme, expected to be in place by 1 January 1995. For all its virtues, the defence analyst of the *Neue Zürcher Zeitung* pointed to a crucial contradiction at the core of the new strategy:

The new Swiss conception and the new Swiss army structure are supposed to permit flexibility. Flexibility presupposes mobility of troops . . . In the light of this can it seriously be argued, as the chief of the general staff has, that our army 'can never be more than a modernised infantry army'? The argument that in spite of substantial cuts the existing preponderance of infantry corresponds to our financial means loses its substance in the light of the recent events and developments.[12]

During the 1990s reforms proceeded rapidly. A new military law was passed on 3 February 1995 and, as punctually as a Swiss timepiece, new structures went into operation. The obligation to serve was shortened to twenty-two years from thirty. An absolute ceiling was set on the number of days any citizen-soldier might be expected to serve in that period. The contrast between the old and the new obligation of service is shown in schematic form in Figure 3.

Officers' training involves months of schooling, admittedly spread out over several years, and training at staff college takes even longer. One general staff officer, the managing director of a successful medium-sized firm, told me that he had never been through anything more gruelling in his life than staff college and that he had several times been on the point of throwing in the sponge.[13]

Every soldier in the Swiss army keeps his equipment at home. This includes uniform, weapon, live ammunition and other supplies. Since he keeps his weapon at home he is legally and financially responsible for its maintenance. The same regulations would apply to a military bicycle and used to apply to the cavalry-man's horse. It may even extend to a military vehicle. The Military Department has no objection if the soldier uses his equipment or means of transportation in his peace-time occupation as long as it is ready when it is needed. This arrangement extends to the main-tenance of specified amounts of food reserves by the supermarkets. It saves a great deal of money. The individual or the firm bears a cost which would otherwise fall on the state. Paperwork by officers, when they are not on active duty, must be done by the officer in his

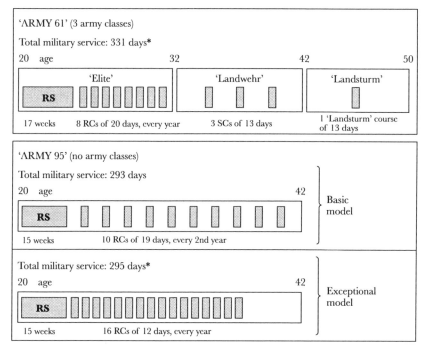

Figure 3 Cycle of military service

private capacity. Large firms which may have a great many high-ranking officers among their senior personnel not uncommonly provide at the company's expense a military secretary whose job it is to do the correspondence of all the officers in the building.

Because the Swiss army reaches so deeply into civil society, it is paradoxically more vulnerable to unrest than a professional army would be. Every citizen serves and forms his own ideas about how good or bad the army is. As social values change, they collide with the army's traditions. The demand for more democracy in society at large catches the Swiss army in an awkward position. In theory, it is perfectly democratic. The professor may be a private and the brick-layer a captain. The social structure of the army is supposed to give men a chance to succeed in one field who have been less successful in others. In practice, no such thing occurs. The general structure of society is faithfully reflected in the army. Hard information on these matters is almost impossible to get. The class structure of the army belongs among the many taboos of public life. In August 1973 the *National-Zeitung* broke ranks and published the civil employments of the officers of Border Division 2, which some radical soldiers had stolen. It will not have changed much in the two decades since these revelations. There were forty-seven directors of firms among the officers, thirty-nine senior employees of large Swiss industrial companies, twenty-nine self-employed, twenty lawyers and accountants, twelve heads and agents of insurance company branches, twelve doctors and chemists, eight senior executives of foreign companies, five directors of employers' and trade associations, four senior police officers, four clerks, and three students. There were, of course, no workers. The firms represented were a *Who's Who* of Swiss business and included: Ciba-Geigy, Esso, Bulova, Lonza, Ebauches, Dubied, Swissair, Swissboring, Nestlé, Landis and Gyr, Holderbank, Hoffmann–La Roche, First National City Bank, the Union Bank, the Swiss Bank Corporation, Crédit Suisse, Volksbank, von Roll, IBM, Honeywell, etc. The authors of the pamphlet concluded simply: 'The bosses in civilian life are the bosses in the army. We are still in the same boat: some row, others steer.'[14]

The first weeks of recruit school are the periods in which the social selection takes place. Cadre NCOs and training officers are always on the look-out for the right sort of chap, and inevitably class and other biases creep in at this point. To be an officer involves a lot of time. A man has to have a long-suffering employer or private means to be able to afford the absences from work. Administrative and technical skills are more likely to be found in recruits from middle-class backgrounds than among working-class conscripts. The problem for the training personnel is to convince likely recruits that the extra time and effort needed to become an officer is worth it. A man can be ordered to accept higher rank, but no commander would try such methods. A much more common device is to point out the practical advantages in civil life which will accrue to those who become officers. Most Swiss know in general terms what the *National-Zeitung* revealed in detail. Swiss officers and Swiss senior executives tend to be the same men. If two equally qualified men apply for a job, and one is and one is not an officer, most Swiss accept that the officer will get it. The argument runs that since Swiss companies know what goes into the making of an officer they tend to prefer someone who has survived that to someone who has not. Disaffected, middle-aged men frequently tell you that they would be at head office, not branch managers, if they had become officers. I know a man who has been litigating with a federal department for years, who is convinced that, had he been an officer, he would have been able to settle the case ages ago.

None of this is surprising but it does shake some myths. The army is not now and never has been perfectly democratic, because Switzerland never was either. We saw in Chapter 2 that even the armed free peasants of William Tell's day recognised the local gentry as their natural leaders. In modern times distinctions between officers and men were rigidly maintained. During the first world war, both the government and the army leadership ignored the severe hardships which long periods of mobilisation imposed on the working classes. During the second world war the army was much less rigid and more egalitarian in temper. Efforts through operation *Heer und Haus* (the army and the home) were made to enlist the full psychological as well as physical support of the home front. Soldiers who lost wages during military service got better compensation. The people saw the need for defence and the *réduit* mentality included everyone. Class distinctions were not obliterated even in the second world war. Max Frisch recalled that his fellow soldiers could not understand how *ein Studierter* was not an officer. His working-class comrades felt his presence in the ranks as slightly improper. Their attitudes to officers, he recalls, were similar. No worker dreamt of becoming an officer. What would he say to officers in the evening in the mess? 'From the workers' point of view officers were genuinely educated or at least well off, hence entitled to lead troops and sleep in beds. They knew how to use foreign words. What they might be worth under fire had nothing to do with it.'[15]

Distinctions of class merged with assumptions about style. The Swiss army, more than any other area of Swiss German life, accepted the primacy of Prussian models during the great days of Imperial Germany. The Swiss German officers borrowed the code of honour and personal style of the aristocratic Junkers and in a fascinating fusion of images the Swiss officer sought to combine the deep respect which the Swiss accord to earned rank, to the

Herr Doktor and *Herr Direktor*, with the Prussian respect for inherited rank, *Exzellenz von und zu X*. Since both models were profoundly authoritarian, the Swiss officer corps absorbed a double dose of values essentially inappropriate to the serene management of a little militia in a bourgeois democracy. The collapse of the Prussian model in the second world war and the erosion of traditional Swiss deference has stripped the officer corps of its code of behaviour at the moment when it needs one most.

A possible alternative to the Germanic models of the past might be the Israeli citizen-soldier of the present. After all, the Israelis consciously adopted Swiss methods and especially mobilisation procedures. The Israeli officer shuttling between desert command and the lecture room comes closer to the Swiss ideal than any other contemporary officer. The Swiss undoubtedly admire and feel close to the Israelis in many ways and are on balance more pro-Israel than any other European country. Still they hesitate to emulate, if that were possible, the turbulent, noisy, shirt-sleeved, egalitarian style of the Israel Defence Force. The spectacle of generals shouting at one another in public forums and being bawled at by hysterical crowds of pushing citizens is not the Swiss way.

Since the Israeli model cannot be transplanted, the Swiss officer corps faces the turbulence of the young dissidents with very little inner confidence. The historic language of command has lost its purchase. The values embedded in words like *Ehre* (honour), *Pflicht* (duty) or *Zucht* (discipline) have evaporated so completely that contemporary young people can hardly make sense of the terms at all. There are no words to use which are common to both sides of the generation gap or which transcend the division in styles of life. *Report 90* summed the problem up by describing it as a 'transformation of values':

The will to self-defence is not as marked as it was. Indifference towards the state is growing. How one is personally affected becomes the standard by which to measure the readiness to engage in public affairs.[16]

The alienation of the young has led to a new problem. Attacks on the undemocratic character of the army carry over to more general attacks on society as a whole. The citizen may well be 'alienated' from civilian society even before he joins the colours. In that moment, the very pervasiveness of the militia system becomes its undoing. With a professional army remote from the populace a

Plate 29 Swiss army generals with Kaiser Wilhelm II

government can do what it likes and commit all sorts of blunders. A citizen army is more vulnerable. It operates, as does the democratic state, on consent.

Yet the difficulties represented by army reform go deeper than simply clashes of style among the generations in Switzerland. Defence and identity go back to the very beginning of Swiss history.

After all, the main purpose of the pact of 1291 was, as the text puts it, 'ut se et sua magis defendere' (to defend themselves and their goods better). For centuries Switzerland defended itself against external threats and internal strife. All Swiss institutions reflect this history of defensiveness, armed neutrality and its militia army particularly so. Some Swiss like to compare the country to the dogged, little hedgehog, a prickly mouthful for the unwary predator.

The fall of the Berlin Wall, the collapse of the Soviet Union, and Austrian accession to the European Union have created a new situation. From 1 January 1995 Switzerland was again surrounded, as in the second world war, but this time by members of the European Union. Designed to resist enemies, Switzerland finds itself encircled by 'friends'. The enemy no longer has a clear profile, and the absence of a definable enemy has unsettled both government and people. This in turn has generated an increasingly nervous sense that Swiss identity has been seriously eroded, that the country is about to disintegrate or simply disappear into the amorphous mass of Europe. The question – is there a 'Swiss identity'? – has suddenly become acute.

The newspapers are full of discussions about Swiss identity: what is it? how did it arise? can it be preserved? When they publicly search their souls in this way, the Swiss begin by assuming that they are not like other European peoples. The central argument of this book is that they are right. There is, or was, a *Sonderfall Schweiz*, a Swiss special case, which emerged from the fusion of geographic factors, the evolution of the micro-economy, the survival of archaic, communal forms, the early commercialisation of meat and milk products, the physical strength of mountaineers, the accumulation of urban wealth, neutrality, the peculiar religious mosaic, the use of direct democratic devices, federalism, communal autonomy, multilingualism, and those unwritten rules of behaviour which lead to concordance and magic formulae, conflict avoidance and tolerance. This specialness makes the Swiss feel both superior and uneasily inferior to other states. By comparison with their more homogeneous neighbours like the French, Germans or Italians, they feel somehow abnormal.

All of them feel 'Swiss' outside Switzerland. As one Swiss friend put it to me, 'Swissness, which is strong in New York, evaporates in the train from Zürich to Solothurn.'[17] Inside the country they disintegrate into all sorts of micro-identities – cantonal such as Basler, Zürcher, Vaudois, Jurassien or regional like the Italian Swiss who divide into *Sottocenerini* and *Sopracenerini* (those who live below and those who live above Monte Ceneri) or ultimately into identities as citizens of one of the 3,000 communes.

Outsiders find this hard to understand. There is something unnatural about a country without a proper national identity. Ever since the French Revolution, nationalists of every colour have attempted to seduce or browbeat the three main Swiss linguistic communities into surrendering their apparently unnatural allegiance to Switzerland. Nowhere is that more true than in the Italian-speaking Canton of Ticino. The Swiss Italian historian, Raffaele Ceschi, cites an anonymous proclamation issued in Milan in 1859 which urged the residents of Ticino to detach themselves from what it called the 'bizarra ed informe federazione elvetica' (the bizarre and shapeless Helvetic Confederation).[18] The fact that Italian Swiss have consistently said 'No' to siren voices from across the border has historical explanations, but such explanations are complicated, not easily expressed in a few words. What remains is the idea that Switzerland is both 'bizarre' and 'shapeless', not natural or organic.

The Swiss react to this by citing their determination to remain Swiss, a determination which finds its verbal representation in the phrase *Willensnation*, a 'nation by will'. In this sense the Swiss see themselves not as a multinational entity but as a fragile set of communities held together by a sort of *volonté générale*. After all, the phrase was invented by Rousseau, who signed his famous work *Du contrat social* simply as 'J. J. Rousseau, citoyen de Genève'.

The idea that Switzerland exists only as long as its citizens will it cannot be dismissed as absurd. The crisis in the army reflects just such a slackening of will. In the passage from *Report 90* cited above, the Federal Council defined the issue by arguing that *Selbstbehauptungswille* (the will to self defence or self-maintenance) had declined. Service in the army requires what they call 'engagement'. The army acts as a shorthand for all other public duties, from the office of secretary of the local political party to service on a *Gemeinderat*, a *Kirchgemeinderat*, the social welfare board, the education board, the committee to manage the local road, the cantonal parliament and even the two chambers of the national parliament, which are not yet fully 'professional'. All these are normally referred to by the term 'militia', that is, the voluntary service by free citizens in the self-determination of their lives.

The will to self-defence is the military equivalent of the will to self-determination in the organisation of personal and communal life. The Federal Council notes with concern that this will has also slackened and with it the tightness of allegiance to the Swiss form of government. Without the engagement of citizens, no democracy, even one as successful as Switzerland, can long survive.

On the other hand, the sheer complexity of modern life leads inexorably to government by full-time professionals. Gradually and reluctantly cantons have accepted that their executive, the *Regierungsrat*, must be full-time and paid. Recent reforms in the national parliament have introduced a more demanding set of standing committees. Attendance in both houses has become more frequent; the volume of business more intimidating. Switzerland exploits its parliamentarians by asking them to serve on endless bodies and boards. As Ständerätin Rosemarie Simmen explained to me, this is particularly the case with women in public life.[19] Swiss unwritten rules require the most important boards, commissions and committees to reflect the spectrum of public life. There must be the right proportion of French, German and Italian Swiss, a balance between Catholic and Protestant, the right number of women, an exact reflection of the party political balance from right to left, employers and trade unionists and so on. A female, Catholic, French-speaking, trade union general secretary, if such a person existed, could spend her days doing nothing but serving on such boards and bodies. Here too, the will to serve the public, 'engagement', must be present.

When Walter Gut became *Fichendelegierte*, it happened in a typically Swiss way. Federal Councillor Arnold Koller, head of the Swiss federal department of justice and police, simply rang up and asked if he would serve. Herr Gut, who had been a member of the Luzern *Regierungsrat* for sixteen years, had served as the head of the equivalent cantonal department and before that had been a state prosecutor. Of course, as he explained to me, if the highest executive office in the land asks for your service, you have to have 'overwhelmingly powerful reasons to say "No"'. There was no contract, indeed, not even a letter to confirm the appointment. Herr Gut went to Bern to do his civic duty.[20]

If public life inside Switzerland depends on this will to serve in order to maintain the state, neutrality and the militia army express that will towards the outside world. Historic Switzerland may be seen as an equilibrium system with 'armed' neutrality as its outer casing. Universal suffrage and universal service in a militia army reinforced each other and erected a protective shell against external threats. That is why mythology focuses on images like William Tell or more recently the heroic resistance to Nazism during the second world war. According to popular mythology, the *réduit national*, fortress Switzerland, convinced Adolf Hitler not to invade the country. However questionable the claim may be as history, it is deeply and widely believed. Hence not to will the continued existence of the army is in a real sense to will the end of historic Swiss identity.

Yet there is another sense in which the Swiss view of themselves as a community of citizens who will the continued existence of the state cannot be right. It is true that Switzerland is not a multinational state but is not a conventional national state either. Its institutions have evolved in a matrix of conflict – religious, ideological, linguistic, economic, social and military – and have turned into systems of concordance and conflict-resolution. The preservation of the autonomy of even the tiniest of authorities gives the system a uniquely 'bottom-up' character, quite unlike the 'top-down' authorities of traditional states like France and Britain. Its complex representative machinery, its magic formulae and multi-member executives, its referenda and initiatives, its jigsaw puzzle of territories, turn the political machinery into an acute and sensitive device for registering, channelling and resolving the movements caused by twitches of the body politic. Identity crises and conflicts, however sharp in one micro-unit of politics, may not be so fierce in the unit next door. Around and through the entire set of structures the values – longevity in service, anonymity, a certain populist cosiness, a general awareness of how things are done according to the 'unwritten rules' – unify behaviour across all the differences. Switzerland is Swiss from Chiasso in the south to Basel in the north, and every visitor feels it the moment he or she crosses the border.

Swiss national identity arises from these shared values and attitudes. A strong rootedness in place marks every Swiss. The former deputy chairman of Ciba-Geigy explained to me that thirty-five years in Basel had not made him less a Zürich man, and a

world-travelling management consultant told me that he is still a
Thurgauer although born and raised in Zürich. Switzerland's long
historic evolution has marked its citizens more deeply than they
imagine. The idea that Switzerland will simply crumble if the
citizens stop willing it to continue is not plausible.

The structures to control and compartmentalise conflict grew
out of the resolution of conflicts within society. Catholic and
Protestant faced each other across the religious trenches. Urban
and rural communities fought for control of politics, as did liberals
and conservatives. There was a near revolution in 1918 when Swiss
socialists tried to mount a general strike and imitate the successful
Bolsheviks. Switzerland escaped none of the disturbing currents
which troubled other European societies. Its 'bottom-up' system of
representation, the confines of tiny, homogeneous units, the cat's-
cradle of overlapping identities, ensured that lines of ideology or
interest rarely coincided. Not all German Swiss were Catholic,
conservative, rural, democrats; only some were. Not all French
Swiss were Protestant, liberal, urban, patricians, though some
were. Not all Italian Swiss were clerical or rural and so on.

Switzerland today faces a double identity crisis. Internally, the
ebbing of commitment to the great ideologies of the twentieth
century, instant communication with the outside world, physical
mobility and the disintegration of the historic 'milieus' have
hollowed out the compartments of Swiss domestic politics. None of
the old structures stands as firmly as in the past because the old
conflicts which those structures redirected have lost power.
Catholic cantons are less Catholic, rural life less rural, trade unions
less solid and so on. The Swiss behave more like their neighbours
because they have become less idiosyncratically Swiss.

On the other hand, Switzerland faces an external identity crisis.
The European Union, which now surrounds it, has begun to develop
into a loose, multinational confederation not unlike what
Switzerland was at an earlier stage. State Secretary Franz Blankart,
who negotiated with the European Union, sees in these
negotiations an irony of history: the long struggle from 1291 to free
the Swiss Confederation from the Holy Roman Empire may end
with Switzerland joining that Empire's unlikely successor, the
European Union.[21]

My guess is that Switzerland will join the European Union. The
sovereign may vote 'No' a few more times but will vote 'Yes' in the

end. Then Switzerland will gradually lose some of its distinctive features as its citizens make their way into European community politics. Nothing lasts forever, and the Helvetic Confederation has no inherent right to permanence. A Confederation which has resisted its enemies for seven hundred years may well surrender to its friends.

Yet if Switzerland loses some of its specialness, it will not lose all. Switzerland is no less 'natural' or 'unnatural' than its neighbours. The Swiss have lived for centuries under a characteristic set of institutions and have run them, as we have seen, in a characteristically Swiss way. These habits and assumptions are deeply etched in the behaviour of all products of that society. Opponents of the army use Swiss German and in so doing absorb those intangible but profound cultural behaviour patterns which create an inner world recognisably Swiss. The European Union will force changes, even if Switzerland stays out. The absolute right of the people to thumb its nose at authority will be limited. The erosion of the cellular structures of Swiss life will continue as the Swiss come to live in Baccini and Oswald's great suburban space, but essential Swissness will remain. The mysterious vitality which seems to glow inside even the tiniest European cultures will ensure that.

CHAPTER 8

Why Switzerland matters

The reader who has followed me this far will not need to be convinced that Switzerland is unusual. He or she may even have begun to find Switzerland interesting. I now want to suggest that what happens in Switzerland matters. Switzerland is not simply another rich, small state in the heart of Europe. It is the living expression of a set of ideas, which may be summed up: although the will of the majority makes law and constitutes the only true sovereign authority, the minorities, however small, have inalienable rights. The dilemma of majority will and minority rights can be overcome by the ingenuity of men. There is nothing startling or very new about these ideas, but it is striking how little they are observed. The Swiss believe that there will always be a political compromise or bit of constitutional machinery which will get round a given difficulty, whether it is the rights of the Jurassiens or conscientious objectors. That the Jurassiens have rights seems to them so obvious that they hardly need to emphasise it. They also believe that no machinery is sacred. The Constitution of 1848 underwent total revision in 1874, and, as we saw in Chapter 3, it is being revised again today. When something does not work, the Swiss tinker with it for a while, sometimes even for decades, and, if it cannot be got working, they scrap it.

The United States pays a heavy price for neglecting the need for constitutional change. The Constitution of 1787 has been turned into a sacred piece of parchment, above politics and beyond the reach of men. Jefferson who had doubts about the document wanted something less remote. He refused to be alarmed in the 1780s by the turbulence of the mob. 'A little rebellion now and then is a good thing, and as necessary in the political world as storms in the physical', he wrote. In his *Notes on the State of Virginia* of 1784 he argued that since the people were the only legitimate fountain of power, government should return to it whenever necessary to remodel the pieces of the constitutional apparatus. Unfortunately, his friend Madison, and many other advocates of the new constitution, had no such optimism. Madison put the opposite view in *The Federalist Papers*, No. 49: 'It may be considered as an objection inherent in the principle that as every appeal to the people would carry an implication of some defect in the government, frequent appeals would, in great measure, deprive the government of that veneration which time bestows on everything and without which perhaps the wisest and freest governments would not possess the requisite stability.'

Against Madison, the Swiss in their lumpish, practical way assert the defectiveness of all government at all times, and they are right to do so. Government must always be defective by precisely that gap in time which separates the date of the creation of a given set of institutions from the present moment. The United States now struggles to operate within the dusty mechanisms of an antique. Checks and balances, wheels and pulleys, designed to mesh for an agrarian, decentralised and thinly settled federation seize up under the pressure of an industrial, cosmopolitan, world empire. The prospect for the future is unpleasant. Madison was certainly not wrong about the other issue: the creation of stability. Time does bestow a lustre on institutions which helps to make them permanent, but real stability is the cause of that lustre, not the other way round. If the foundations are stable, the constitutions will last. Real stability comes from below.

English readers may feel that these lessons, however relevant to their ill-advised American cousins foolish enough to write things down, need have no application in Great Britain. I think they would be wrong. Take the hallowed House of Commons. Is it today more than an empty debating chamber in which a very large number of restless men and women play at political games, while real decisions are made elsewhere? The only function which parliament now performs is to select the people who will eventually be ministers and to ratify the decisions of those who already are. The nominating function is an important one. The selection of leadership within the parliamentary party provides a useful and flexible device for ensuring that those selected can govern with the full support of the rank and file. By rewarding loyalty with promotion and punishing independence with banishment to the darker back benches, it ensures that the majority rarely crumbles and that decisions once taken are suitably rubber-stamped. The average citizen (or his or her MP for that matter) has very little chance to find out what is going on and practically no chance to alter it. In Great Britain, the people get not the government they deserve but what the senior civil service and front bench of the governing party think they ought to have. Imagine what would happen if the Swiss initiative and referendum were regularly used in the United Kingdom, and not just to evade divisions within the governing parties. Would capital punishment have been abolished? Would the poll tax have become law? Would water and gas have been privatised? Would the UK have signed the Maastricht Treaty? Suppose the answer to all these had been 'No'. How would you, my English reader, feel about such outcomes? I suspect that, depending on political preference, you would settle for a system without such eruptions of popular will. The truth is that the United Kingdom is no democracy and the majority of voters from left to right do not want it to be. They share, in secret, Alexander Hamilton's belief that 'your people, Sir, are a great beast'.

The Swiss have always operated on a different premise. The people, they think, are themselves. The ancient Fundamental Law of Canton Schwyz recognised 'that the May *Landsgemeinde* is the greatest power and prince of the land and may without condition do and undo, and whoever denies this and asserts that the *Landsgemeinde* be not the greatest power nor the prince of the land and that it may not do and undo without condition is proscribed. Let a price of one hundred ducats be set on his head.'

The man who denies the sovereignty of the community is no member of it. He is proscribed, outlawed and subject to a severe penalty. Harsh certainly but utterly democratic. The community makes and unmakes laws, and there is no law outside it. The Swiss cannot imagine that the people should not have a say on virtually everything. The results are often tiresome, obstructive or even reactionary, but not always. We have seen examples both of stubborn truculence and enlightened good sense. The people turn down one set of proposals but vote for the revised packet later.

I am not so foolish as to set one society up to be imitated by another. The reasons why the Swiss trust the people and the British do not go deep into the very different histories of the two societies. The US Constitution has ossified because the USA has developed in its own special way. The illusions of the eighteenth-century *illuminati* that one could write a constitution for one state which would do quite well in another have long since been shattered. Yet the study of Switzerland has its uses. Because the Swiss are so different, they serve as a mirror in which we see our own assumptions more clearly. For example, Switzerland reminds us of the reality of frontiers and the national state. The Swiss nation state is very present and its influence can be seen in the astonishing 'Swissness' of every part of the country, regardless of language, religion, geography or economic features. Where a political frontier has existed for any length of time, culture develops differently on either side of it. What was once an imperceptible grading of one region into another becomes an absolutely basic difference of kind. I can illustrate this by an example of a frontier in Switzerland. One Sunday in 1972 I took the little local train from Lugano to Ponte Tresa on the Italian–Swiss border. The train rattled along the sun-drenched, manicured Val d'Agno through silent, deserted villages. The streets of the Swiss Ponte Tresa were also absolutely empty, save for the steady stream of traffic pouring across the frontier. The heavily barred windows of the banks and jewellery shops glittered respectably in the hot Italian sun. I walked the bridge crossing the Tresa, and found myself in the cacophony of Ponte Tresa (Italy). The streets were jammed with noisy, jostling people. I bought a newspaper and sat for half an hour in an overcrowded sidewalk café gulping down great draughts of bad news: strikes, scandals, murders, kidnappings, governmental and financial collapse, speculation against the lira, the usual disastrous record of daily life in the Republic of Italy. I browsed in a bookshop and thumbed through self-serving accounts by fascist field officers of their role in the Africa Campaign and paperback histories of the battles of the first world war. The books were awful but alive, the newspapers shocking but engrossing. By contrast the *Corriere del Ticino* or the *Giornale del Popolo*, the two main Italian Swiss papers on sale on the other bank of the river, had no news in them: a fire in Mendrisio, an exhibition of modern painting in Bellinzona, the problems of the new cantonal library in Lugano. There was no scrap of evidence in any Italian shop of the presence of that Switzerland three hundred yards away. The *New York Herald Tribune* was on sale at the kiosks, but not Swiss papers.

As I crossed back into Switzerland where the plumbing works and the trains run to time, I began to reflect on the mystery of frontiers. The little railway stations with the *Jugendstil* ornaments in wrought iron could have been anywhere in the Germanic world. The Ticinese railwaymen belong to the same stock as the men of the Varesotto on the other bank, but they look different, trimmer, more reserved. Swiss Italians do not behave in public like Italians. On a hot, starry southern evening I went to watch F.C. Lugano play La Chaux-de-Fonds in the Swiss First Division, a very tense game in a beautiful, tropical stadium. The crowd were as docile and quiet as they used to be at Wimbledon. There is more passion, Latin temperament and violence at Stockport County v. Doncaster Rovers than there was in that apparently 'Italian' stadium.

The Swiss Italians and French are Swiss because they live on one side of a frontier, not because they belong to a different people or even, on one level, to a different culture from the people on the other side. Over time, the political institutions, laws, economic arrangements, educational processes, social structures on one side have transformed the inhabitants. They become, as Denis de Rougemont noticed about the Swiss French, part of a Germanic community by a kind of osmosis. The smallest artifacts of daily life, doors, window frames, coins, pencils, street signs, price tags in shops began to 'look' Swiss, as the invisible walls of tariffs and customs barriers gradually created a national market. Swiss towns look Swiss because for so many years all architects were either trained at, or influenced by, the Eidgenössische Technische Hochschule in Zürich. A small regulation, such as the one which required Swiss architects to train in Switzerland if they wished to practise, created the uniformity of townscape which makes its own subtle but very real contribution to the national community. As long as the effective frontier is that which divides members of the European Union from each other, there will be no united European state. As that frontier gradually disappears, as it did in Swiss history, an imperceptible European atmosphere will emerge.

Switzerland matters, because it is genuinely sceptical about the European Union. It doubts whether Brussels and its authoritarian, centralist, francophone, bureaucracy will govern the country better than its own democracy. The chances are that it will not. The Swiss oppose the 'top-down' *dirigisme* of the European Union and offer in its place the 'bottom-up' democracy of the *Gemeindeautonomie*, the self-governing village. 'People power' works in Switzerland. The

Swiss get the government they deserve, good and hard, but, if they do not like it, they can change it. That example offers Europe an alternative to the swollen, self-perpetuating bureaucracy of Brussels.

The existing model of the European Union has failed. The new members have made it more difficult than ever to govern Europe as if it were France. It will be necessary very soon to learn to govern Europe as if it were Switzerland. The European Union must loosen its grip, democratise its decision-making and decentralise its institutions. The more it moves to a looser union the more like Switzerland it will become.

Finally Switzerland by its very differences from the European norm reminds us how contingent and limited our certainties are. The words we use are terrible oversimplifications. What is a language? What is a state? What is a people? What is an economy? Sometimes we are inclined to the view that we know the answers. When that happens, we ought to think about Switzerland for a moment. Switzerland has survived as the 'Europe that did not happen', the Europe which flourished without the national state and without strong central government. It gives us an alternative way of seeing ourselves. Why Switzerland? Because it shows us by reflection who we are.

Appendix: *How to vote for the lower house of parliament* (Nationalrat) *in Switzerland*

The information and examples given in this Appendix are based on the official guide to voting, *Die Politischen Rechte der Schweizerin und des Schweizers* (Bundeskanzlei, Bern, 1971). I am grateful to the Federal Chancellor for permission to reproduce the examples.

Every canton and half-canton makes up a constituency for the elections to the *Nationalrat*. Registered voters have as many members to elect as their canton or half-canton is entitled to in proportion to the population. Some cantons have only one member because of the size of their populations while others may have several. Single-member cantons (Uri, Obwalden, Nidwalden, Glarus and Appenzell I.-R.) elect members by simple majority. In multi-member cantons the election is based on proportional representation based on the procedures described in Chapter 3 (pp. 75–7). After the number of seats to which each party is entitled has been calculated, the members themselves who had the highest number of votes on their party's list are elected.

Each party which wishes to take part in an election submits a list of candidates to each voter, the so-called 'party list', which contains a number of candidates not exceeding the number of members for that canton. The electoral authorities also provide voters with a blank list as well, which contains as many spaces as there are members to elect. The voter can use the prepared party list or the blank list. Below are some examples of the possibilities open to a voter in a canton with seven *Nationalrat* members.

Parties A and B have made full use of the lists by nominating seven candidates while Party C has chosen to nominate four only. A voter is free to fill out the remaining spaces on that list or not, as he or she chooses.

PARTEI A	PARTEI B	PARTEI C	LISTE: ....
Hans B.	Arnold A.	Rudolf B.	1. ....
Trudi D.	Emil F.	Erwin G.	2. ....
Fritz E.	Marie H.	Eva H.	3. ....
Rolf J.	François K.	Andreas L.	4. ....
Peter M.	Karl M.		5. ....
Urs M.	Therese P.		6. ....
Thomas S.	Walter S.		7. ....

IF YOU USE A PARTY LIST

You have a variety of possibilities open to you: you can put a straight party list into the ballot box.

PARTEI A
Hans B.
Trudi D.
Fritz E.
Rolf J.
Peter M.
Urs M.
Thomas S.

If a voter puts Party A's list into the box, Party A gets *seven party votes* and each individual candidate gets *one candidate vote*.

You can strike out the name of any candidate you do not want to vote for on Party A's list.

PARTEI A
Hans B.
Trudi D.
~~Fritz E.~~
Rolf J.
Peter M.
Urs M.
Thomas S.

The candidate omitted (Fritz E.) gets *no candidate votes*, while the others get one each.

The party still gets *seven party votes*, even though you have crossed out one name, because you have used a party ballot.

You can cross out several names on the list.

Party A still gets *seven party votes*, but only those candidates whose names appear get a *candidate vote*.

'CUMULATION'

If you want to give a particular candidate more chance of being elected, you can *cumulate*, that is, put him or her down *twice*. A name which is already on the list will be repeated.

PARTEI A
Hans B.
Trudi D.
Fritz E.
Rolf J.
~~Peter M.~~ *Rolf J.*
Urs M.
Thomas S.

The candidate whom the voter has so preferred is *cumulated*. He gets *two candidate* votes (i.e. Rolf J. in the example).

The candidate whom the voter does not want to see elected is crossed out and gets *no candidate votes* (i.e. Peter M.).

Party A gets *seven party votes*.

No name may be written three times. If it is, the third vote will not be counted.

If empty spaces exist on the list, you can cumulate without crossing out anybody, as in the case of Party C.

Warning: Only names which appear on a list can be written in, and, to be valid, a list must show at least one name on it.

'PANACHAGE'

You can also vote for candidates of other parties by altering your party list to include them, as in the examples below. This process is called *panachage*. The altered party list will only yield as many party votes as there are candidates of that party still on the list. Your votes for candidates transferred from other lists will be added to the number of party votes of the parties to which they belong. There are several options:

(a) Take one or more candidates from another party's list and put them on the list of your own party by crossing out some of the printed names. In the example given, Party A gets *five party votes* and surrenders one to each of the other parties. All seven names on the Party A list get *candidate votes*.

PARTEI B	PARTEI A	PARTEI C
Arnold A.	Hans B.	Rudolf B.
Emil F.	~~Trudi D.~~ *Arnold A.*	Erwin G.
Marie H.	Fritz E.	Eva H.
François K.	Rolf J.	Andreas L.
Karl M.	~~Peter M.~~ *Eva H.*	
Therese P.	Urs M.	
Walter S.	Thomas S.	

(b) Take candidates from other lists and *cumulate* them, as in the example below:

PARTEI B	PARTEI A	PARTEI C
Arnold A.	~~Hans B.~~ *Emil F.*	Rudolf B.
Emil F.	~~Trudi D.~~ *Emil F.*	Erwin G.
Marie H.	Fritz E.	Eva H.
François K.	~~Rolf J.~~ *Andreas L.*	Andreas L.
Therese P.	Peter M.	
Walter S.	~~Urs M.~~ *Andreas L.*	
	Thomas S.	

In this example, Party A only gets *three party votes*, losing two each to Party B and Party C; Emil F. and Andreas L. get *two candidate votes* each, while Fritz E., Peter M. and Thomas S. get one.

IF YOU USE A BLANK LIST

You will find that there are as many spaces as there are vacant seats to be filled and that there is also space for the party label. You need not place anything in the place for the party's name. If you do not, no party gets credit for any blank spaces you choose to leave, as in the case below:

LISTE: ....
Karl M.

In this case Karl M. gets *one candidate vote* and his party *one party vote*. The other six spaces do not count.

You can put several candidates down who are taken from different lists (A and C):

LISTE: ....
Erwin G.
Eva H.
Hans B.

In this case each of the candidates written in gets *one candidate vote* and brings the party to which he or she belongs a *party vote* as well. Party C gets *two votes* (Erwin G. and Eva H.) while Party A gets *one vote* (Hans B.). The four blank spaces do not count.

You can write in the names of candidates you take from other lists once or twice (i.e. you can *cumulate* them). Below you will find an example:

LISTE: ....
Hans B.
Hans B.
Arnold A.
Eva H.
Eva H.

Candidate Hans B. (from List A) and Eva H. (from List C) get *two candidate votes* each, while Arnold A. (from List B) gets *one*. Parties A and C get *two party votes* each and Party B *one*. The two blank spaces do not count.

You may, of course, use all the spaces in this way and thus lose no chance to vote for a person or party.

If you choose to fill in the blank space at the top, you guarantee that any blank spaces not given to candidates will count toward the total number of party votes of the party of your choice. You still have the same possibilities of writing in the names of candidates from other lists as if you had not designated a particular party. You may write in the names of candidates you choose to *cumulate* as well. In the example below, you designate your ballot as a party list but take names from other parties:

LISTE:
Partei B
Arnold A.
Emil F.
Trudi D.
Rudolf B.
Rudolf B.

Here you write the names of two candidates from Party B, two candidates from other parties, one of whom you *cumulate*. The reckoning works out as follows: Arnold A., Emil F., and Trudi D., get *one candidate vote* each, and Rudolf B. gets *two*.

For the parties the result is:

Party A: 1 party vote (Trudi D.)
Party C: 2 party votes (Rudolf B.)
Party B: 4 party votes of which
          1 is from Arnold A.
          1 is from Emil F.
          2 are from 2 blank spaces

WHO MAY VOTE?

1. Every Swiss citizen, male or female, who has reached his or her twentieth birthday and who, according to the laws of the canton in which he or she resides has not been deprived of his civil rights, may vote.

2. To vote a registration card is required. In some cantons this may be issued for a long period of time; in others it will be issued before each election.

3. The right to vote is exercised where one lives regardless of the place where one is specifically enrolled as a citizen (*Ortsbürger*).

4. In contrast to the regulations in some cantonal elections, no deputy may cast your vote in a federal election.

Notes

1. WHY SWITZERLAND?

1 Boswell's *Life of Johnson*, ed. R. W. Chapman (Oxford 1970), p. 113.
2 *Statistisches Jahrbuch der Schweiz 1973* (Bern, 1973), 'Arbeitstreitigkeiten', p. 319; *Die Volkswirtschaft* (Bern, February 1975), p. 64; *Statistisches Jahrbuch der Schweiz 1995* (Bern, 1995), Table 3.21, p. 110.
3 Ibid., Table 16.1, p. 352.
4 F. R. Allemann, *25 mal die Schweiz* (Munich, 1965), p. 547.
5 Urs Altermatt, *Der Weg der Schweizer Katholiken ins Ghetto* (Zürich and Einsiedeln, 1972), p. 21.
6 Quoted in Edgar Bonjour, *Geschichte der schweizerischen Neutralität*, 6 vols. (Basel, 1965–71), Vol. I, p. 133.
7 Edgar Bonjour, *Die Gründung des schweizerischen Bundesstaates* (Basel, 1948), Part II, Doc. 8, pp. 206–7.
8 Boswell's *Life*, p. 112.

2. HISTORY

1 François de Capitani, Ch. 5, 'Beharren und Umsturz (1648–1815)', in *Geschichte der Schweiz und der Schweizer* (Basel, 1983), Vol. II, pp. 164–7. This remarkable 'new' history of Switzerland is also available in French and Italian.
2 Georg Thürer, *St Galler Geschichte. Aufklärung bis Gegenwart* (St Gallen, 1972), Vol. II, p. 107.
3 François de Capitani, 'Beharren', pp. 168–70.
4 F. R. Allemann, *25 mal die Schweiz* (Munich, 1965), pp. 572–3.
5 Francesco Quirici, *Lineamenti di storia ticinese e svizzera* (Bellinzona and Lugano, 1969), pp. 117–19.
6 Cited in Hans Kohn, *Nationalism and Liberty: The Swiss Example* (London, 1956), pp. 81–2.
7 Giovanni Bonalumi, *La giovane Àdula (1912–1920)* (Scrittori della Svizzera Italiana, XIII) (Chiasso, 1970), pp. 202–3.
8 Kurt Spillmann, 'Zwingli und die zürcherische Politik gegenüber der

Abtei St Gallen', *Mitteilungen zur vaterländischen Geschichte des Kantons St Gallen*, 44, 1965, p. 16, n. 30.

9 Perry Anderson, *Passages from Antiquity to Feudalism* (London, 1974), p. 203, n. 15.

10 Jean-François Bergier, *Guillaume Tell* (Paris, 1988), p. 11. For a general survey of the new writing cf. *Geschichtsforschung in der Schweiz. Bilanz und Perspektiven – 1991*, ed. Boris Schneider and Francis Python (Basel, 1992).

11 Werner Meyer, '700 Jahre Schweiz im Wandel', *Schweizerische Zeitschrift für Geschichte* (abbreviated hereafter as *SZG*), 44, 1994, No. 3, pp. 314–15.

12 Hans-Conrad Peyer, 'Wurde die Eidgenossenschaft 1291 gegründet?', *Neue Zürcher Zeitung* (abbreviated hereafter as *NZZ*), 4 January 1991, pp. 29–30.

13 Olivier Pavillon, 'Du débat à l'anathème. A propos de l'exposition "Nos ancêtres les Waldstaetten. La Suisse centrale au XIIIe siècle. Mythes et histoire"', *SZG*, 44, 1994, No. 3, pp. 311–14.

14 Schiller to Körner, 9 September 1802, *Schillers Werke* (Frankfurt/Main, 1966), Vol. II, ed. Hans Mayer, p. 570.

15 E. L. Stahl, *Friedrich Schiller's Drama Theory and Practice* (Oxford, 1954), p. 146.

16 Guy P. Marchal, 'Die "alpine Gesellschaft"', in *Geschichte der Schweiz*, Vol. I, pp. 151–4.

17 Hans-Conrad Peyer, 'Frühes und Hohes Mittelalter. Die Entstehung der Eidgenossenschaft', *Handbuch der Schweizer Geschichte* (Zürich, 1972), Vol. I, pp. 169–70.

18 Adolf Gasser, *Geschichte der Volksfreiheit*, 2nd edn (Aarau, 1947), pp. 104–6.

19 Walter Müller, 'Die Öffnungen der Fürstabtei St Gallen', *Mitteilungen zur vaterländischen Geschichte*, 43, 1964, p. 50.

20 Perry Anderson, *Passages*, p. 191.

21 Hans-Conrad Peyer, 'Frühes Mittelalter', pp. 202–3. Jean-François Bergier, *Guillaume Tell*, pp. 207–31.

22 Perry Anderson, *Passages*, p. 202.

23 Leonhardt von Muralt, 'Renaissance und Reformation', *Handbuch*, Vol. I, p. 395. Cf. Anselm Zurfluh, *Un monde contre le changement. Une culture au coeur des Alpes. Uri en Suisse* (Paris, 1993), pp. 153–4.

24 Hans-Conrad Peyer, 'Frühes Mittelalter', p. 201 and Jean-François Bergier, *Guillaume Tell*, pp. 323–6.

25 Perry Anderson, *Passages*, p. 153.

26 Jean-François Bergier, *Guillaume Tell*, p. 334.

27 Text in the translation of G. Bohnenblust, *Schweizer Brevier* (Bern, 1972), p. 89.

28 Walter Ullmann, 'Zur Entwicklung des Souveränitätsbegriff im Spätmittelalter', in *Festschrift für Nikolaus Grass*, 2 vols. (Innsbruck, 1974/5), Vol. I, p. 22.

29 Benjamin Barber, *The Death of Communal Liberty. A History of Freedom in a Swiss Mountain Canton* (Princeton, N.J., 1973), p. 92.

30 Walter Schaufelberger, *Der Wettkampf in der alten Eidgenossenschaft. Zur Kulturgeschichte des Sports vom 13. bis ins 18. Jahrhundert* (Bern, 1972), pp. 62–3; Guy P. Marchal, 'Die "alpine Gesellschaft"', p. 153.

31 Nicholas Morard, 'Auf der Höhe der Macht', *Geschichte der Schweiz*, Vol. I, p. 307.

32 Perry Anderson, *Passages*, pp. 197–205 for a brilliant analysis of the elements of the general crisis of the fourteenth century.

33 Georg Thürer, *St Galler Geschichte*, Vol. II, p. 27.

34 Benjamin Barber, *The Death of Communal Liberty*, pp. 34–6.

35 Hans-Conrad Peyer, 'Frühes Mittelalter', p. 222.

36 For a vivid account of popular pressure to maintain the *Eidgenossenschaft* as more than just a military alliance at the time of the *Sempacherbrief*, Bernhard Stettler, 'Der Sempacher Brief von 1393 – ein verkanntes Dokument aus der älteren Schweizer Geschichte', *SZG*, 35, 1985, No. 1.

37 Ibid., p. 12.

38 Jean-François Bergier, *Naissance et croissance de la Suisse industrielle* (Bern, 1974), pp. 28–9.

39 Georg Thürer, *St Galler Geschichte*, Vol. II, p. 26.

40 Leonhardt von Muralt, 'Renaissance und Reformation', *Handbuch*, Vol. I, p. 398.

41 Giuseppe Chiesi, 'Venire cum equis ad partes Lombardie. Mercanti confederati alle fiere prealpine nella seconda metà del XV secolo', *SZG*, 44, 1994, No. 3, pp. 254–5.

42 Maurice de Tribolet, 'Le Comte de Neuchâtel, l'empire et le modèle confédéré au XVe siècle: aspects institutionnels', *SZG*, 44, 1994, No. 3, p. 243.

43 Bernhard Stettler, 'Reichsreform und werdende Eidgenossenschaft', *SZG*, 44, 1994, No. 3, p. 208.

44 Leonhardt von Muralt, 'Renaissance und Reformation', *Handbuch*, Vol. I, p. 408.

45 Peter Blickle, 'Markstein der Schweizer Geschichte', a review of Ernst Walder, *Das Stanser Verkommnis* (Beiträge zur Geschichte Nidwaldens Heft 44), Stans, 1994 in *NZZ*, 24 April 1995, p. 26.

46 For an analysis of the military failure and its political roots, Walter Schaufelberger, *Marignano. Strukturelle Grenzen eidgenössischer Militärmacht zwischen Mittelalter und Neuzeit* (Frauenfeld, 1993).

47 Kurt Spillmann, 'Zwingli', pp. 77–8.

48 Cited in Edgar Bonjour, *Geschichte der schweizerischen Neutralität*, 6 vols. (Basel, 1965–71), Vol. I, p. 25.

49 Cited in H. Nabholz *et al.*, *Geschichte der Schweiz* (Zürich, 1932), Vol. II, p. 6.

50 William L. Shirer, *Berlin Diary* (New York, 1941), p. 234.

51 Carl Spitteler, *Unser Schweizer Standpunkt* (Zürich, 1915), p. 21.

52 The 1990s turned out to be an uncomfortable decade for Swiss self-definition. 1991 marked the 700th anniversary of the signing of the original *Bundesbrief*. The various fiftieth anniversaries of events during the second world war revived some episodes which many Swiss would prefer to forget, and 1998 became an anniversary nightmare: the three hundred and fiftieth of the Peace of Westphalia, the two hundredth of the establishment of the Helvetic Republic and the one hundred and fiftieth of the establishment of the modern, federal state in 1848. In June 1995 the lower house of parliament, the *Nationalrat*, debated whether all three of the events, 1648, 1798 and 1848 should be remembered and how. After considerable discussion the house voted to concentrate on 1848, to subordinate 1798 to that concentration and to ignore 1648. See *NZZ*, 10/11 June 1995, pp. 17–18 and Franz Egger, 'Johann Rudolf Wettstein – ein erfolgreicher Unterhändler der Schweiz', *NZZ*, 30 March 1995, p. 27.

53 For an examination of the fall in prices after 1648, Walter Bodmer, 'Die Bewegungen einiger Lebensmittelpreise in Zug zwischen 1610 und 1821 verglichen mit denjenigen in Luzern und Zürich', *SZG*, 34, 1984, No. 4, pp. 454 ff.

54 Perry Anderson, *Lineages of the Absolutist State* (London, 1974), p. 20.

55 Ibid., p. 425.

56 David Lasserre, *Etapes du fédéralisme* (German ed. trans. by A. Gasser) (Zürich, 1963), p. 102.

57 Abraham Stanyan, *An Account of Switzerland* (London, 1714), p. 144.

58 On Geneva see Angela C. Bennett, 'Continuity and Conflict: the Struggle for Political Rights in Eighteenth-century Geneva' (University of Kent, Ph.D., 1995) and Rudolf Braun, *Das ausgehende Ancien Régime in der Schweiz* (Göttingen and Zürich, 1984), pp. 114–22.

59 Rudolf Braun, *Das ausgehende Ancien Régime*, pp. 34 and 45–6 and Charles Hurni, 'Vom Bauernkrieg bis zum Untergang der alten Eidgenossenschaft', in *Flühli-Sörenberg 1836–1986* (Gemeinde Flühli, 1986), pp. 20–3. Hurni points out that in 1784 in the Entlebuch district of Luzern 313 out of a male population of 3,707 had been forced to emigrate.

60 Rudolf Braun, *Das ausgehende Ancien Régime*, pp. 125 ff.

61 Walter Bodmer, 'Die Bewegungen einiger Lebensmittelpreise', pp. 461–2.

62 Georg Thürer, *St Galler Geschichte*, Vol. ii, p. 212.

63 François de Capitani uses diagrams in his chapter on politics in the old regime to illustrate the workings of these complex machines. François de Capitani, 'Beharren', pp. 130–3.

64 R. R. Palmer, *The Age of the Democratic Revolution*, 2 vols. (Princeton, N.J., 1959 and 1964), Vol. i, p. 128. Angela Bennett argues that the lost rights of the general assembly of the citizens of Geneva played a greater part in the ideology behind the unrest than general

democratic ideas as argued by Palmer. Cf. Angela C. Bennett, 'Continuity and Conflict', chs. 7–9.

65 Alfred Stoecklin, 'Constantin Siegwart-Müller. Ein Übergang vom liberalen zum ultramontanen Katholizismus', *SZG*, 39, 1989, No. 1, pp. 15–17, and *Ökumenische Kirchengeschichte der Schweiz*, ed. Lukas Vischer, Lukas Schenker and Rudolf Dellsperger (Fribourg, 1994), p. 224 and p. 247.

66 Edgar Bonjour, *Die Gründung des schweizerischen Bundesstaates* (Basel, 1948), Part II, Doc. 4, p. 196.

67 Ibid., Doc. 20, p. 246.

68 Stoecklin, 'Constantin Siegwart-Müller', pp. 18–19 and Georges Andrey, 'Auf der Suche nach dem neuen Staat (1798–1848)', in *Geschichte der Schweiz und der Schweizer*, Vol. II, pp. 250–7.

69 J. H. Plumb, *The Growth of Political Stability in England, 1675–1725* (London, 1967), pp. xvi–xvii.

70 *Briefwechsel Philipp Anton von Segesser (1817–1888)*, ed. Victor Conzemius (Zürich and Fribourg, 1983–95), Vol. I, p. 494.

71 A. Lawrence Lowell, *Governments and Parties in Continental Europe*, 2 vols. (Cambridge, Mass., 1896), Vol. II, p. 241.

72 Georg Thürer, *Free and Swiss. The Story of Switzerland* (London, 1970), p. 114.

73 *Briefwechsel Philipp Anton von Segesser*, Vol. I, p. xiii.

74 Ibid., Vol. IV, pp. 215–16.

75 Thomas Gauly, *Katholiken. Machtanspruch und Machtverlust* (Bonn, 1991), p. 181.

76 Urs Altermatt, *Katholizismus und Moderne. Zur Sozial- und Mentalitätsgeschichte der Schweizer Katholiken im 19. und 20. Jahrhundert* (Zürich, 1989), p. 146. See also Urs Altermatt, *Der Weg der Schweizer Katholiken ins Ghetto* (Zürich and Einsiedeln, 1972).

77 *Briefwechsel von Segesser*, Vol. I, p. 494.

78 *Bundesverfassung der Schweizerischen Eidgenossenschaft* (of 29 May 1874), Part I, Article 3.

79 Cavour to G. Durando, 6 June 1860, in Denis Mack Smith, *Cavour and Garibaldi* (Cambridge, 1954), p. 29.

80 André Allaz, *L'Helvétisme: péril national* (Fribourg, 1914), p. 5. There has been a revival of interest in this group of French-speaking intellectuals. Two studies have appeared which explore in depth their relations as a coterie and place in politics: Alain Clavien, *Les Helvétistes. Intellectuels et politique en Suisse romande au début du siècle* (Lausanne, 1993) and Aram Mattioli, *Zwischen Demokratie und totalitärer Diktatur. Gonzague de Reynold und die Tradition der autoritären Rechten in der Schweiz* (Zürich, 1994). Closer examination does not make these figures more attractive.

81 Carl Spitteler, *Kritische Schriften*, ed. Werner Stauffacher (Zürich, 1965), p. 179.

82 Carlo Salvioni, 'Le condizioni della cultura italiana nel cantone Ticino', 25 April 1914, in G. Bonalumi, *L'Àdula*, p. 211.

83 Romberg to Bethmann Hollweg in E. Bonjour, *Neutralität*, Vol. II, p. 590.

84 Bundesrat Karl Scheurer, *Tagebücher 1914–1929*, ed. Hermann Böschenstein (Bern, 1971), p. 50.

85 Ibid., p. 150.

86 Paul Stauffer, 'Die Affäre Hoffmann/Grimm', *Schweizer Monatshefte*, Supplement 1, 1973/74, p. 22. See also E. Bonjour, *Neutralität*, Vol. II, pp. 613 ff.

87 Willi Gautschi, *Der Landesstreik 1918* (Zürich and Einsiedeln, 1968), p. 32.

88 Erich Gruner, *Die Parteien in der Schweiz* (Bern, 1969), p. 183 and Table 10, pp. 184–5.

89 Paul Bairoch uses different definitions but arrives at the same conclusion. He points to this 'sous-urbanisation' as a characteristic feature of Swiss industrialisation. Whereas in terms of the level of industrialisation per inhabitant, Switzerland in 1913 ranked third in Europe behind Britain and Belgium, in terms of urbanisation Switzerland ranked seventh. Paul Bairoch, 'L'Economie suisse dans le contexte européen: 1913–1939', *SZG*, 34, 1984, No. 4, p. 471 and Tables 1 and 8.

90 *Statistisches Jahrbuch der Schweiz 1995* (Bern, 1995), Table 3.6, p. 102 and Table 3.25, p. 112.

91 Willi Gautschi, *Landesstreik*, p. 108.

92 Hans Ulrich Jost provides vivid detail of the 'white' reaction to the 'red' strike and the extreme bitterness which followed the end of it in *Geschichte der Schweiz*, Vol. III, pp. 138–40.

93 Ibid., p. 142.

94 Pierre Jeanneret, 'Le Parti socialiste suisse des années 20 à la croisée des chemins', *SZG*, 34, 1984, No. 4, p. 513.

95 Hans Ulrich Jost, *Geschichte der Schweiz*, Vol. III, p. 143, for the figures of the collapse of Swiss business and trade in the early 1920s.

96 Erich Gruner, *Die Parteien in der Schweiz*, Table 19, p. 216.

97 From the introduction of proportional representation, the Socialist Party had gained 23.5% of the vote, which by 1928 had grown to 27.4%. Pierre Jeanneret, 'Le Parti socialiste', Table B, p. 520.

98 The Radicals had been in steady decline, along with other European bourgeois liberal parties, since the economic crises of the late nineteenth century. Erich Gruner describes this process in his *Die Parteien in der Schweiz*, pp. 86–90.

99 Hans Ulrich Jost, *Geschichte der Schweiz*, Vol. III, pp. 163–4.

100 For a detailed analysis of the text of the agreement and the subsequent amendments, J. Murray Luck, *History of Switzerland* (Palo Alto, Calif., 1985), pp. 543–6.

101 *Documents diplomatiques suisses*, Vol. VII–II, *28.6.1919–15.11.1920*, eds. Antoine Fleury, Gabriel Imboden and Daniel Bourgeois (Bern, 1984), Doc. No. 11, 9 July 1919, pp. 22–3.

102 Ibid., 'Die Schweiz und der Völkerbund. Militärisches Gutachten', Doc. 24, annexe 2, 14/18 July 1919, pp. 67–8.

103 Ibid., Chef du Département de Justice et Police, E. Müller, au Conseil Fédérale, Doc. 25, 28 July 1919, p. 88 and for the popular vote, Doc. No. 322, pp. 649–50.

104 *Documents diplomatiques suisses*, Vol. XII, *1.1.1937–31.12.1938*, eds. Oscar Gauye (†), Gabriel Imboden and Daniel Bourgeois (Bern, 1994), Le Président de la Confédération, G. Motta, au Conseil national, Doc. 169, 22 December 1937, pp. 356–7.

105 Ibid., L'ancien Conseiller fédérale, E. Schulthess, au Président de la Confédération, G. Motta, Doc. 37, 23 February 1937, Annexe, p. 75.

106 Ibid., Chef de la Division de la Police au Département de Justice et Police, H. Rothmund, au Conseiller national Guido Müller, Doc. 471, 7 December 1938, p. 1,082.

107 Ibid., Le Consul de Suisse à Venise, F. Imhof, au Chef de la Division des Affaires étrangères du Département politique, Doc. 460, 30 November 1938, p. 1,057.

108 Ibid., Le Chef de la Division de la Police du Départment de Justice et Police, H. Rothmund, et le Conseiller de Légation, F. Kappeler, au Président de la Confédération, J. Baumann, Doc. 414, 1 October 1938, pp. 933 ff.

109 Stefan Keller, *Grüningers Fall. Geschichten um Flucht und Hilfe* (Zürich, 1993).

110 Federal Councillor Kaspar Villiger, 7 May 1995 in parliament, *NZZ*, 8 May 1995, p. 11.

111 *Documents diplomatiques suisses*, Vol. XIII, *1.1.1939–31.12.1940*, eds. Jean-François Bergier, André Jäggi and Marc Perrenoud (Bern, 1991), Le Sous-Chef de l'Etat, J. Huber, au Chef de l'Etat, J. Labhart, 18 March 1939, Doc. 45, p. 111.

112 Edgar Bonjour, *Neutralität*, Vol. V, p. 440.

113 Guido Calgari, 'L'Umanità di Giuseppe Motta – Commemorazione alla Radio svizzera', 24 January 1940, reprinted in *Schweizer Rundschau*, 70, November/December 1971, pp. 394–5.

114 Edgar Bonjour, *Neutralität*, Vol. IV, p. 53.

115 William Shirer, *Berlin Diary*, p. 235.

116 Edgar Bonjour, *Neutralität*, Vol. V, p. 437.

117 *Documents diplomatiques suisses*, Vol. XIII provides the full text in Doc. 318, 25 June 1940, pp. 760–2. The editors reproduce in addition Pilet-Golaz's handwritten notes for several other speeches in which *apaisement*, as he put it on 25 June, is not quite so apparent. The Pilet-Golaz who emerges from the documents is a secretive and cunning

man who does not easily commit his thoughts in writing ('le papier est toujours indiscret', he observed on 30 May 1940, p. 701).

118 Georg Kreis, *Auf den Spuren von La Charité. Die schweizerische Armeeführung im Spannungsfeld des deutsch-französischen Gegensatzes 1936–1941* (Stuttgart and Basel, 1976) provides evidence of the close cooperation between Swiss and French staffs. Kreis points out shrewdly that neutrality functions at least as much at home as it does abroad: as a means to avoid conflict between the linguistic groups (p. 155).

119 On the vexed question of 'appeasement' and 'resistance', see Philip Wanner, *Oberst Oscar Frey und der schweizerische Widerstandswille* (Münsingen, 1974), esp. pp. 107 ff. where the author reproduces Colonel Frey's bulletins to his troops in Inf. Regt. 22; André Lasserre, *La Suisse des années sombres. Courants d'opinion pendant la Deuzième Guerre mondiale 1939–45* (Lausanne, 1989) sees the Swiss government as essentially defeatist in May 1940, and sees in Pilet-Golaz's speech a *mentalité pétainiste*, pp. 87 ff.; Philippe Marguerat, *La Suisse face au IIIe Reich. Réduit national et dissuasion économique* (Lausanne, 1991) plays down both the 'appeasement' and the 'resistance', pp. 17–26.

120 Edgar Bonjour, *Neutralité*, Vol. v, p. 154.

121 *Documents diplomatiques suisses*, Vol. XIII, Le Chef de la Division des Affaires étrangères du Département politique, P. Bonna, au Ministre de Suisse à Berlin, H. Fröhlicher, No. 353, 31 July 1940, pp. 862–3 contains an attempt to diminish the significance of the *geste symbolique* and to mollify German irritation. As an appendix, M. Bonna sends the ambassador the official text of the speech itself. The speech ends with the following ringing phrases: 'Soldats du Premier Août 1940 . . . Aujourd'hui, sur la prairie du Rütli, berceau de notre liberté, j'ai réuni vos chefs supérieurs pour leur passer la consigne et je les charge de la passer à leur tour. Courage et confiance: le Pays compte sur vous.' The origins of the famous *Rütlischwur* remain as obscure as ever. The editors of the volume tell us that no copy of General Guisan's actual notes has been found and probably none ever existed (No. 353, n. 1). Where Guisan does offer opinions, he is much less forthright than his corps commanders and almost as subtle and devious in dealing with the Federal Council as Pilet-Golaz himself.

122 This controversial episode took place in Arosa in March 1943. Willi Gautschi has reconstructed the events and even found the bills and guest books signed by the Germans and the Swiss. He concludes that Guisan dishonestly concealed his actions from his own government. Willi Gautschi, 'Der Kontakt General Guisans mit SS-Standartenführer Schellenberg', *SZG*, 39, 1989, No. 2, pp. 152 ff.

123 Alfred Ernst, *Die Konzeption der schweizerischen Landesverteidigung 1815–1966* (Frauenfeld, 1971), p. 204.

124 Edmund Wehrli, 'Wehrlose Schweiz – eine Insel des Friedens?', *Allgemeine Schweizerische Militärzeitschrift*, No. 9, September 1973, pp. 10–14.

125 Ulrich Schlie, *Kein Frieden mit Deutschland. Die geheimen Gespräche im zweiten Weltkrieg 1939–1941* (Munich and Berlin, 1994), pp. 260–2.

126 *Documents diplomatiques suisses*, Vol. xv, *8 septembre 1943–8 mai 1945 (avec annexes 21 juin 1945–11 juin 1946)*, eds. Philippe Marguerat, Louis-Edouard Roulet, Roland Blättler, Catherine Krüttli-Tüscher, Marc Perrenoud, Maurice Peretti and Marie-Jeanne Steiner (Bern, 1992), Le Conseil fédéral aux Gouvernements britannique et américain, Doc. 9, 30 September 1943, pp. 20 ff.

127 Ibid., Rapport de la Direction générale de la Banque nationale sur les relations de la Banque nationale et de la Reichsbank pendant la Guerre mondiale (1939–1945), Doc. 446, 16 May 1946, pp. 1,117 ff.

128 Oswald Inglin, *Der stille Krieg. Der Wirtschaftskrieg zwischen Grossbritannien und der Schweiz im Zweiten Weltkrieg* (Zürich, 1991), p. 199.

129 Jean-Claude Favez, *Une mission impossible? Le CICR, les déportations et les camps de concentration nazis* (Lausanne, 1988), pp. 160–4 for the full text of the minutes of the fateful meeting.

130 Hans Ulrich Jost, in *Geschichte der Schweiz*, Vol. iii, p. 179.

3. POLITICS

1 Interview with Dr Albert Bodmer, former Vice-Chairman, Ciba-Geigy AG, Basel, 4 April 1991.

2 Clive H. Church, 'Where is Switzerland? Explaining the position of a small country in post-Maastricht Europe', School of European and Modern Language Studies, University of Kent, Occasional Paper No. 5, 1994, p. 17.

3 Christopher Hughes, *The Parliament of Switzerland* (London, 1962), p. 39.

4 For a neat and clear description of how referenda work, René Rhinow and Annemarie Huber-Hotz, 'Die Zukunft des schweizerischen politischen Systems', in *Blickpunkt Schweiz. 27 Ansichten*, eds. Kurt R. Spillmann and Rolf Kieser with Thomas Köppel (Zürich, 1995), pp. 53 ff. In a survey the *Neue Zürcher Zeitung* (abbreviated hereafter as *NZZ*) calculated that since its introduction in 1874 the optional or *fakultativ* referendum has never rejected more than seven bills per decade and is not now used more often than in the past. What has changed is the number of obligatory referenda (constitutional changes) and initiatives; cf. *NZZ*, 'Vertrauen in den misstrauischen Bürger', 19 January 1991, p. 23.

5 *Statistical Data on Switzerland*, Swiss Federal Statistical office (Bern, 1991), Table 1, p. 2 and Table 4, p. 7. Also interview with Dr Hans Windlin, Landschreiber des Kantons Zug, Zug, 5 April 1991.

6 *Verfassung, Gemeinde- und Wahlgesetz*, Herausgegeben von der Staatskanzlei des Kantons Zug, 1985.

7 After the elections of 1994 the eighty were divided among the parties as follows (1990 results in brackets): Christian Democratic People's Party (CVP) 33 (36), Radical Party (FDP) 28 (25), Socialist Party of Switzerland (SPS) 9 (11), Swiss People's Party (SVP) 3 (0), Socialist–Green Alternative 3 (4), FB (Fresh Breeze) 2 (2), G 3 (Track 3) 1 (1), Critical List/Forum Oberägeri 1 (0), Colourful List 0 (1): source, Staatskanzlei des Kantons Zug. Cf. 'Linkrutsch bei den Zuger Wahlen', *NZZ*, 13 November 1990, p. 21.

8 'Gesetz über die Organisation und die Verwaltung der Gemeinden (Gemeindegesetz) (vom 4. September 1980)', in *Verfassung. Gemeinde- und Wahlgesetz*, p. 110.

9 *Statistisches Jahrbuch der Schweiz 1995* (Bern, 1995), Table 18.1, p. 383.

10 Interview with Gemeindeschreiber Herr Josef Geisseler, Malters, 2 June 1995.

11 Interview with Landschreiber Dr Hans Windlin, Zug, 5 April 1991.

12 *Statistisches Jahrbuch der Schweiz 1995*, Table 1.3, p. 26.

13 Ibid., Section 17.5.5, pp. 378–9.

14 Anita von Arx-Fischler, 'Der Grosse Rat von Luzern', in Paul Stadlin, ed., *Les Parlements des cantons suisses* (Zug, 1990), p. 256; 'Die SVP als Gewinnerin der Luzerner Wahlen', *NZZ*, 3 April 1995, p. 19. The CVP had 85 seats in 1987, 80 in 1991 and 73 in 1995, whereas the Liberals had 56 (1987), 57 (1991) and 51 (1995).

15 Information from Herr dipl. arch. Benno Baumeler, Entlebuch, 8 June 1995.

16 Amtliches Ergebnis der Volksabstimmung, Gemeinde Malters, 6 December 1992 and 'Resultate der Grossrats- und Regierungswahlen vom 2. April, 1995', *Malters Informiert*, Gemeinde Malters, No. 76/4, 1995, p. 15.

17 *Rechnung und Verwaltungsbericht 1994*, Stadt Grenchen, Approved 22 June 1995, p. 4; *Rechnung 1994*, Gemeinde Malters, 1995, p. 4.

18 *Grenchen* (Grenchen, 1992), p. 9; interview with Stadtschreiber Herr Rolf Enggist, 16 June 1995.

19 *Gemeindeordnung*, Stadt Grenchen, Ausgabe Februar 1993, Para. 36, p. 12, and interviews with Herrn Enggist and Geisseler.

20 Jürg Haefelin, 'Wie Zürich zur Grosstadt wurde. Der Weg zur Stadtvereinigung vom 1. Januar, 1893', *NZZ*, 31 December 1992, p. 33 and *Statistisches Jahrbuch der Schweiz 1995*, Table 1.8, p. 31.

21 'Die städtische Rechnung 1993', *NZZ*, 24 June 1994, p. 35; 'Rote Zahlen und sechsmal ein "blaues Auge" Knapp akzeptable Ostschweizer Kantonsbudgets', *NZZ*, 31 December 1992, p. 23.

22 'Pro Sitz 11.9 Bewerberinnen und Bewerber. Immer mehr Frauen kandidieren für den Zürcher Gemeinderat', *NZZ*, 15 January 1994, p. 37; 'Statistische Übersicht zu den Zürcher Wahlen',

'Wahlbeteiligung bei den Gemeinderatswahlen 1928–1994', *NZZ*, 8 March 1994, p. 32.

23 'Arthur Gilgen – Politiker mit unverwechselbaren Profil', *NZZ*, 6 May 1995, p. 31.

24 Alfred Cattani, 'Erinnerung an Emil Landholt', *NZZ*, 21 April 1995, p. 32.

25 Interview with Landschreiber Dr Hans Windlin, Zug, 5 April 1995.

26 Adolf Gasser, *Der Jura im Kanton Bern* (Basel, n.d.), p. 7.

27 Ibid., p. 31.

28 Bernard Prongué, *Nouvelles composantes de l'identité jurassienne 1974–1989*, Programme national de recherche 21 (Basel, 1991), p. 8; Jean-Claude Montavon, 'Le Parlement jurassien', in Paul Stadlin, *Les Parlements des cantons suisses* (Zug, 1990), pp. 459–60; Kurt Müller, 'Der lange Weg zum Selbstbestimmungsrecht. Zwanzig Jahre nach dem 23. Juni 1974', *NZZ*, 24 June 1994, p. 29.

29 Benjamin Barber, *The Death of Communal Liberty. A History of Freedom in a Swiss Mountain Canton* (Princeton, N.J., 1973), pp. 173–4.

30 Ibid., p. 176.

31 Georg Kreis, *Der Weg zur Gegenwart. Die Schweiz im neunzehnten Jahrhundert* (Basel, Boston and Stuttgart, 1986), p. 150.

32 Ibid., p. 159.

33 Daniel Brühlmeier, *Auf dem Weg zu einer verfassten nationalen Identität*, Nationales Forschungsprogramm 21 (Basel, 1991), p. 15.

34 Wolf Linder, 'Die Zukunft der schweizerischen Demokratie', in *Die Schweiz: Aufbruch aus der Verspätung* (Zürich, 1991), p. 25.

35 Ibid., p. 26.

36 *Reform der Bundesverfassung. Mitlesen, Mitdenken, Mitreden* (Bern, 1995), p. 9.

37 Ibid., p. 11.

38 Ibid., p. 15.

39 *Verfassung, Gemeinde- und Wahlgesetz*, Staatskanzlei des Kantons Zug. I am grateful to Landschreiber Dr Hans Windlin of Canton Zug for checking the labels in Figure 1.

40 Urs Altermatt, *Fundamentalistische Strömungen in den neuen Oppositionsbewegungen 1965–1985*, Nationales Forschungsprogramm 21 (Basel, 1991), p. 17.

41 A. Lawrence Lowell, *Governments and Parties in Continental Europe*, 2 vols. (Cambridge, Mass., 1896), Vol. II, pp. 291–2.

42 Denis de Rougemont, *La Suisse ou l'histoire d'un peuple heureux* (Paris, 1965), p. 125.

43 Figures from *Statistisches Jahrbuch der Schweiz 1995*, pp. 374–5, Table 17.10, 'Eidgenössische Volksabstimmungen seit 1993'. Cf. Jean Meynaud, *La Démocratie semi-directe en Suisse* (Lausanne, 1970), p. 14; Max Imboden, *Helvetisches Malaise* (Zürich, 1964), p. 7.

44 René Rhinow and Annemarie Huber-Hotz, 'Die Zukunft des schweizerischen politischen Systems', p. 55.

45 Ibid., p. 44.
46 Jürg Steiner, Erwin Bucher, Daniel Frei and Leo Schürmann, *Das politische System der Schweiz* (Munich, 1971), pp. 146–7.
47 Georg Kreis, 'Die Illusion einer Revision des Staatsvertragsreferendums', *NZZ*, 10 July 1995, p. 13.
48 Sophie de Skowronski, 'Switzerland and the European Community; the EEA Referendum of 1992' (Cambridge University, M.Phil. Dissertation, 1994), p. 20.
49 Interview with Staatssekretär Franz Blankart, Bundesamt für Aussenwirtschaft, Bern, 11 April 1991.
50 Sophie de Skowronski, 'Switzerland', p. 21.
51 'Die Schweiz stellt EG Beitrittsgesuch' and 'Kein Schicksal sondern Chance. Der Bundesrat zur europäischen Zukunft der Schweiz', *NZZ*, 20 May 1992, p. 27 and 22 May 1992, p. 29.
52 VOX, *Analyse de la votation fédérale du 6 décembre 1992*, GfS, Publication No. 47, February 1993.
53 Ibid., ch. 4, 'Le Profil du vote', pp. 31–41; 'Mehrere Gräben in der Europapolitik', *NZZ*, 28 February 1993, p. 26.
54 'Die Ergebnisse der eidgenössischen Abstimmung' and 'Die Ergebnisse der eidgenössischen Abstimmung in Stadt und Kanton Zürich', *NZZ*, 26 June 1995, p. 12.
55 Max Frenkel, 'Ein Nein, das Konsequenzen haben muss', ibid., p. 11.
56 Marliss Buchmann and Stefan Sacchi, 'Lebensstandard in der Schweiz', *Blickpunkt Schweiz*, p. 204.
57 Erich Gruner, *Die Parteien in der Schweiz* (Bern, 1969), p. 29.
58 François Masnata, *Le Parti socialiste et la tradition démocratique en Suisse* (Neuchâtel, 1963), p. 244.
59 Bundesrat Karl Scheurer, *Tagebücher 1914–1929*, ed. Hermann Böschenstein (Bern, 1971), p. 42.
60 Christopher Hughes, *The Parliament*, p. 98.
61 Max Frisch, *Mein Name sei Gantenbein* (Frankfurt, 1964), p. 36.
62 A. Lawrence Lowell, *Governments and Parties*, Vol. II, p. 193.
63 Christopher Hughes, *The Parliament*, p. 80.
64 *Documents diplomatiques suisses*, Vol. IV, *1.1.1890–31.12.1903*, eds. Yves Collart, Marco Durer, Verdiana Grossi, Martin Ludi and Ronald Dreyer (Bern, 1994). Switzerland hardly seemed to need a separate 'Département des affaires étrangères' and, in fact, until 1887 had not had one. True democrats distrust the fancy manners and aristocratic pretensions of diplomats and hence Swiss politicians found the so-called 'système Droz' deeply unnatural. Numa Droz, an authoritarian Federal Councillor, had invented the Swiss Ministry of Foreign Affairs and placed himself at its head from 1887 to 1892. His retirement gave the Federal Council a chance to consider the place of professional diplomacy in democratic Switzerland. Among the most interesting of the documents reproduced in this volume is the lengthy protocol of

the debate on 8 February 1894 in which the Federal Council actually decided to abolish the ministry and return to a system by which the Federal President during his one-year term acted as foreign secretary. As Federal Councillor Schenk put it, 'diplomacy does not need to be so developed among us . . . if things go on as they are, we shall soon have a staff of officials demanding to be used, especially in the consular service' (Doc. No. 128, p. 284).

65 Interview with Bundesrat Otto Stich, Bern, 12 April 1991.
66 Interview with Consigliere federale Flavio Cotti, 12 April 1991.
67 'Ersatz Wahl in den Bundesrat als Hauptattraktion', *NZZ*, 28 February 1993, p. 25.
68 'Bundesratswahl mit offenem Result', ibid., 5 March 1993; ibid., 13 March 1995, p. 29.
69 Giovanni Orelli, *La Festa del Ringraziamento* (Milan, 1972), p. 62.
70 A. Lawrence Lowell, *Governments and Parties*, Vol. II, p. 205.
71 'Weniger vertrauen zu Behörden', *NZZ*, 6 June 1995, p. 13.
72 Interview with Bundesrat Otto Stich, Bern, 12 April 1991.
73 *Statistisches Jahrbuch der Schweiz 1995*, Figure 17.2 and Table 17.9, pp. 372–3.
74 'Chancengleichheit statt gesetzliche Hilfen', *NZZ*, 28 July 1995, p. 23; 'Keine Frauenquote in Berner Stadtparlament', *NZZ*, 11 September 1995, p. 13.
75 *Statistisches Jahrbuch der Schweiz 1995*, Table 1.8, p. 31.
76 Werner Haug, 'Wachsende Vielfalt – Wege zur Integration. Ausländer und Ausländerinen – Zahlen und Fakten', *NZZ*, 29 June 1995, p. 27.
77 *Statistisches Jahrbuch der Schweiz 1995*, Table 1.26, p. 52.
78 Ibid., Table 1.27, p. 53.
79 Rolf Weibel, *Schweizer Katholizismus heute: Strukturen, Aufgaben, Organisationen der römisch-katholischen Kirche* (Zürich, 1989), pp. 62–3.
80 'Stände-Schranken für "Schweizer" Ausländer', *NZZ*, 14 June 1994, p. 23.

4. LANGUAGE

1 Tullio de Mauro, *Storia linguistica d'Italia unita* (Bari, 1972), p. 43.
2 Perry Anderson, *Passages from Antiquity to Federalism* (London, 1974), p. 127.
3 For a useful, if technical, introduction to these matters, cf. R. E. Keller, *German Dialects* (Manchester, 1961).
4 Ibid., pp. 6–7.
5 Ludwig Fischer, *Luzerndeutsche Grammatik* (Zürich, 1960), p. 32.
6 J. A. Cremona, 'The Romance Languages', in *Literature and Western Civilisation*, ed. David Daiches and Anthony Thorlby, Vol. II, *The Medieval World* (London, 1973), p. 62.

7 Olga Neversilova, 'Schweizerdeutsch: Abenteuer der Sprache', *National-Zeitung*, Basel, 29 July 1972.

8 Peter Bichsel, *Des Schweizers Schweiz* (Zürich, 1969), pp. 43–4.

9 Cited in Hermann Burger, 'Schreiben in der Ich-Form', *Schweizer Monatshefte*, 53, No. 1, April 1973, p. 50.

10 Ibid., p. 51.

11 Peter Ruedi, 'Gflickt, aber suuber', *Die Weltwoche*, No. 9, 5 March 1975.

12 Dieter Fringeli, *Dichter im Abseits. Schweizer Autoren von Glauser bis Hohl* (Zürich, 1974), p. 8.

13 T. de Mauro, *Storia*, pp. 129–35.

14 Gottfried Keller, *Der grüne Heinrich*, in *Gottfried Kellers Werke*, Vol. 1 (Basel, n.d.), p. 10.

15 *Zustand und Zukunft der viersprachigen Schweiz*, Arbeitsgruppe des Eidgenössischen Departementes des Innern zur Revision des Art. 116 der Bundesverfassung (Bern, 1989), p. 140.

16 The peculiar dominance of the Frisch and Dürrenmatt generation in German letters seems to have been temporary. No living Swiss German writer enjoys anything like the same prestige among German-speaking readers, although a small cult has formed around Gerhard Meier, whose curious telegraphic style in poetry and prose and his roots in his Bernese village of Niederbipp make him into what one writer calls 'the provincial as world citizen' (Daniel Weber, 'Der Provinzler als Weltbürger. Friedrich Kappelers Dokumentarfilm "Gerhard Meier – Die Ballade vom Schreiben"', *Neue Zürcher Zeitung* (abbreviated hereafter as *NZZ*), 21 April 1995, p. 35). It may be that Frisch and Dürrenmatt enjoyed the benefits of a post-war German culture, hungry for writers not tainted by Nazism and hence able to write of it without ambivalence and/or guilt. Whatever the causes, Swiss German writing has turned inwards and lost its foreign audience.

17 J. A. Cremona, 'The Romance Languages', p. 59.

18 I am grateful to Dr Spiess for allowing me to quote an unpublished lecture. See also F. Spiess, 'Lingua e dialetti nella Svizzera italiana', *Dal dialetto alla lingua*, Atti del IX Convegno per gli Studi Dialettali Italiani (Pisa, 1974).

19 F. Spiess, 'Lingua', pp. 360–1. Dr Cremona drew my attention to the French parallel.

20 *Annuario statistico del cantone Ticino* (Bellinzona, 1971), p. 84; Angelo Rossi, 'Ipotesi del lavoro', *Ticino Management*, Anno III, No. 3, 1991, pp. 58–62. Rossi shows how dependent Italian Switzerland has become on its *frontalieri* and how much more so it will be in 2005.

21 In 1980 six of the 250 Ticino communes had more than 35% of German-speakers and for the areas of Locarno and Lugano communities with 30% were not uncommon. The government survey expects the process to accelerate: *Materialenband zum Schlussbericht der*

Arbeitsgruppe zur Revision von Artikel 116 der Bundesverfassung (Bern, 1989), Maps 14–16, with commentaries.

22 Ursula Zenger, 'Die vier Sprachgruppen in der Bundesverwaltung', *Die Weltwoche*, 22 August 1973.

23 Flavio Zanetti, 'Il Ticino all'inizio degli anni settanta', *Jahrbuch der eidgenössischen Behörden* (Bern, 1971), p. 192.

24 Heinrich Schmid, 'Über die Lage des Rätoromanischen in der Schweiz' (1983), cited in *Zustand und Zukunft*, pp. 264–5.

25 'Rumantsch grischun kann gemeinsame Schriftsprache werden', *NZZ*, 19 December 1991.

26 Iso Camartin, *Nichts als Worte? Ein Plädoyer für Kleinsprachen* (Zürich and Munich, 1985), p. 129.

27 Andri Peer and John Pult, *Die Rätoromanische Sprache* (Zürich, 1972), p. 11.

29 *Zustand und Zukunft*, pp. 159 ff. The history of the constitutional amendments covering linguistic status is neatly surveyed by the working party.

29 The lower house approved a version of the new Article 116 on 22 September 1993 which omitted both the territorial and the freedom of language principles. For the debate, see 'Eidgenössische Räte', *NZZ*, 24 September 1993, p. 31. In June 1994, the upper house restored the territorial principle to the text of the constitutional amendment but not the freedom of language use principle. They also elevated Romansch to the dignity of 'official' language. For the text, cf. *NZZ*, 17 June 1994, p. 32. In March 1995, the upper house referred the matter back to committee, where at this moment the matter rests. 'Letzte Chance für den Sprachenartikel', *NZZ*, 15 March 1995, p. 25. On the court decision, see 'Aus Territorialitätsprinzip', *NZZ*, 4 May 1995, p. 27.

30 Denis de Rougement, *La Suisse ou l'histoire d'un peuple heureux* (Paris, 1965), p. 173.

31 Ibid., pp. 189–90.

32 Pierre Cordey, in Erich Gruner, ed., *Die Schweiz seit 1945* (Bern, 1971), p. 248; *Statistisches Jahrbuch der Schweiz 1995* (Bern, 1995), Table 16.8, p. 358.

33 Ernst Bollinger, 'Pressekonzentration in der Westschweiz. Der Trend zur überregionalen Tageszeitung', *NZZ*, 12 February 1994, p. 29.

34 *Zustand und Zukunft*, p. 64.

35 *Statistisches Jahrbuch der Schweiz 1995*, Figure 16.1, p. 351.

36 Forschungsinstitut der schweizerischen Gesellschaft für Marketing, as reported in the *NZZ*, 27 August 1992, p. 42.

37 *Statistisches Jahrburh der Schweiz 1995*, Table 16.2, p. 352. The exact figures are German 29.7%, French 61.0%, Italian 1.9% and 'other' 7.5%.

38 J. A. Cremona, 'The Romance Languages', p. 61.

39 J. W. von Goethe, *Dichtung und Wahrheit* (Munich, 1961), Part I, p. 246.

40 Johann Gottfried Herder, *Abhandlung über den Ursprung der Sprache* (Berlin, 1772; reprinted Stuttgart, 1966), pp. 104 and 109.

5. WEALTH

1 'Reiche Schweiz. Problematische Einkommensstatistik der Weltbank', *Neue Zürcher Zeitung* (abbreviated hereafter as *NZZ*), 31 December 1994.

2 Pierre Bairoch, 'L'Economie suisse dans le contexte européen: 1913–1939', *Schweizerische Zeitschrift für Geschichte* (abbreviated hereafter as *SZG*), 34, 1984, No. 4, Table 12, p. 494.

3 Hektor Ammann, *Schaffhauser Wirtschaft im Mittelalter* (Thayngen (SH), 1950), pp. 256–8; Hajo Holborn, *A History of Modern Germany*, Vol. I, *The Reformation* (London, 1965), p. 79 and pp. 72–6.

4 What constitutes intolerable inequality? For a fascinating study into this difficult terrain by an economist, see J. E. Meade, *Efficiency, Equality and the Ownership of Property* (London, 1964), especially pp. 27–33.

5 Georg Thürer, *St Galler Geschichte. Aufklärung bis Gegenwart* (St Gallen, 1972), Vol. II, p. 92.

6 Ibid., pp. 212–14.

7 Ibid., p. 229.

8 Rudolf Braun, *Das ausgehende Ancien Régime in der Schweiz* (Göttingen and Zürich 1984), pp. 33–4, 49–50, 61 and 124–7.

9 Karl Marx, *Das Kapital* (Vol. XXIII of *Marx und Engels Werke* (Berlin, 1962)), Book I, Section IV, ch. 12, p. 365.

10 Ibid., pp. 362–3.

11 R. A. G. Miller, 'The Watchmakers of the Swiss Jura, 1848–1900' (unpublished D.Phil. dissertation, Oxford, 1974), pp. 10–18.

12 Ibid., p. 355.

13 Pierre Bairoch, 'Les Spécificités des chemins de fer suisses des origines à nos jours', *SZG*, 39, 1989, No. 1, pp. 36–8.

14 Pierre Bairoch, 'L'Economie suisse', Tables 1 and 2, pp. 470 and 472.

15 Ibid., Table 3, p. 475.

16 D. S. Landes, *Revolution in Time. Clocks and the Making of the Modern World* (Cambridge, Mass., 1983), pp. 326, 378.

17 Pierre Bairoch, 'L'Economie suisse', p. 479.

18 Ibid., Table 9, p. 486, Table 11, p. 490, p. 492.

19 R. A. G. Miller, 'The Watchmakers', p. 212.

20 P. A. Kropotkin, *Memoirs of a Revolutionary* (New York, 1966), p. 281.

21 Ibid., pp. 285–6.

22 David Landes, *The Unbound Prometheus. Technological Change and Industrial Development in Western Europe from 1750 to the Present* (Cambridge, 1969), pp. 168–9.

23 Georg Thürer, *St Galler Geschichte*, Vol. ii, pp. 460–5.
24 Ibid., p. 462.
25 R. A. G. Miller, 'The Watchmakers', p. 12.
26 J.-F. Bergier, *Naissance et croissance de la Suisse industrielle* (Bern, 1974), p. 128.
27 K. Marx, *Das Kapital*, p. 363, n. 32.
28 *Statistisches Jahrbuch der Schweiz 1995* (Bern, 1995), Table 2.6, p. 66.
29 Ibid., Table 7.1, p. 176.
30 Rudolf Braun, *Ancien Régime*, pp. 68–9.
31 G. Thürer, *St Galler Geschichte*, Vol. ii, p. 205.
32 Gottfried Keller, *Der grüne Heinrich*, in *Gottfried Kellers Werke*, Vol. i (Basel, n.d.), p. 203.
33 David Landes, *Unbound Prometheus*, p. 276.
34 Rudolf Wackernagel, *Geschichte der Stadt Basel* (Basel, 1924), Vol. ii, pp. 166–77. See also Paul Burckhardt, *Geschichte der Stadt Basel* (Basel, 1942), p. 4, pp. 81–2, 202, 217 and *The Story of the Chemical Industry in Basle: 75th Anniversary of CIBA* (Basel, 1959).
35 Jacob Burckhardt, *Briefe an Gottfried und Johanna Kinkel*, ed. Rudolf Meyer-Kraemer (Basel, 1921), no. 15, 24 November 1843, p. 63.
36 David Landes, *Prometheus*, p. 275.
37 Figures on turnover taken from company reports published in the *NZZ* as follows: Sandoz, 26 April 1995, p. 14; Ciba, 21 April 1995, p. 11; Hoffmann, 28 April 1995, p. 12. The figures on Swiss federal expenditure from *Statistisches Jahrbuch der Schweiz 1995*, Table 18.1, p. 383; interview with Dr Albert Bodmer, 4 April 1991. In 1991 the Bank Bär studied the share ownership of 114 leading quoted Swiss companies and found that only 19 had a substantial public participation, whereas the rest were controlled tightly by the use of shares with special rights. Foreigners owned 36% of shares quoted, of whom foreign institutional investors (pension funds etc.) at 21% were by far the most important: 'Die Besitzverhältnisse bei kotierten Schweizer Aktien', *NZZ*, 12 July 1991, p. 15.
38 'Kein Königsweg in der Pharmabranche', *NZZ*, 13 May 1995, p. 9.
39 Branco Weiss, 'Die Zukunft der Schweizer Industrie', in *Blickpunkt Schweiz. 27 Ansichten*, eds. Kurt R. Spillmann and Rolf Kieser with Thomas Köppel (Zürich, 1995), p. 130.
40 Thomas P. Gasser, 'Gefährdeter Standort Schweiz', *NZZ*, 28 December 1994.
41 'Die schweizerische Konjunktur im Jahre 1974 und ihre Aussichten für 1975', Mitteilung No. 231, Kommission für Konjunkturfragen, January 1975.
42 D. S. Landes, *Revolution in Time*, p. 353.
43 Ibid., p. 342.
44 Ibid., Appendix A, p. 377.
45 Ibid., p. 352.

46 Ibid., p. 359.

47 1975 figures in 'Die schweizerische Konjunktur', p. 5; export figures for 1993 from *Statistisches Jahrbuch der Schweiz 1995*, Table 6.8, p. 163; currency indices from 1981 to 1994, ibid., Table 12.4, p. 266.

48 A. M. Schütz, interview, Grenchen, 9 April 1991.

49 'Nicholas Hayek als Motor der Unruhe', *NZZ*, 29 July 1995, p. 37.

50 'Atemloser SMH-Uhrenkonzern', *NZZ*, 31 May 1995, p. 21.

51 Georg Thürer, *St Galler Geschichte*, Vol. II, p. 463.

52 Ibid., pp. 470–2; J. Früh, *Géographie de la Suisse*, Vol. II, *Géographie humaine* (Lausanne, 1939), p. 260.

53 Peter G. Rosse, 'Die Zukunft der mittleren Industriebetriebe in der Schweiz', *Schweizer Monatshefte*, 52, No. 10, January 1973, pp. 711–21.

54 These statistics are drawn from Wilhelm Bickel, 'Wachstum und Strukturwandel der Wirtschaft', in Erich Gruner, ed., *Die Schweiz seit 1945* (Bern, 1971); *Statistical Data on Switzerland*, Swiss Federal Statistical Office (Bern, 1973); *Die Volkswirtschaft*, April 1975, p. 205; *Statistisches Jahrbuch der Schweiz 1995*, Table 18.1, p. 383.

55 *Statistisches Jahrbuch der Schweiz 1995*, Table 12.4, p. 266.

56 Peter Gilg and Peter Halblützel, 'Beschleunigter Wandel und neue Krisen (seit 1945)', in *Geschichte der Schweiz und der Schweizer*, 3 vols. (Basel, 1983), Vol. III, p. 214.

57 *Statistisches Jahrbuch der Schweiz 1995*, Table 18.1, p. 383, Table 18.2, p. 385.

58 Interview with Herr Bundesrat Otto Stich, Bern, 12 April 1991.

59 Ibid. and *Statistisches Jahrbuch der Schweiz*, Table 18.1, p. 383 and Table 4.1, p. 117.

60 Ibid., Figure 18.5, p. 389.

61 Marliss Buchmann and Stefan Sacchi, 'Lebensstandard in der Schweiz', *Blickpunkt Schweiz*, Figure 1, 'Einkommensverteilung in ausgewählten Industrieländern (1979–1987)', pp. 196–7.

62 Ibid., p. 204.

63 Christoph Brunner, 'Erfolgreiche Schweizer Bankübernahmen?', *NZZ*, 28 July 1994, p. 9; *Statistisches Jahrbuch der Schweiz 1995*, Table 12.8, p. 268.

64 'Offerte der CS Holding für die NAB', *NZZ*, 22 September 1994, p. 11.

65 'Ein von Personalabbau geprägtes Grossbankenjahr!', *NZZ*, 12 March 1993, p. 13; 'Die Bankgesellschaft unter Zinsdruck', ibid., 4 August 1995, p. 9.

66 *Documents diplomatiques suisses*, Vol. XI, *1934–1936*, eds. Mauro Cerutti, Jean-Claude Favez and Michèle Fleury-Seemüller (Bern, 1989), Doc. No. 66, 26 September 1934, p. 214.

67 J. Murray Luck, *History of Switzerland* (Palo Alto, Calif., 1985), p. 634.

68 Christine Hirszowicz, 'Banken und Bankgeheimnis in der Schweiz', *Blickpunkt Schweiz*, p. 141.

69 'Aufreibender Kampf gegen Geldwäscherei: ein Seminar der Bankier-vereinigung', *NZZ*, 31 May 1995, p. 25.
70 Rolf Zimmermann, *Volksbank oder Aktienbank. Parlamentsdebatten, Referendum und zunehmende Verbandsmacht beim Streit um die National-bankgründung, 1891–1905* (Zürich, 1987), p. 215.
71 *Statistisches Jahrbuch der Schweiz 1995*, Table 16.4, p. 355.
72 Urs Dürmüller, 'Englisch in der Schweiz', *Materialienband zum Schluss-bericht der Arbeitsgruppe zur Revision von Artikel 116 der Bundesverfassung* (Bern, 1989), pp. 4 ff.
73 'EG-Beitritt oder EWR? Bundesrat Felber vor den Zürcher Sozial-demokraten', *NZZ*, 27 November 1990, p. 27.
74 Interview with Staatssekretär Franz Blankart, Bern, 11 April 1991.

6. RELIGION

1 *Statistisches Jahrbuch der Schweiz 1995* (Bern, 1995), Table 16.3, p. 353.
2 *Ökumenische Kirchengeschichte der Schweiz*, ed. Lukas Vischer, Lukas Schenker and Rudolf Dellsperger (Fribourg, 1994), pp. 94–5. Randolph C. Head argues that by the late fifteenth century, Swiss political ideas had become 'antiaristocratic . . . to a degree unimaginable in most of Europe'. These ideas rested on a concept of political will which justified the Swiss cantons in exercising 'tighter control over their clergy than even the German cities': Randolph C. Head, 'William Tell and his comrades: association and fraternity in the propaganda of fifteenth and sixteenth century Switzerland', *The Journal of Modern History*, 67, No. 3, September 1995, pp. 554–5.
3 *Ökumenische Kirchengeschichte*, p. 117.
4 Ibid., p. 147.
5 Martin Körner, 'Glaubensspaltung und Wirtschaftssolidarität (1515–1648)', in *Geschichte der Schweiz und der Schweizer* (Basel, 1983), Vol. II, pp. 53–4.
6 Cf. Jürgen Habermas, *The Structural Transformation of the Public Sphere* (Cambridge, 1989).
7 Rudolf Braun, *Das ausgehende Ancien Régime in der Schweiz* (Göttingen and Zürich, 1984), pp. 82 f. and 87 ff.
8 Georges Andrey, 'Auf der Suche nach dem neuen Staat (1798–1848)', in *Geschichte der Schweiz und der Schweizer*, Vol. II, p. 249.
9 Walter Gut, *Politische Kultur in der Kirche* (Fribourg, 1990), pp. 25–6.
10 Ibid., p. 27.
11 Interview with Regierungsrat Dr Walter Gut, 13 April 1991.
12 Quoted in *Ökumenische Kirchengeschichte*, p. 219.
13 Klaus Scholder, *Die Kirchen und das Dritte Reich*, Vol. I, *Vorgeschichte und Zeit der Illusionen 1918–1934* (Frankfurt/Main, 1977), p. 50.
14 Ibid., p. 51.
15 *Ökumenische Kirchengeschichte*, p. 263.

16 Victor Conzemius, 'Katholische Kirche und Demokratie', *Schweizer Monatshefte*, 71, No. 4 (April 1991), p. 308.

17 *Briefwechsel Philipp Anton von Segesser (1817–1888)*, ed. Victor Conzemius (Zürich and Fribourg, 1983–95), Vol. I, p. 494.

18 Ibid., Vol. II, p. 324.

19 Ibid., Vol. IV, p. 90.

20 Ibid., Vol. IV, pp. 215–16.

21 Ibid., Vol. III, p. 207.

22 Ibid., Vol. VI, p. 58; see also Georg Kreis, *Der Weg zur Gegenwart. Die Schweiz im neunzehnten Jahrhundert* (Basel, Boston and Stuttgart, 1986), pp. 166–9.

23 'Rücktritt Bischof Vogels von Basel', *Neue Zürcher Zeitung* (abbreviated hereafter as *NZZ*), 3/4 June 1995, p. 13.

24 'Misstöne am *Dies academicus* der Universität Freiburg. Keine Verleihung theologischer Ehrendoktoren', *NZZ*, 13 November 1990, p. 22.

25 Walter Gut, *Politische Kultur*, pp. 46–7 and p. 112.

26 Gonsalv K. Maienberger, 'Zwischen vernünftigem Vermuten und verordneten Glauben', in *Die Schweiz: Aufbruch aus der Verspätung* (Zürich, 1991), pp. 332–3.

27 'Ruf nach Amtsenthebung von Bischof Haas', *NZZ*, 10 March 1995, p. 30.

28 'Mängel an der Theologischen Hochschule Chur, "Ultimatum" der Bündner Regierung an Bischof Haas', *NZZ*, 29 June 1995, p. 25.

29 'Erzbischof Lefebvre gestorben', *NZZ*, 27 March 1991, p. 27.

30 *Hans Urs von Balthasar 1905–1988* (private publication; La Tour de Peilz, 1989), p. 68.

31 This account rests on information provided to me by Herr J. Frey, legal officer of the Evangelical–Reformed Church of Canton Bern, interview, 15 April 1991, and on the new *Verfassung des Kantons Bern*.

32 'Wohnbevölkerung der Schweiz nach Konfessionen 1920–1970', in *Ökumenische Geschichte der Schweiz*, p. 304.

33 '50 bis 60 Kirchenaustritte pro Tag', *NZZ*, 27 March 1993, p. 43.

34 'Die Jahresberichte der Landeskirchen: Ökumenischer Unterricht auf gutem Weg', *NZZ*, 6 June 1995, p. 53.

35 'Demokratische Staat – demokratische Kirche?', *NZZ*, 15 January 1991, p. 23.

36 Rolf Weibel, *Schweizer Katholizismus heute: Strukturen, Aufgaben, Organisationen der römisch-katholischen Kirche* (Zürich, 1989), pp. 53–5.

37 'Die Jahresberichte', *NZZ*, 6 June 1995.

38 'Gegen die Privatisierung der Kirche', *NZZ*, 22 May 1995, p. 17.

39 Rolf Weibel, 'Seelsorger im Dienst der Bistümer', *Schweizer Katholizismus*, p. 25.

40 'Die Jahresberichte', *NZZ*, 6 June 1995.

41 Peter Baccini and Franz Oswald, 'Achtung: die Schweiz – Eine Replik auf einen Aufruf von 1955', *NZZ*, 17 August 1995, p. 25.

7. IDENTITY

1 Interview with Divisionär a.D. Gustav Däniker, Bern, 15 April 1991.

2 Marko Milivojević, 'The Swiss Armed Forces', in Marko Milivojević and Pierre Maurer, *Swiss Neutrality and Security. Armed Forces, National Defence and Foreign Policy* (New York, Oxford and Munich, 1990), p. 3 and Table 1.1, p. 48.

3 Cited in Martin Merki, 'Auch wenn Gelehrte streiten, es lebe unser Tell – Die Einweihung eines Nationaldenkmals vor 100 Jahren', *Neue Zürcher Zeitung* (abbreviated hereafter as *NZZ*), 19/20 August 1995, p. 27.

4 On the *Fichenaffäre* see 'Zum Abschluss der Fichenaffäre', *NZZ*, 27 July 1991. Hansjörg Braunschweig, *Freiheit kleingeschrieben* (Basel, 1990), pp. 90 ff. In May 1990 the Federal Council established an historical investigating committee under the Basel modern historian, Georg Kreis, to study the activities of counter-intelligence and state security from 1935 to the present; cf. 'Die Fichenaffäre historisch beleuchtet. Publikation des Berichts der Arbeitsgruppe Kreis', *NZZ*, 13/14 June 1993, p. 21. An 81-year-old Zürich book-seller, Theo Pinkus, apparently enjoyed the dubious distinction of having the largest fiche: 252 A4 pages. The first entry dated from 1936 and bore the entry 'Jew'. The last, from 15 May 1990, stated: 'P. is included on the list of closed dossiers.' This grotesque invasion of privacy led the ombudsman, Herr Arthur Haefliger, to write Herr Pinkus a formal letter of apology: 'By these inappropriate measures you have been substantially injured in your personal rights.' Cf. *Sonntagszeitung für Heute*, Zürich, 7 April 1991.

5 Max Frisch, *Dienstbüchlein* (Frankfurt/Main, 1974), p. 47.

6 'Arbeitsdienst für Militärverweigerer? Eine Übergangslösung – nicht mehr nichts weniger', *NZZ*, 19/20 May 1991, p. 23; 'Sieg der Vernunft in Sachen Dienstverweigerung – Resultate der Eidgenössischen Abstimmung', *NZZ*, 4 June 1991, p. 21.

7 'Der Zivildienst wird endlich Wirklichkeit'; 'Anteile der Ja-Stimmen in Prozenten und Stimmbeteiligung', both in *NZZ*, 19 May 1992, p. 20. Low voter turnout (38.5%) and the overwhelming 'Yes' vote both suggest that the matter no longer seemed controversial.

8 Marko Milivojević, 'The Swiss Armed Forces', p. 19.

9 'Auslegeordnung zur Armeereform. Alte und unkonventionelle Vorschläge der Arbeitsgruppe Schoch', *NZZ*, 2/3 December 1990, p. 26.

10 *Schweizerische Sicherheitspolitik im Wandel. Bericht 90 des Bundesrates an die Bundesversammlung über die Sicherheitspolitik der Schweiz* (Bern, 1 October 1990), p. 36.

11 Ibid., p. 41.

12 'Auch in Zukunft nur ein modernisiertes Infanterieheer?', *NZZ*, 16 May 1991, p. 27.

13 Higher commands have had their terms of service shortened and their number of days reduced. Platoon leaders now serve 750 instead of 900 days, and unit commanders 940 instead of 1,100 days: Federal Military Department, *Armed Forces in Transition – Summary of Swiss Armed Forces' White Paper* (Bern, 1995), p. 11; *Bundesgesetz über die Armee und Militärverwaltung (Militärgesetz, MG) vom 3 Februar 1995*, especially Article 14.

14 'Wirtschaftsführer sind oft auch hohe Offiziere – zum Beispiel die Grenzdivision 2', *National-Zeitung Basel*, No. 254, 16 August 1973.

15 Max Frisch, *Dienstbüchlein*, p. 34.

16 *Schweizerische Sicherheitspolitik*, p. 9.

17 Interview with Professor Urs Altermatt, Solothurn, 6 April 1991.

18 Raffaele Ceschi, 'Buoni ticinesi e buoni svizzeri. Aspetti storici di una duplice identità', in *Identità in Cammino*, ed. Remigio Ratti and Marco Badan (Locarno and Bellinzona, 1986), p. 23.

19 Interview with Ständerätin Rosemarie Simmen (CVP, Solothurn), 10 April 1991.

20 Interview with Regierungsrat a.D. Walter Gut, 13 April 1991.

21 Interview with Staatssekretär Franz Blankart, Bern, 11 April 1991.

Index

(Note: Swiss towns have their cantonal location in brackets.)